Frommer's® 99

P O R T A B L E

Sydney

by Marc Llewellyn
with Natalie Kruger

Macmillan • USA

ABOUT THE AUTHOR

Sydney resident **Marc Llewellyn** is one of Australia's premier travel writers and a regular contributor to all of Australia's leading newspaper travel sections and travel magazines. As a member of the Australian Travel Writers' Association, he keeps his suitcase ready-packed beneath his bed.

MACMILLAN TRAVEL

A Simon & Schuster Macmillan Company
1633 Broadway
New York, NY 10019

Find us online at **www.frommers.com**

ISBN 0-02-862440-8
ISSN 1097-654X

Editor: Suzanne Roe Jannetta
Production Editor: Christina Van Camp
Photo Editor: Richard Fox
Design by Michele Laseau
Digital Cartography by Roberta Stockwell and Ortelius Design
Page Creation by Carrie Allen, John Bitter, Natalie Evans, and Laura Goetz

SPECIAL SALES

Bulk purchases (10+ copies) of Frommer's and selected Macmillan travel guides are available to corporations, organizations, mail-order catalogs, institutions, and charities at special discounts, and can be customized to suit individual needs. For more information write to Special Sales, Macmillan General Reference, 1633 Broadway, New York, NY 10019.

Manufactured in the United States of America

Contents

List of Maps

AN INVITATION TO THE READER

In researching this book, we discovered many wonderful places—hotels, restaurants, shops, and more. We're sure you'll find others. Please tell us about them, so we can share the information with your fellow travelers in upcoming editions. If you were disappointed with a recommendation, we'd love to know that, too. Please write to:

Frommer's Portable Sydney '99
Macmillan Travel
1633 Broadway
New York, NY 10019

AN ADDITIONAL NOTE

Please be advised that travel information is subject to change at any time—and this is especially true of prices. We therefore suggest that you write or call ahead for confirmation when making your travel plans. The authors, editors, and publisher cannot be held responsible for the experiences of readers while traveling. Your safety is important to us, however, so we encourage you to stay alert and be aware of your surroundings. Keep a close eye on cameras, purses, and wallets, all favorite targets of thieves and pickpockets.

WHAT THE SYMBOLS MEAN
✪ Frommer's Favorites

Our favorite places and experiences—outstanding for quality, value, or both.

The following abbreviations are used for credit cards:

AE	American Express	ER	enRoute
BC	Bankcard	EURO	Eurocard
CB	Carte Blanche	JCB	Japan Credit Bank
DC	Diners Club	MC	MasterCard
DISC	Discover	V	Visa

FIND FROMMER'S ONLINE

Arthur Frommer's Outspoken Encyclopedia of Travel (www.frommers.com) offers more than 6,000 pages of up-to-the-minute travel information—including the latest bargains and candid, personal articles updated daily by Arthur Frommer himself. No other Web site offers such comprehensive and timely coverage of the world of travel.

Planning a Trip to Sydney

By Natalie Kruger

The land "Down Under" is a modern nation coming to terms with its identity. The umbilical cord with mother England has been cut, and the nation is still trying to find its position within Asia. One thing it realized early on, though, was the importance of tourism to its economy. Millions of visitors flock to Australia every year. The most populated state, New South Wales, is also the one most visited by tourists. Principally they come to see Sydney, which in addition to having spectacular offerings of it's own, is a good base to discover the magnificent Blue Mountains.

Sydney, the "emerald" city, sits majestically around the greenest, most beautiful urban harbor in the world. It's at its best approached at night from the air, when you'll see a million twinkling lights, a vast swath of fluorescent spreading across the water, and the Sydney Opera House and Harbour Bridge lit up like Christmas. And this is not just one Sydneysider's opinion of the city, either. In October 1996, *Condé Naste Traveler* voted Sydney the World's Best City Destination for the second year running, and in 1997 the magazine's readers voted it the World's Friendliest City. In 1998, *Travel & Leisure* readers gave it the thumbs up as the Best City in the World. Beat that Paris, or Venice, or Melbourne, or myriad other hopefuls.

Sydney has something for everyone: miles of beaches, from world-famous Bondi to pretty little Shelly Beach on the North Shore; world-class cuisine that combines the very best of many cultures; outdoor adventures literally at the city's back door, in the Blue Mountains and beyond; historic pubs where you can buy a "shout" for your new Aussie mates; city strolls; harbour cruise; top-notch hotels; and more. Sydney is also, of course, gearing up for the 2000 Olympic Games, when the city will be the focus of the world's attention. Preparations are well underway, and you can even tour the Sydney Olympic Park, in Homebush Bay, where the opening and closing ceremonies and many events will be held.

No matter what your interests, what your budget, or what your reason for journeying to the land Down Under, this chapter will give you everything you need to get you on your way.

Australia

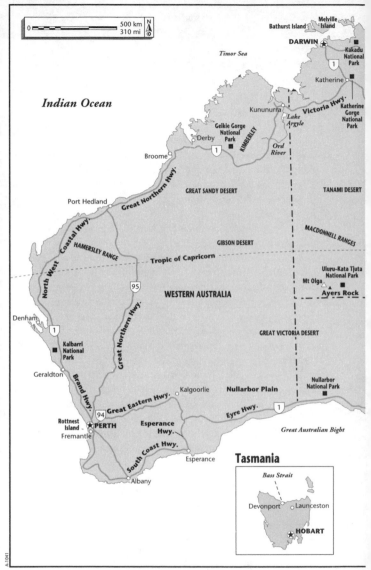

Thursday Island

Coral Sea

Great Barrier Reef Marine Park

Arnhem Land

Gulf of Carpentaria

Cape York Peninsula

Cooktown

Port Douglas

CAIRNS

South Pacific Ocean

NORTHERN TERRITORY

Stuart Hwy.

Barkly Hwy

66

QUEENSLAND

Townsville

Proserpine

Mackay

87

Mt. Isa

Flinders Hwy. 78

Landsborough Hwy.

ALICE SPRINGS

SIMPSON DESERT

Longreach

66

Capricorn Hwy.

GREAT DIVIDING RANGE

Rockhampton

Gladstone

Fraser Island

Simpson Desert National Park

Mitchell Hwy.

15

Sunshine Coast

Bruce Hwy.

87

Coober Pedy

SOUTH AUSTRALIA

71

Lightning Ridge

BRISBANE

Gold Coast

Lamington Natl. Pk.

1

Stuart Hwy.

Flinders Ranges National Park

Barrier Hwy.

Darling River

Oxley

Coffs Harbour

New England Hwy.

Pacific Hwy.

Broken Hill

Tamworth

Dubbo

Blue Mtns. Natl. Pk.

32

Port Macquarie

32

NEW SOUTH WALES

Newell Hwy.

Newcastle

ADELAIDE

Mildura

20

Murray River

Hume Hwy.

SYDNEY

Kangaroo Island

Port Pirie

Princes Hwy.

Dukes Hwy.

39

Wodonga

CANBERRA

Prince's Hwy.

A.C.T.

Mt. Gambier

8

VICTORIA

31

Albury

Mt. Kosciusko

1

SNOWY MOUNTAINS

Ballarat

MELBOURNE

Geelong

Apollo Bay

SEE INSET

Tasman Sea

3

1 Visitor Information & Entry Requirements

VISITOR INFORMATION

AUSTRALIAN TOURIST COMMISSION   For specific help on planning your itinerary in Australia, contact the Australian Tourist Commission's (ATC) **Aussie Helpline** at ☎ **805/775 2000** or fax 805/775 4448 in the United States and Canada; ☎ 0990/022 000 (Aussie Helpline), 0990/561 434 (to order brochures), or fax 0171/940 5221 in the United Kingdom and Ireland; and ☎ 0800/65 0303 or fax 09/527 1629 in New Zealand.

The ATC has a network of "Aussie Specialist" travel agents in several hundred cities across North America, Canada, the United Kingdom, and New Zealand. You're sure to find these guys a great help, as they're committed to a continuous training program on the best destinations, hotels, deals, and tours in Oz. They will know better than most agents how to package an itinerary that's right for you. To find the Aussie Specialist closest to you, call the Aussie Helpline.

The Australian Tourist Commission's Web site (www.aussie.net.au) is excellent, with more than 10,000 pages of listings for tour operators, hotels, car-rental companies, specialist travel outfitters, and much more. You can also access an on-line version of the Aussie Helpline that answers most of your questions within 24 or 48 hours, locate Aussie Specialist travel agents, and order brochures. The pages are well organized, but if you are keen on a particular activity, go straight to the Special Interests page.

You can write to the Australian Tourist Commission at Level 4, 80 William St., Wolloomooloo, Sydney, NSW 2011 (☎ **02/9360 1111;** fax 02/9331 2538).

STATE TOURIST OFFICE   You can also obtain information from **Tourism New South Wales** (www.tourism.nsw.gov.au). In **Australia:** Tourism House, 55 Harrington St., The Rocks, Sydney, NSW 2000 (☎ 02/9931 1111; fax 02/9931 1490). In the **United States:** 13737 Fiji Way, Suite C-10, Marina Del Ray, CA 90292 (☎ 310/301 1903; fax 310/301 0913). In the **United Kingdom:** Gemini House, 10/18 Putney Hill, London SW15 6AA (☎ 0181/789 1020; fax 0181/789 4577).

OTHER USEFUL WEB SITES   The Australian Embassy in Washington, D.C. has a very handy Web site at www.austemb.org. The embassy posts loads of links to sites on tourism; cultural and educational matters; the official Sydney 2000 Olympic Games pages (www.sydney.olympic.org); briefings on the economy, trade, sport, geography, and the people; major newspapers; events listings; and more mundane stuff, like all the governmental bodies (including Customs and Quarantine) and the *Yellow* and *White Pages*. It's written with North Americans in mind, though much of the information is relevant no matter where you are traveling from.

ENTRY REQUIREMENTS

DOCUMENTS   The Australian government requires a visa from visitors of every nation except New Zealand. This gets up the noses of the United States and other countries who do not ordinarily make the same demand of Australians entering their own borders, so in 1996 the Australian government introduced the **Electronic Travel Authority (ETA)**—an electronic or "paperless" visa that takes the place of a rubber stamp in your passport. This is how it works: You give your passport details to your travel agent, or, if you are not using an agent, to your airline reservationist at the time you make your travel booking. These will be typed into the travel agent's or airline's reservations system, which is linked to the Australian Department of Immigration and Multicultural Affairs' computer system. Assuming you are not wanted by Interpol, your ETA should be approved in about 6 to 8 seconds while you wait. The beauty of this system is that you can do all this over the telephone without having to stand in a line at the embassy or mail your passport to the embassy with a visa application form. You can also apply for an ETA at Australian embassies, high commissions, and consulates, as they are connected to the same system.

If you are visiting as a tourist, ask for a **Tourist ETA,** which is free of charge and valid for multiple stays of up to 3 months each within a 1-year period. If you are visiting for business, you will have to pay A\$50 (U.S.\$35) for a **Long Validity Business ETA** that entitles you to as many 3-month stays as you like for as long as your passport is valid. You can pay for it by credit card when you apply. Business travelers who are U.S., Canadian, French, or Spanish citizens can apply for a **Short Validity Business ETA** valid for a single visit of 3 months within a 1-year period. This ETA is free of charge. The difference between the Tourist ETA and the Short Validity Business ETA is that with the latter you will be given an Australian Business Access Card, which speeds you through Immigration desks at Australian airports.

There are a few catches with the ETA system. One is that travel agents and airlines must modify their computer systems to use it, so you will need to find an agent and airline that has done so. In the

United States, Canada, and the United Kingdom, most agents and major airlines are ETA-compatible.

There are still some situations where you will need to apply for a visa the old-fashioned way—by mailing your passport and a visa application form to your nearest Australian embassy or consulate. This will be the case if your airline is not connected to the ETA system or if you are arriving in Australia by cruise ship, as most cruise lines are not connected to the ETA system yet. In this case, you will be charged a A$50 (U.S.$35) processing fee, or A$110 (U.S.$77) if you want to stay in Australia longer than 3 months. A business visa applied for this way will cost A$50 (U.S.$35) for a stay of up to 3 months, and A$145 (U.S.$101.50) for stays between 3 months and 4 years. You can apply via the Internet at the Australian Department of Immigration and Multicultural Affair's Web site (www. immi.gov.au). This site also has a good explanation of the ETA system.

Australian embassies, consulates, and high commissions in the **United States** are located at 1601 Massachusetts Ave. NW, Washington, DC 20036-2273 (☎ 202/797-3000) and at 2049 Century Park East, Level 19, Los Angeles, CA 90067-3238 (☎ 310/229-4840); in **Canada** at 50 O'Connor St., #710, Ottawa, ON KIP6L2 (☎ 613/783 7619 for Immigration matters); in the **United Kingdom** at Australia House, The Strand, London WC2B 4LA (☎ 171/379 4334 and after hours 171/887 5181 or 171/887 5186), and at Chatsworth House, Lever St., Manchester M1 2QL (☎ 0161/228 1344); and in **Ireland** at Fitzwilton House, Wilton Terrace, Dublin 2, Ireland (☎ 1/676 1517).

CUSTOMS & QUARANTINE   Anyone over 18 can bring into Australia no more than 250 cigarettes or 250 grams of cigars or other tobacco products, 1.125 liters (41 fl. oz.) of alcohol, and "dutiable goods" to the value of A$400 (U.S.$280), or A$200 (U.S.$140) if you are under 18. Broadly speaking, "dutiable goods" are luxury items like perfume concentrate, watches, jewelry, furs, plus gifts of any kind. Keep this in mind if you intend to come bearing presents for family and friends in Australia. If the items are your own personal goods and you're taking them with you when you leave, they are usually exempt from duty. If you are not sure what is dutiable and what's not, contact the **Customs** representative at the Australian Embassy in Washington (☎ **202/797-3000**).

Because Australia is an island, it is free of many agricultural and livestock diseases. To keep it that way, strict quarantine applies to importing plants, animals, and their products. You will have to declare to Customs all organic products, including items made from wood, shell, seeds, coral, feathers, rawhide, or bone (such as jewelry, souvenirs, and ornaments); fresh and packaged food (such as chocolate, cheeses, or dried fruit); plant cuttings and seeds (South Pacific bead jewelry is often made from seeds); and even straw packing. Although it may seem mind-boggling to list all the items you are carrying and wearing that come from animals or plants, most things get cleared without a problem. A few items may be taken for treating and returned to you. Don't be alarmed if, just before landing, the flight attendants spray the aircraft cabin (with products approved by the World Health Organization) to kill flying insects that entered the cabin in a foreign country. If you are worried that certain of your belongings may not be allowed entry, contact the nearest Australian embassy or the **Australian Quarantine and Inspection Service** in Sydney (☎ **02/9364 7222**).

You cannot bring weapons of any kind, including handguns, into Australia.

For U.S. Citizens   You can take back into the United States $400 (U.S. dollars) worth of goods (per person) without paying a duty. The first $1,000 worth of goods over $400 you pay a flat 10% duty on. Beyond that, it works on an item-by-item basis. There are a few restrictions on amount: 1 liter of alcohol (you must be over 21), 200 cigarettes, and 100 cigars. Antiques over 100 years old and works of art are exempt from the $400 limit, as is anything you mail home. Once per day, you can mail yourself $200 worth of goods duty-free; mark the package "for personal use." You can also mail to other people up to $100 worth of goods per person, per day; label each package "unsolicited gift." Any package must state on the exterior a description of the contents and their values. You cannot mail alcohol, perfume (it contains alcohol), or tobacco products.

For more information on regulations, check out the U.S. Customs Service Web site (www.customs.ustreas.gov), or write to them at P.O. Box 7407, Washington, DC 20044 to request the free *Know Before You Go* pamphlet.

To prevent the spread of diseases, you cannot bring into the United States any plants, fruits, vegetables, meats, or other foodstuffs. This includes even cured meats like salami (no matter what the shopkeeper in Europe says). You may bring in the following: bakery goods, all but the softest cheeses (the rule is vague, but if the cheese is at all spreadable, don't risk confiscation), candies, roasted coffee beans and dried tea, fish (packaged salmon is OK), seeds for veggies and flowers (but not for trees), and mushrooms. Check out the USDA's Web site (www.aphis.usda.gov/oa/travel.html) for more information.

For British Citizens   If you're returning home from a non–European Union country, or if you buy your goods in a duty-free shop, you're allowed to bring home 200 cigarettes, 2 liters of table wine, plus 1 liter of spirits or 2 liters of fortified wine. Get in touch with **Her Majesty's Customs and Excise Office,** New King's Beam House, 22 Upper Ground, London SE1 9PJ (☎ **0171/620-1313**), for more information.

For Canadian Citizens   For a clear summary of Canadian rules, write for the booklet *I Declare,* issued by **Revenue Canada,** 2265 St. Laurent Blvd., Ottawa K1G 4KE (☎ **800/461-9999** or 613/993-0534). Canada allows its citizens a $500 exemption, and you're allowed to bring back duty-free 200 cigarettes, 2.2 pounds of tobacco, 40 imperial ounces of liquor, and 50 cigars. In addition, you're allowed to mail gifts to Canada from abroad at the rate of C$60 a day, provided they're unsolicited and aren't alcohol or tobacco (write on the package "unsolicited gift, under $60 value"). All valuables should be declared on the Y-38 form before departure from Canada, including serial numbers of, for example, expensive foreign cameras that you already own. *Note:* The $500 exemption can only be used once a year and only after an absence of 7 days.

For New Zealand Citizens   Most questions are answered in a free pamphlet available at New Zealand consulates and Customs offices: *New Zealand Customs Guide for Travellers, Notice no. 4.* For more information, contact **New Zealand Customs,** 50 Anzac Ave., P.O. Box 29, Auckland (☎ **09/359-6655**).

DEPARTURE TAX   Australia's A$27 (U.S.$18.90) departure tax, euphemistically disguised by the authorities as a "Passenger Movement Charge," will rise to A$30 (U.S.$21) in mid-1999. It is included in the price of your airline ticket. Children under 12 are exempt.

2 Money

CASH & CURRENCY   The Australian dollar is divided into 100 cents. Coins come in 5¢, 10¢, 20¢, and 50¢ pieces (all silver in color) and $1 and $2 pieces (gold in color). The 50¢ piece is 12-sided. When you're ferreting through your purse in the

The Australian Dollar, the U.S. Dollar & the British Pound

For U.S. Readers The rate of exchange used to calculate the dollar values given in this book was U.S.$1 = approximately A$1.43 (or A$1 = U.S.70¢).

For British Readers The rate of exchange used to calculate the pound values in the accompanying table was £1 = A$2.50 (or A$1 = 40p).

Note: International exchange rates can fluctuate markedly. Check the latest rate when you plan your trip. The table below should only be used as a guide.

A$	U.S.$	U.K.£	A$	U.S.$	U.K.£
0.25	0.17	0.10	30.00	21.00	12.00
0.50	0.35	0.20	35.00	24.50	14.00
1.00	0.70	0.40	40.00	28.00	16.00
2.00	1.40	0.80	45.00	31.50	18.00
3.00	2.10	1.20	50.00	35.00	20.00
4.00	2.80	1.60	55.00	38.50	22.00
5.00	3.50	2.00	60.00	42.00	24.00
6.00	4.20	2.40	65.00	45.50	26.00
7.00	4.90	2.80	70.00	49.00	28.00
8.00	5.60	3.20	75.00	52.50	30.00
9.00	6.30	3.60	80.00	56.00	32.00
10.00	7.00	4.00	85.00	59.50	34.00
15.00	10.50	6.00	90.00	63.00	36.00
20.00	14.00	8.00	95.00	66.50	38.00
25.00	17.50	10.00	100.00	70.00	40.00

dark, or if you're visually impaired, it's useful to keep in mind that the $2 coin is the heaviest, and it's smaller than the $1 piece. Prices in Australia often end in a variant of 1¢ and 2¢ (for example, 78¢ or $2.71), a relic from the days before 1¢ and 2¢ pieces were phased out (prices are rounded to the nearest 5¢). Bank notes come in denominations of $5 (light purple), $10 (blue-green), $20 (orange), $50 (yellow-green) and $100 (pale blue). Most Australian bank notes are made from a sturdy plastic.

What Things Cost in Sydney	U.S. $
Taxi from the airport to the city center	12.60
Bus from Central Station to downtown	.91
Local telephone call from a pay phone	.28
Double at the Park Hyatt (very expensive)	427.00
Double at the Russell (moderate)	140.00
Double at the Lord Nelson (inexpensive)	77.00
Lunch for one, without wine, at Capitan Torres (moderate)	13.30
Lunch for one at Sketches (inexpensive)	9.00
Dinner for one at Merrony's (deluxe)	38.50
Glass of Fosters beer (285ml)	1.45
Can of Coca-Cola (375ml)	1.05
Cup of coffee (sitting down at a cafe)	1.55
Roll of Kodak ASA 100 film, 36 exposures	4.25
Adult admission to Taronga Zoo	10.50
Movie ticket	8.75
1 liter (.26 U.S. gallon) unleaded petrol (gas)	.55

ATMs, CREDIT CARDS & TRAVELER'S CHECKS   There are three ways to access and carry cash in Australia—using your bank card to withdraw cash from an ATM, paying by credit card everywhere you go, or carrying traveler's checks.

ATMs   One of the fastest, safest, and easiest methods is undoubtedly to withdraw money from your home bank account at an Australian automatic-teller machine (ATM). This allows you to get cash when banks and currency exchanges are closed, and it means your money is safely residing in your bank account back home earning interest until you withdraw it. It also means you get the better bank exchange rate, not the commercial rate charged at currency exchanges. You will be charged a fee for each withdrawal from an ATM, usually A$4 (U.S.$2.80) or so, but this still works out to be less expensive than cashing a traveler's check.

All of the biggest banks in Australia—ANZ, Commonwealth, National, and Westpac—are connected to the Cirrus network.

ANZ, Commonwealth, and National are also connected to Maestro. The Plus network is less common; only two of the big four banks, ANZ and National, are connected to it. ATMs are widely available in cities and the bigger towns, but in remote parts of the country and in small Outback towns, they can be conspicuous by their absence. It's a good idea to have cash (several hundred dollars) and a credit card as back-up when you foray into remote areas. Ask your bank at home for a directory of international ATM locations where your card is accepted. Both the **Cirrus** (☎ **800/424-7787;** www.mastercard.com/atm) and **Plus** (☎ **800/843-7587;** www.visa.com/atms) networks have automated ATM locators that list the banks in each country that will accept your card. ATMs in Australia accept both four- and six-digit PINs (personal identification numbers).

Credit Cards   Credit cards, of course, are another simple and safe way to handle your money. Visa and MasterCard are universally accepted in Australia; American Express and Diners Club less so. Definitely get a Visa or MasterCard before you leave home. Always have some cash on your person, as there are still a few merchants in Australia who do not take credit cards, especially in remote areas. Some merchants will not take cards for purchases under A$5 (U.S.$3.50) or A$10 (U.S.$7). If your credit card is linked to your bank account, you can use it to withdraw cash from an ATM (just keep in mind that interest starts accruing immediately on credit-card cash advances).

Traveler's Checks   While U.S.-dollar traveler's checks are widely accepted at banks, big hotels, and currency exchanges, many smaller hotels, restaurants, and businesses will have no idea what the exchange rate is when you present a U.S. check. For this reason, it is best to buy your checks in Australian dollars, as these will be accepted by most merchants big and small. Shop around for the best exchange rate and the lowest exchange fee. **Westpac** bank cashes traveler's checks for "free" (which means the fee is built into the exchange rate). **ANZ** charges A$6.50 (U.S.$4.55) for amounts under A$3,000 (U.S.$2,100); it cashes amounts over A$3,000 (U.S.$2,100) and all Visa traveler's checks for free. **Commonwealth** charges a A$7 (U.S.$4.90) fee. **National** charges a A$5 (U.S.$3.50) fee. Banks are generally cheaper than currency-exchange booths. Most banks are closed weekends, so it's a good idea to cash your checks Friday afternoon before 5pm.

3   When to Go

THE CLIMATE & HIGH/LOW TRAVEL SEASONS

Lots of things are "upside down" in the land Down Under, including the seasons. Because seasons are created by the earth tilting on its axis, when the United States, the United Kingdom, and other Northern Hemisphere countries have winter, Australia and the Southern Hemisphere have summer, and vice versa. Summer in Australia is officially December through February, fall (autumn) is March through May, winter is June through August, and spring is September through November. Remember the farther south you go, the colder it gets.

Temperatures in Sydney are pleasant year-round. If you visit in the Australian summer, you can take full advantage of the beaches, although March, April, and May are the rainiest months.

Sydney's Average Temperatures (°F) and Rainfall

	Jan	Feb	Mar	Apr	May	June	July	Aug	Sept	Oct	Nov	Dec
Max.	78	78	76	71	66	61	60	63	67	71	74	77
Min.	65	65	63	58	52	48	46	48	51	56	60	63
Days of Rain	8.3	9.1	12.3	12.5	12.3	11.0	11.0	8.4	7.9	7.7	7.9	7.2

Source: Australian Tourist Commission
Australia Vacation Planner.

HOLIDAYS

Aussies love their public holidays. It's fair to say they care more about getting the day off than they do about celebrating the actual holiday. Whenever some well-meaning authority suggests Australians should actually celebrate the holiday on the day it falls, rather than on the Monday following the weekend closest to the holiday to make a long weekend, there is a national outcry.

Try to stay away from Australia from Boxing Day (Dec 26) to the end of January, which is when Aussies take their summer vacations. Hotel rooms and seats on planes get scarce and very expensive. The 4 days at Easter (from Good Friday through Easter Monday) and all school holiday periods are also very busy, so book ahead. Almost everything shuts down on Good Friday, and much is closed Easter Sunday and Monday. Most things are closed until 1pm, if not all day, on ANZAC Day, a World War I commemorative day on April 25.

One of the world's richest horse races is the Melbourne Cup. Melbourne Cup Day might only be an official holiday in

Melbourne, but not a lot of work gets done anywhere in the country after lunchtime on Cup Day (the 1st Tues in Nov). Shops set up TVs for customers to watch the race, restaurants are full, and office workers take over the boardrooms to scoff chicken and champagne before the race starts. Cup Day, rather than Australia Day on January 26, is really Australia's "national day." Try getting a cab around 3:20pm when the horses bolt from the starting gates, and you will see why it's called "the race that stops a nation."

MAJOR NATIONAL HOLIDAYS

New Year's Day	January 1
Australia Day	January 26
Labour Day	1st Monday in March (WA)
Eight Hour Day	1st Monday in March (TAS)
Labour Day	2nd Monday in March (VIC)
Canberra Day	3rd Monday in March (ACT)
Good Friday	Varies
Easter Sunday	Varies
Easter Monday	Varies
ANZAC Day	April 25
May Day	1st Monday in May (NT)
Labour Day	1st Monday in May (QLD)
Adelaide Cup	3rd Monday in May (SA)
Foundation Day	1st Monday in June (WA)
Queen's Birthday	2nd Monday in June (except WA)
Royal National Show Day	2nd or 3rd Wednesday in August (QLD)
Queen's Birthday	Monday in late September/ early October (WA)
Labour Day	1st Monday in October (NSW, SA)
Melbourne Cup Day	1st Tuesday in November (Melbourne only)
Christmas Day	December 25
Boxing Day	December 26

SCHOOL HOLIDAYS

The school year in Australia is broken into four semesters, with 2-week holidays falling around the last half of April, the last week of June and the 1st week of July, the last week of September, and the 1st week of October. There's a 6-week summer/Christmas vacation from mid-December to the end of January.

Sydney 2000 Olympic Games Update

The Games of the XXVII Olympiad will be held in Sydney from September 15 to October 1. Approximately 10,000 athletes from some 200 countries will vie for gold, silver, and bronze in 28 sports. Events will primarily be held in two major Olympic "zones"—the Sydney Olympic Park and the Sydney Harbour Zone.

The Sydney Olympic Park, at Homebush Bay, a 30-minute drive from downtown Sydney, will be the site of the new 110,000-seat Stadium Australia, where the opening and closing ceremonies and soccer and track-and-field events will be held, and the Athletes' Village. Other venues constructed or under construction here include an indoor arena; a velodrome; and centers for tennis, baseball, and archery. Already open and in use at Homebush Bay are the Sydney Showground (where baseball, rhythmic gymnastics, and basketball preliminaries will be held, among other events), the Sydney International Athletic Centre, and the Sydney International Aquatic Centre.

Events to be held in the Sydney Harbour Zone include portions of the marathon, which will begin in North Sydney and head across the Harbour Bridge and through The Rocks, the Botanic Garden, and Darling Harbour before finishing at Stadium Australia; basketball, boxing, and weightlifting at Darling Harbour; and yachting in Sydney Harbour. Sydney's famous Bondi Beach will be the venue for beach volleyball, which was first introduced in Olympic competition in 1996 at the Atlanta Olympic Games.

What's a major sporting event without a mascot? The Sydney 2000 Olympic Games will have three such critters designed to

SYDNEY CALENDAR OF EVENTS

January

✪ **New Year's Eve.** Seeing the Sydney Harbour Bridge light up with fireworks is an event in itself. The main show is at 9pm, not midnight, so young kids don't miss out on the spectacle. Some of the best vantage points around Sydney Harbour are from Mrs. Macquarie's Point in the Royal Botanic Gardens; from New South Head Road on the hill beyond the eastern suburb of Rose Bay; from Cremone Point on the North Shore (the ferry from Circular Quay takes you right to it); and from the Sydney Opera House. You'll have to put up with crowds embody the spirit of the Games (merchandising?). All three are cuddly versions of native Aussie animals: Olly, an "honest, enthusiastic, and open-hearted" kookaburra; Millie, a sharp echidna (it's like a spiny-coated anteater) who's a "techno-whiz and information guru"; and Syd, a "focused, dynamic, and enthusiastic" platypus.

GETTING TICKETS   Details on how Australians can apply for (or, more likely, since the demand for tickets will no doubt be high, enter a national ballot for) Sydney 2000 tickets will be released by the **Sydney Organising Committee for the Olympic Games (SOCOG)** in mid 1999. For more information, contact SOCOG's Web site at www.sydney.olympic.org.

Eighty percent of the approximately 5.5 million tickets will be sold in Australia; residents of other countries should check with their country's National Olympic Committee for details on obtaining tickets.

In the United States, **Cartan Tours, Inc.,** 1334 Parkview Ave., Suite 210, Manhattan Beach, CA 90266 (☎ **800/818-1998** or 310/546-9662; fax 310/546-8433), is the Official Ticket Agent responsible for the exclusive sale of tickets to the general public. To request information or receive *Cartan's Olympic Brochure,* call or visit the agency's Web site at www.cartan.com or contact them via e-mail at sales@cartan.com. Cartan will also offer a variety of exclusive travel packages.

Of course, several events, including the marathon, are open to spectators free of charge.

no matter where you go, but if you can't stand a crush, avoid the hugely popular areas around The Rocks and the Opera House. Pack a picnic and stake your spot around 6pm if you don't want to end up watching the fireworks standing up with the crowds.

- **Sydney Festival.** A summertime visual- and performing-arts festival, with impromptu nightclubs, outdoor cinema by the Opera House, and more. Highlights are the free concerts held Saturday nights in the Domain near the Botanic Gardens. Contact the Sydney Festival, Level 11, 31 Market St., Sydney, NSW 2000 (☎ **02/9265 0444;** fax 02/9264 9495). From January 1 for 1 month.

• **Australia Day.** Australia's answer to July 4 marks the landing of the First Fleet at Sydney Cove in 1788. Most Aussies celebrate by heading to the nearest beach and plopping down on the sand, but every large town and city has some kind of celebration in a major park or public space during the day. In Sydney, there are ferry races on the harbor, free performing arts at Darling Harbour, and fireworks in the evening. January 26 (always celebrated on the nearest Monday as a long weekend).

March

✪ **Sydney Gay and Lesbian Mardi Gras.** A spectacular parade of floats, costumes, and dancers, concentrated on Oxford Street, is the culmination of a month-long gay and lesbian celebration. *A tip:* Find something to stand on (many people bring plastic milk crates); otherwise you'll see nothing more than the tops of heads. Contact Sydney Gay and Lesbian Mardi Gras, 21-23 Erskineville Rd., Erskineville, NSW 2043 (☎ **02/9557 4332;** fax 02/9516 4446). Usually the last Saturday night in February; occasionally the 1st Saturday in March.

June

• **Sydney International Film Festival.** World and Australian premieres of leading Aussie and international flicks are shown in the ornate State Theatre. Tickets start at A$21 (U.S.$14.70) for any three films, or you can pay up to A$245 (U.S.$171.50) for a 2-week subscription to the best seats in the house. Contact the Sydney Film Festival, 405 Glebe Point Rd., Glebe, NSW 2037 (☎ **02/9660 3844;** fax 02/9692 8793; e-mail: info@sydfilmfest.com.au). Runs for 2 weeks from 1st Friday in June.

August

• **Sun-Herald City to Surf,** Sydney. Tens of thousands of Sydneysiders pound the pavement annually on a 14-kilometer (9-mile) "fun run" from the city to Bondi Beach. There are also walking and wheelchair categories. Entry is around A$25 (U.S.$17.50) for adults and A$15 (U.S.$10.50) for kids. For an entry form, write to the Sun-Herald City to Surf, 201 Sussex St., Sydney, NSW 2000 (☎ **02/9282 2822;** fax 02/9282 2360), or enter on the day of the race. Usually the 2nd Sunday in August, but it may be a month earlier in 2000 to avoid clashing with the Olympics.

December

• **Sydney to Hobart Yacht Race.** Find a cliff-top spot near the Heads to watch the glorious show of spinnakers as a hundred or so yachts leave Sydney Harbour for this grueling world-class 5-day event. Contact **Tourism New South Wales** (☎ **02/9931 1111**) or **Tourism Tasmania** (☎ **03/6230 8233**). Starts December 26.

- **Sydney Harbour Jazz Festival.** This recent addition to the Sydney summer scene is really shaping up. Australian and international jazz artists perform at free concerts in front of the Sydney Opera House, in The Rocks, at Star City, and around Darling Harbour. Call ☎ **02/9931 1571** for details. December 26 to December 31.

4 Health & Insurance

You don't have a lot to worry about health-wise on a trip to Sydney. Hygiene standards are high, hospitals are modern, and doctors and dentists are all well educated. No vaccinations are needed to enter the country unless you have been in a yellow-fever danger zone—that is, South America or Africa—in the past 6 days. If you are carrying any kind of medication, bring a letter from your doctor saying what the generic name of the drug is, what it is used for, and why you need it. You are unlikely to use the letter, but it avoids any potential confusion at the Immigration desk. Australia has restrictions on the quantity of prescription drugs you can carry. Usually a 3-month supply is the maximum, so if you are carrying large amounts of medication, it's a good idea to contact the **Australian embassy** in Washington (☎ **202/797 3000**) just to check that your supply does not exceed the maximum allowed amounts of that drug. If you need more medication while you're in Australia, you will need to get an Australian doctor to write the prescription for you.

It's a long trip Down Under (no matter where you're coming from!) so ask your doctor to recommend treatments for common problems like travel sickness, insomnia, jet lag, constipation, and diarrhea. Drink plenty of water on the plane as the air-conditioning dehydrates you quickly.

Some health plans include a modicum of overseas travel insurance, but check exactly what yours does and does not include. You might want to be sure your policy covers the cost to fly you back home in a stretcher, along with a nurse, should that be necessary. A stretcher takes up three coach-class seats. Your travel agent can easily sell you a comprehensive travel policy that will cover cancellation, theft, loss, medical treatment, and medical evacuation. If you hold British or New Zealand citizenship, you are covered for medical expenses (but not evacuation) by Australia's national health system.

A TIP ABOUT THE SUN　The reason Australians have the world's highest skin-cancer death rate is the country's intense sunlight. There are three kinds of ultraviolet (UV) sun rays: UVA, UVB, and UVC. UVC rays, the most dangerous, and half of the UVB rays, are usually kept out by ozone, which is why the largish seasonal hole in the ozone layer over the Antarctic every spring is such a problem. UVB and UVA rays go straight through clouds, so an overcast day is no protection against sunburn. UVA and UVB are most dangerous when they shine together, which is from around 11am to 3pm in summer and 10am to 2pm in winter. Aussies run for the shade during these hours. *Remember:* Scattered UV rays that bounce off surfaces such city walls, the water, and even the ground can burn you, too, even if you are not in direct sunlight. When you are out sightseeing, always wear a broad-brimmed hat that covers the back of your neck, ears, and face (not a baseball cap); sunscreen with a Sun Protection Factor (SPF) of 30 (make sure it's a "broad-spectrum" product that protects you against both UVA and UVB rays); and a long-sleeved shirt to cover your forearms.

Don't even think about coming to Oz without sunglasses, or you'll spend your entire vacation with your eyes shut against Australia's "diamond light," so called because it's so bright it cuts your eyes like a knife.

A NOTE ABOUT SMOKING　Lighting up in public is increasingly likely to draw frowns of disapproval from those around you. Smoking in many public areas, such as offices, cinemas, and theaters, is restricted if not banned. Smokers can take heart that few Oz restaurants are totally nonsmoking yet; they just have smoking and nonsmoking sections, not necessarily effective in keeping the fumes away from the nonsmokers. Pubs are definitely a territorial victory for smokers; after a night in an Aussie pub, nonsmokers go home smelling as if they smoked the whole pack (which they probably did, albeit passively). Australian aircraft on all domestic and international routes are completely nonsmoking, even on long-haul flights to the United States and Europe.

5　Tips for Travelers with Special Needs

FOR TRAVELERS WITH DISABILITIES　Most tour attractions and hotels have wheelchair access, and virtually every chain hotel in Australia has rooms specifically designed for people in wheelchairs. Many smaller lodges and even B&Bs are starting to cater to guests with disabilities. National parks make a big effort to include wheelchair-friendly pathways through their more pictur-esque scenery.

An excellent source of information on all kinds of facilities and services in Australia for people with disabilities is the **National Information Communication Awareness Network (NICAN)**, P.O. Box 407, Curtin, ACT 2605 (☎ **1800/806 769** in Australia or 02/6285 3713; fax 02/6285 3714; e-mail nican@spirit.com.au). This free service can supply you with contact details on accessible ac-commodations and tour attractions throughout Australia and put you in touch with travel agents and tour operators who understand your needs.

FOR GAY & LESBIAN TRAVELERS   Sydney is probably the biggest gay city in the world after San Francisco. Across most of Australia, the gay community has a high profile and lots of support services. The annual Sydney Gay and Lesbian Mardi Gras is a high point on the city's calendar for people of all sexual persuasions and attracts a lot of gay visitors from around the world.

The **International Gay & Lesbian Travel Association (IGLTA)**, 4331 N. Federal Hwy., #304, Fort Lauderdale, FL 33308 (☎ **954/776 2626;** fax 954/776 3303), can put you in touch with gay-friendly travel agencies, hotels, tour operators, and other travel-related companies that specialize in or welcome gay business. The IGLTA has an **Australia/New Zealand chapter** in Sydney at P.O. Box 1397, Rozelle, NSW 2039 (☎ **02/9818 6669;** fax 02/9818 6660). One of the biggest travel agencies specializing in gay travel in Australia is **Jornada Travel,** 263 Liverpool St., Darlinghurst, NSW 2010 (☎ **02/9360 9611;** fax 02/9326 0199; www.jornada. com.au).

The *Sydney Star Observer* is Australia's premier weekly gay news-paper available free from newsagents, clubs, and cafes. *Outrage* is a monthly glossy magazine sold in newsagents. Some services you may find useful are the **Gay And Lesbian Counselling Service of NSW** (☎ **02/9207 2888** for the administration office), which runs a hot line from 4pm to midnight (☎ 02/9207 2800) and a 24-hour re-corded information line (☎ 02/9207 2822). **The Albion Street Centre** in Surry Hills in Sydney is an AIDS clinic and information service. Its information line is ☎ **1800/451 600** in Australia or 02/9332 4000.

FOR SENIORS   Aussies call their seniors by the rather unlovely term "pensioner," so if you see "discounts for pensioners" offered anywhere and you're over 55, it's referring to you! Unfortunately, seniors visiting Australia from other countries don't always qualify for the discounted entry prices to tours, attractions, and events that Australian seniors enjoy. Always flash some ID and ask, however, as this policy varies from one operator to the next. Many smaller tour operators change their discount policy for seniors as often as they change their underwear, depending on how well business is doing that week. The best ID is something that marks you as an "official" senior, like a membership card from the **American Association of Retired Persons (AARP),** 601 E St. NW, Washington, DC 20049 (☎ **800/424-3410** in the U.S.). Membership in AARP is open to working or retired people over 50 and costs U.S.$8 a year.

Elderhostel, 75 Federal St., Boston, MA 02110-1941 (☎ **617/ 426 8056**), is a nonprofit organization that sells educational package tours, including ones to Australia, for travelers 55 years and over. It also has a Canadian office at 4 Cataraqui St., Kingston, Ontario K7K 1Z7 (☎ 613/530 2222).

The Australian College for Seniors at the University of Wollongong, south of Sydney (☎ **02/4221 3531;** fax 02/4226 2521; e-mail acfs@uow.edu.au), runs about 20 trips a year within Australia, including some tailored specifically from North America. The college is the Australian representative for Elderhostel.

Senior Tours, Level 2, 32 York St., Sydney, NSW 2000 (☎ **02/ 9262 6140;** fax 02/9262 2085), is a travel company specializing in vacations for seniors in Australia.

If you need help or advice on any matter at all once you get to Sydney, contact the **Seniors Information Service** (☎ **13 1244** in New South Wales) for free assistance.

FOR FAMILIES   Your kids will love you forever if you bring them to Australia for a holiday. Most Australian vacations are outdoorsy, fun, action-oriented, and relaxed, which suits kids down to the ground. They will get a big kick out of cuddling up to koalas and kangaroos, too.

If there is one drawback to taking children Down Under, it's enduring the time it takes to get here. The flight is a long one, so it's important to keep the kids comfortable and amused—for your sake, if not for theirs! Ask your airline what facilities it has onboard for kids. It should have diaper-changing tables for babies, coloring books and the like, and kids' menus. Most airlines are in the process of installing in-seat videos in all classes, if they have not done it already, so check on that too—it could make the difference between a tolerable flight and the journey from hell. If you are traveling with a baby, airlines often let you request a bulkhead seat with more room. If you fly business or first class, check to see if the airline allows kids up there with you. They may have to go coach instead.

An increasing number of big hotel chains are cottoning to the fact that children travel, and are offering free or inexpensive kids' clubs that take the little ones out of your hair for a while—or all day and all evening if you like! The **Southern Pacific Hotels** chain, which operates Travelodge, Parkroyal, and Centra hotels in Australia, has A$7 (U.S.$4.90) two-course children's menus at all its hotels and extensive kids' clubs at a few of its resorts. **Accor Asia Pacific,** which operates Sofitel, Novotel, Mercure, and Ibis hotels in Australia, has a Gecko Club for kids at a number of popular family destinations.

Most hotels in Australia accommodate children free in your room if they use existing beds; if a hotel does charge extra for a child, it's usually only A$20 (U.S.$14) at the most. Don't forget to ask what other services the hotel offers—nearly all of them have high chairs, bottles, and cribs (called cots), and many will arrange baby-sitting given a day's notice. Consider taking a serviced apartment if you have two or more children. These are a great idea for families because they often cost considerably less than a hotel room, yet give you an ample living room, a kitchen to keep meal costs down, often two bathrooms, and the privacy of a separate bedroom for adults.

Rascals in Paradise, 650 Fifth St., San Francisco, CA 94107 (☎ **800/U RASCAL** or 415/978 9800; fax 415/442 0289; e-mail: trips@RascalsInParadise.com), tailors family vacation packages to Australia that suit both the kids and you.

FOR STUDENTS It's cheap, sporty, laid-back, has stunning scenery, great weather, fun pubs, and beautiful beaches—in other words, paradise for students. The Australian Tourist Commission identified student travelers or "backpackers" as one of its biggest-spending markets, and publishes a groovy vacation guide just for them called *Australia Unplugged* (see "Visitor Information," earlier in this chapter).

STA Travel (☎ **1800/637 444** in Australia, 800/781-4040 in the U.S., 171/361 6161 in the U.K., or 09/307 0555 in New Zealand) is a good source of tips and advice for traveling Down Under as a student. It specializes in discounted airfares for students and any traveler under 26. It also sells Australian rail passes, its own brand of travel insurance, and, most important of all, International Student Identity Cards (ISIC), an essential item for any globe-trotting student. The ISIC is the most widely recognized proof in

Australia that you really are a student. Flash one of these and you are usually assured a discount to a wide variety of tours and attractions. It costs U.S.\$20 and is available to any student over 12 years of age who is enrolled in a diploma or degree program at an accredited secondary or tertiary institution. Check out STA Travel's Web site at www.sta-travel.com.

If you want to join a package tour with people your age, **Connection Holidays** (☎ 02/9262 2444, or call Australian Travel Vacations at ☎ 888/287-8728 in the U.S. or Goway Travel at ☎ 800/387-8850 in Canada) and **Contiki Holidays** (☎ 800/CONTIKI in the U.S. and Canada or 02/9511 2200 in Australia) specialize in packages for 18- to 35-year-olds. These trips attract a lot of Australians, too, so they are a good way to meet locals. Vacations for the 18-to-35 age bracket are renowned in Australia for involving lots of alcohol (mostly consumed by Australian passengers, we should add), so be prepared for a few raucous nights.

Students have plenty of choices when it comes to finding cheap accommodation in hostels and backpacker lodges across Australia, where you can get a bed dirt cheap—as little as A\$11 (U.S.\$7.70)—if you don't mind sharing with strangers. Part of the fun of traveling is meeting other funsters like yourself, anyhow, so backpacking makes a lot of sense.

The **Australian Youth Hostels Association (YHA),** the Australian arm of Hostelling International, has 130 hostels in Australia. Despite the name, people of any age can stay at the hostels. Although quality and facilities may vary, all YHA hostels keep to a high standard of cleanliness and all have communal kitchens and 24-hour access. To stay at a YHA property you need to join the association. Ideally, do this before you arrive in Australia. In the United States, contact **Hostelling International,** P.O. Box 37613, Washington, DC 20013-7613 (☎ **202/783-6161**), or join at any of the 150 hostels in the United States. Membership is U.S.\$10 if you are 17, U.S.\$25 if you are 18 to 54, and U.S.\$15 if you are 55 years or older. Membership is valid for 12 months and gives you access to 5,000 or so hostels worldwide. You can download a membership application form from the Hostelling International Web site at www.hiayh.org. It is possible to join once you arrive in Oz—for A\$27 (U.S.\$18.90)—at some but not all Australian hostels and at YHA Membership and Travel Centres in all state capital cities. In Sydney, go to 422 Kent St., Sydney (☎ **02/9261 1111**). Ring the YHA national administration office in Sydney (☎ **02/9565 1699**) for the locations of membership centers in other states. Membership gets you worthwhile discounts on other kinds of travel and travel-related stuff, too. In 1998, these included 30% discounts on Avis and Budget rental cars; discounts on Hertz rental cars, a 10% discount on Greyhound Pioneer and McCafferty's bus travel and on train travel including the Indian Pacific, The Ghan, and the Overlander; 10% off AAT Kings tours; and up to 10% off Paddy Pallin camping gear and outdoor clothing.

It is generally a good idea to book a hostel at least a day in advance, especially in high season. To do this, you need to pay in full, either by credit card over the phone—the simplest method—or by writing or faxing the hostel with a check or credit-card details. If you want to book more than one hostel in advance, you pay a A$2 (U.S.$1.40) fee. To book a hostel from outside Australia, you can either call or fax the hostel direct with payment, or call the International Booking Network (IBN) at Hostelling International in Washington (see above). Through the IBN, you pay in Australian dollars and skip the currency exchange fees, although IBN will charge you a small booking fee. Note that YHA properties are nonsmoking.

YWCA (☎ **1800/249 124** in Australia or 03/9329 5188) has comfortable budget hotels with private rooms, not dormitories, that are a cut above the average backpacker hostel. Rates for a double range from A$35 to $80 (U.S.$24.50 to $56).

The **Homestay Network** (see "Tips on Accommodations," later in this chapter) specializes in placing students with Sydney families on a bed-and-breakfast or three-meals-a-day basis. This is a nice way to be part of Australian daily life and is a great way to settle into Sydney if you are staying on a long-term basis. Student placements will cost around A$185 (U.S.$129.50) a week with all meals included. There is a A$120 (U.S.$84) booking fee if you stay for 4 weeks or more.

6 Flying to Australia

There's no doubt about it—Australia is a lo-o-o-ng flight from anywhere except New Zealand. Sydney is a 14-hour nonstop flight from Los Angeles, longer if your flight stops in Honolulu. From the East Coast, add $5^1/_2$ hours. If you're coming from the states via Auckland, add transit time in New Zealand plus another 3 hours for the Auckland-Sydney leg. The real killer, though, is coming from the United Kingdom. Prepare yourself for a flight of more or less 12 hours from London to Asia, then a long day in transit, as flights to

Australia have a nasty habit of arriving in Asia early in the morning and departing around midnight. And the 8- to 9-hour flight to Sydney is still ahead of you!

THE MAJOR CARRIERS   **United** has daily nonstop flights from Los Angeles and San Francisco to Sydney, a daily nonstop from Los Angeles to Melbourne, and daily Los Angeles–Auckland-Melbourne service. **Qantas** operates two daily nonstop flights from Los Angeles to Sydney, and daily Los Angeles–Melbourne service via Auckland. **Air New Zealand** has 13 nonstop flights from L.A. to Sydney a week, and makes 24 flights a week from L.A. to Auckland, where you can connect to Sydney, Melbourne, Brisbane, Perth, and Cairns. **Canadian Airlines** operates a daily codeshare service with Qantas, which means you will fly a Canadian Airlines aircraft to Honolulu and continue on your journey, with the same flight number, on a Qantas aircraft to Sydney. Smokers, and those with a low tolerance for cigarette smoke, should note that all Qantas flights worldwide are totally nonsmoking.

British Airways and Qantas both operate daily one-stop flights from London to Sydney, Melbourne, Brisbane, and Perth. More than a dozen carriers fly between London or Manchester and Australia.

Here are toll-free reservations numbers for the major international airlines serving Australia. The "13" prefix in Australia means the number is charged at the cost of a local call from anywhere in the country.

Major carriers flying from the United States:

- **Air New Zealand** (☎ **800/262-1234** in the U.S., 800/663-5494 in English and 800/799-5494 in French in Canada, 0800/737 0000 in New Zealand, or 13 2476 in Australia)
- **Canadian Airlines** (☎ **800/665-1177** in Canada and the U.S. or 1300/655 767 in Australia)
- **Qantas** (☎ **800/227-4500** in the U.S. and Canada or 13 1211 for international flights or 13 1313 for domestic flights in Australia)
- **United Airlines** (☎ **800/241-6522** in the U.S. and Canada or 13 1777 in Australia)

  Major carriers flying from the United Kingdom:

- **British Airways** (☎ **0345/222 111** in the U.K. or 02/9258 3300 in Australia)
- **Cathay Pacific** (☎ **0171/747 8888** in the U.K. or 13 1747 in Australia)

- **Malaysia Airlines** (☎ **0171/341 2020** or 0181/740 2626 in the U.K., 13 2627 in Australia)
- **Qantas** (☎ **0345/747 767** in the U.K., 13 1211 for international flights or 13 1313 for domestic flights in Australia)
- **Singapore Airlines** (☎ **0181/747 0007** in London, 0161/830 8888 in Manchester, 13 1011 in Australia except Cairns, or 07/4031 753 in Cairns)
- **Airways International** (☎ **0171/491 7953** in the U.K. or 13 1960 in Australia)

FINDING THE BEST AIRFARE   When you discover how high airfares are to Australia, you will freak out. They can easily be a third of the cost of your whole trip. For example, at the time this book was published, a regular Qantas fare from Los Angeles to Sydney was U.S.$3,920. That's just to sit in zoo class, as Australians unkindly refer to coach. Business class was U.S.$6,582 and first class was a steal at U.S.$10,426.

You can, however, minimize the hole in your wallet by purchasing a less expensive "restricted" ticket, which all of the airlines offer. Your best bet is a 21-day advance-purchase Super APEX fare, which can drop the fare to just U.S.$1,058 in low season, U.S.$1,308 in shoulder season, and U.S.$1,558 in high season. The catch is you must stick to a 7-day minimum and 1-month maximum stay in Australia, no stopovers are allowed (so no Hawaii or New Zealand interludes), and you can't change the routing once you have paid for the ticket.

If you are coming from America, **high season** is December through February. **Shoulder season** is September through November, and again from March to mid-April. **Low season** is mid-April to the end of August—happily, this happens to be the best time to travel most parts of Australia.

One step up from the Super APEX is what Qantas calls its Custom APEX fare, which for U.S.$150 extra will give you one free stopover and the option to buy more and the freedom to change your routing as long as you give 14 days' notice and pay a U.S.$75 fee. You are also allowed a maximum 3-month stay and the option to stay 6 months for an extra U.S.$150. These tickets need to be bought at least 14 days in advance. Super APEX and Custom APEX fares are U.S.$60 cheaper if you depart Monday to Thursday.

Keep an eye out for spot special deals, too. Unexpected lows in airline passenger loads often lead airlines to put cheap offers on the market. The catch is these usually have a short lead time, requiring you to travel in the next 6 weeks or so. Some deals involve taking a circuitous route, via Fiji or Japan for instance. Some travel agents that specialize in cheap fares to Australia include **Austravel** (☎ **800/ 633-3404** in the U.S.); **DownUnder Direct,** which is a division of Swain Australia (☎ **800/642-6224** in the U.S.); **Goway Travel** (☎ **800/387-8850** in the U.S. and Canada); and **South Pacific Travel Shops** (☎ 800/894-7722 in the U.S.).

The typical passenger ends up paying about U.S.$75 per person on top of their airfare to cover U.S. departure tax; Australian departure tax, which is included in the cost of your ticket when you buy it rather than paid at the Australian airport on your way home; agricultural taxes; and the like.

7   Booking a Package Tour

Many Australians get around their own country by taking a package tour because it's cheaper, and a package may be a good idea for you, too. There are two kinds of "package tours"—independent and escorted—and there are pros and cons of each.

Independent packages usually include some combination of airfare, accommodations, and car rental, with an occasional tour or shopping discount voucher book thrown in. The main advantage is that you get to travel around at your own pace and according to your own interests, rather than having to stick to a group schedule. You can travel safe in the knowledge that your car and hotel arrangements are already booked, leaving you free to get on with your day instead of fussing about finding a hotel for the night. Plus, each element of the package, airfare, hotel, or car rental, should cost less than if you had booked the same trip on your own.

Escorted tours have different advantages—you don't have to carry your own luggage, for starters. Nor do you need to constantly plan ahead, because your day is already planned for you. Plus, if you do have free time, there is someone to advise you on fun things to do and sometimes even make your tour bookings for you. A significant argument for escorted tours is that you usually have a well-informed guide who can offer interesting tidbits about the country as you go along, so that you'll probably learn more about the country than you would on your own. You also get to meet and travel with other people.

When choosing a package, think carefully about what you want to get out of your vacation. If you fancy an independent tour, think about whether you really want to book your own tours day after day, do all the driving yourself (on the wrong side of the road, don't forget!), and carry your own luggage. If you're considering joining an escorted tour, think about whether you really want your magical bushwalk in the Blue Mountains cut short because the schedule says at noon we all have to be back in Sydney for opal shopping. And can you stand the thought of traveling with strangers for days or weeks on end?

The following American companies offer independent packages Down Under: **Antipodes** (☎ 800/354-7471 in the U.S.), **Austravel** (☎ 800/633-3404 in the U.S.), **Inta-Aussie South Pacific** (☎ 800/531-9222 in the U.S. and Canada), **Qantas Vacations** (☎ 800/532-6709 in the U.S. or 800/268-7525 in Canada), and **Sunmakers Tours** (☎ 800/841-4321 in the U.S. and Canada).

Escorted tours are available from **Collette Tours** (☎ 800/340-5158 in the U.S. and Canada), **Globus & Cosmos** (☎ 800/338-7092 in the U.S. and Canada), **Maupintours** (☎ 800/255-4266 in the U.S. and Canada), **Premiere Vacations** (☎ 800/321-6720 in the U.S.), and **Sunbeam Tours** (☎ 888/955-G'DAY in the U.S.).

The following companies offer both independent and escorted tours: **ANZA Travel** (☎ 800/292-2399 in the U.S. and 800/667-G'DAY in Canada), **ATS Tours** (☎ 800/423-2880 in the U.S.), **Destinations Downunder** (☎ 312/332-1222), **Goway Travel** (☎ 800/387-8850 in the U.S. and Canada), **Kristensen International Travel & Tours** (☎ 800/635-5488 in the U.S. and Canada), and **Swain Australia Tours** (☎ 800/22-SWAIN in the U.S. and Canada). Swain Australia is owned and largely staffed by Aussies.

8 Tips on Accommodations

You'll find a wide range of accommodation choices in Sydney to suit every taste and budget. Some of the terms used in Australia may not be familiar to international visitors, so here's a brief rundown.

HOTELS   You will recognize many of the major hotel chains in Australia, including Hilton, Holiday Inn, Hyatt, Ibis, Inter-Continental, Marriott, Novotel, Radisson, Ramada, Ritz-Carlton, Sheraton, Sofitel, and Travelodge. Australia has a few hotel chains of its own, too, such as the deluxe Parkroyal; Centra, Gazebo, and Rydges, which cater to business travelers; Mercure, which varies widely in style and quality according to location; the boutique Sir Stamford; and the honest and affordable Country Comfort. The Australian company Mirvac Hotels runs an assortment of chains, including the boutique Sebel hotels; glamorous Quay West apartments in Sydney, Brisbane, and Auckland; and some stylish but affordable hotels in convenient city-fringe locations. Travelodge, incidentally, is a smarter, more midrange product Down Under than its U.S. counterpart. Novotel is an upscale but still affordable chain.

If you are prepared to forego the convenience and predictability of a chain, there are any number of moderately priced, individually run hotels that often offer a little more personal warmth and style than the big guys.

Amenities   It's a rare hotel room that does not have reverse-cycle air-conditioning for heating and cooling, a telephone, color TV, clock-radio, a minirefrigerator if not a minibar, an iron and ironing board, and self-serve tea and coffee. Private bathrooms are standard, although they often have only a shower, not a tub.

Rates & Deals   Australians are never shy to ask for a discount, so why should you be? As is the case all over the world, city hotels empty out on weekends when their business clientele deserts them. So appealing are some of the consequent weekend packages hotels offer to lure guests—free breakfasts, theater tickets, champagne, and so on—that many Aussies move three suburbs from home to a hotel for the weekend for a miniholiday! Country and seaside resorts, on the other hand, drop their rates to attract business during the middle of the week, when everyone is at work. The key to getting these good rates is simple—ask for them. If you don't ask, the hotel may try to sell you the most expensive "rack" rate, the official published rate, first.

Reservations   See the Appendix at the back of the book for a list of U.S., Canadian, U.K., and Australian reservations numbers for the major chains in Australia.

MOTELS & MOTOR INNS   You can usually rely on Australia's plentiful motels to be neat, clean, and bright. You can count on them having air-conditioning, a telephone, color TV, clock radio, a minirefrigerator or minibar, and self-serve tea and coffee. Most have only showers, not bathtubs. Some have a restaurant attached, and many have a swimming pool. Motor inns offer a greater range of facilities and fancier rooms than motels, without losing their down-to-earth touch or their affordability. Some of the big chains are **Best Western** (☎ **13 1779** in Australia, 800/780-7234 in the U.S. and Canada, 0800/39 3130 in the U.K., or 0800/237 893 in New Zealand); **Flag International** (☎ **13 2400** in Australia, 800/ 624-3524 in the U.S. and Canada, 0800/892 407 in the U.K., or

0800/803 524 in New Zealand); and **Sundowner Motor Inns** (☎ **1800/654 576** in Australia or 02/9747 8188). The **Country Comfort** chain listed above in "Hotels" also has motor inns.

BED & BREAKFAST INNS   Some B&Bs in Australia are a modest suburban home whose owners rent out a room to travelers; others are charming historical houses converted to accommodations; others still are purpose-built homes with several rooms designed for traveling guests, often with private bathrooms. Some larger commercial inns, with maybe 10 or 15 rooms, call themselves B&Bs. Whatever the style of building, the accommodation is usually cozy and the welcome warm. Staying in B&Bs is a terrific way to meet other travelers, and of course you get to meet your real Aussie hosts. Because you are staying in someone's home, there are a few considerations to take into account—you probably won't have access to a telephone unless the hosts let you use theirs; you may not have a TV, clock-radio, minibar, or other accoutrements you are used to in hotels and motels; they may not take credit cards; and your hosts, who have their own lives to live, may not be there to receive you 24 hours a day. Generally, check-in is usually in late afternoon and checkout at 10am or so. Bath facilities are usually shared with other guests, although quite a few B&Bs have at least one room with a private attached bathroom. A few offer dinner, but mostly you will need to eat out. Another plus of staying in B&Bs is the cost—rarely will you pay more than A$110 (U.S.$77) a double per night.

Travel agents rarely list B&Bs because the establishments are not big enough to pay commission. One excellent source is **Bed & Breakfast Australia,** P.O. Box 408, Gordon, NSW 2072 (☎ **02/9498 5344;** fax 02/9498 6438; www.bnba.com.au; e-mail: bnb@bnba.com.au). This Sydney-based booking service has hundreds of B&Bs on its books in cities, on farms, near beaches, and in wine regions all over the country. Accommodations are graded Economy (simple and clean with shared facilities), Quality (separate shared bathroom for guests and a desirable location), Superior (spacious rooms and private attached bathroom in most cases), and Superior Plus (usually private bathroom, somewhat luxurious). Rates range from A$85 to $120 (U.S.$59.50 to $84) double, including breakfast. Owners Carolyn and Cory Moore know their properties well and try to suit you to compatible hosts, houses, and locations. They can also find you lodgings in larger guesthouses and inns, suggest itineraries, and make car-rental bookings for you. If you like the idea of staying somewhere private, but don't really want to stay under the same roof as your host, they offer self-catering cottages with off-site hosts. The company requires a minimum booking of 2 nights, which can be spent at two separate locations. Cory and Carolyn also offer **Home Hosted Dinners,** where you get to have dinner with Aussie hosts at their home. Your host usually picks you up from your hotel and serves you a three-course home-cooked meal with wine. The price is A$65 (U.S.$45.50) per person.

Another good source is **The Australian Bed & Breakfast Book,** distributed by South Pacific Traveler's Booksource, Box 55, Wooster, OH 44691 (☎ **800/234-4552;** ☎ and fax 330/262 7821). It retails for U.S.$16.95. In the United Kingdom, contact **The Bed & Breakfast Book,** 16 Blenheim St., Hebden Bridge, West Yorkshire, HX7 8BU (☎ **01422/845 085;** fax 01422/845 875).

PUBS   Aussie pubs are really made for having a drink, not spending the night, but many do offer rooms upstairs, usually with shared facilities. Because most pubs are over 100 years old, the rooms can often either be old-fashioned in a cute kind of way—wrought-iron beds, pretty lace bedcovers, dark wood furniture, French doors onto wide verandas—or they can be just old, plain, and depressing. Pub accommodations are dying out in the cities, but pubs are a common enough place to stay in the country. Australians are rowdy drinkers, so sleeping over the front bar can be hellishly noisy, but the pub's saving grace is incredibly low rates. Most charge per person, not per room, and you would rarely pay more than A$50 (U.S.$35) per person a night. It is not hard to find a bed for as little as A$20 (U.S.$14) a night.

HOMESTAYS   If you want to stay with an Aussie family and really get involved in their life, even down to sitting at their table and eating three meals a day with them, ♦ **Homestay Network,** 5 Locksley St., Killara, NSW 2071 (☎ **02/9498 4400;** fax 02/9498 8324; www.citysearch.com.au/sydney/homestaynetwork; e-mail: thenetwork@bigpond.com), can place you in one of 1,400 homes in the wider Sydney area. Director Claudia Kohler says her customers appreciate being "part of the scene" right away instead of just wandering a new city as a tourist or stranger. Her service can match couples, singles, families, seniors, students, academics, and all kinds of travelers with Sydneysiders of like age and even like interest and profession. Prices vary widely depending on the grandeur of the home you want to stay in, and whether you want no meals, three meals, or just breakfast; as a rough guide, expect to pay about A$150

(U.S.$105) double with breakfast. Homestay Network will also arrange dinners or Aussie BBQs in Australian homes, which average A$40 (U.S.$28) per person, depending on how lavish you want the occasion to be. Another great service the Homestay Network offers is finding you a companion to take you shopping, to the theater, to a football match, or just out exploring the city. Expect to pay around A$50 (U.S.$35) per hour for your escort's time.

2

Getting to Know Sydney

*I*t would take you more time than you probably have to learn all the ins and outs of the Emerald City, with its numerous beaches, neighborhoods, and sprawling suburbs. Luckily, this book has done the legwork for you. What follows in this chapter is a crash course to get you oriented and on your way.

1 Orientation

ARRIVING   By Plane   Sydney International Airport is 8 kilometers (about 5 miles) from the city center. The International and Domestic terminals are separate but are linked by regular free shuttle buses. In both terminals you'll find free luggage carts, wheelchairs, a post office (open Mon to Fri from 9am to 5pm), mailboxes, duty-free shops (including one before you go through customs on arrival), restaurants, bars, stores, showers, luggage lockers, and tourist information desks. Caffé Italia on the Departures Level regularly wins awards for the best coffee in Sydney. There is also an Olympic Store here selling Sydney 2000 Olympic Games–related goods. The airport is completely nonsmoking. There is no phone number for the airport.

Getting into Town   Green and yellow **Airport Express buses** (☎ **131 500** in Australia) operated by State Transit travel to and from the city center and both the International and Domestic terminals between 5am and 11pm, stopping at various points along the way. The no. 300 bus runs to and from Circular Quay, The Rocks, Wynyard, and Town Hall every 20 minutes; the trip to Circular Quay takes about 45 minutes. Bus no. 350 runs to and from Kings Cross, Potts Point, and Elizabeth Bay every 20 minutes and takes around 30 minutes to reach Kings Cross. Both buses travel via Central Station (around 20 minutes from the International terminal). One-way tickets cost A$6 (U.S.$4.20) for adults, A$4 (U.S.$2.80) for kids under 16, and A$15 (U.S.$10.50) for a family (any number of children); round-trip is A$10 (U.S.$7) for adults, A$5 (U.S.$3.50) for kids, and A$25 (U.S.$17.50) for a family. You must

Greater Sydney

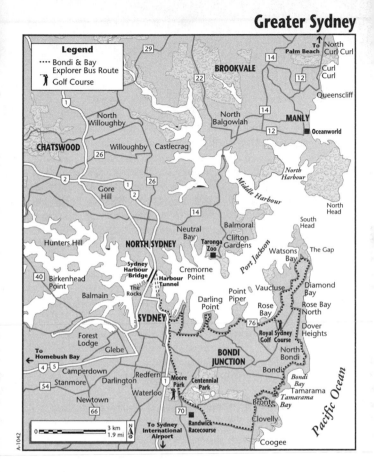

use the return portion within 2 months. A regular State Transit bus, no. 100, provides new rapid service from the airport to the northern beaches.

Kingsford Smith Airport Coach also operates to the city center, from bus stops outside the terminals. This service will drop you off (and pick you up) at your hotel (pickups require at least 1 hour's advance notice; call ☎ **02/9667 3221**). Tickets cost A$6 (U.S.$4.20) one-way and A$10 (U.S.$7) round-trip (the return portion can be used at any time in the future).

Privately operated shuttle buses also connect the airport with city center, Kings Cross, Darling Harbour, and Glebe hotels.

These buses depart when they're full and run from the city to the airport between 5am and 8pm and from the airport to the city between the first and last flights each day. Each company requires advance reservations for pickups from your hotel to the airport. Fares are A$6 (U.S.$4.20) one-way and A$10 (U.S.$7) round-trip.

The **Bondi Jetbus** (☎ **02/9664 2366** or 0500 886008; fax 02/9487 3554) will deliver you anywhere on the eastern beaches, including Bondi and Bronte. The trip costs A$8 (U.S.$5.60) for adults and A$4 (U.S.$2.80) for children. Call when you arrive at the airport, and they'll come pick you up within 15 minutes. The **Pittwater Airport Shuttle** (☎ and fax **02/9973 1877**) will take you to any of the northern beaches. A trip to Manly, for example, costs A$20 (U.S.$14) for the first person, A$10 (U.S.$7) for the second, and A$5 (U.S.$3.50) for each subsequent passenger. It leaves the airport around six times a day, so it may not be worth your while hanging around. Reservations (a day in advance) are essential; travel agents can make reservations.

A **taxi** from the airport to the city center costs between A$16 (U.S.$ 11.20) and A$20 (U.S.$14).

Premier Limousines (☎ **02/9313 4277**; fax 02/9313 5404) offers transportation to and from the city center in a sedan (for up to three people with luggage) for A$49 (U.S.$34.30), and in a stretch limo (for up to four people with luggage) for A$88 (U.S.$61.60).

A **rail link** from the airport to Central Station is due to be completed in time for the Olympics.

Taxi Tip

Especially in busy periods, cab drivers may try to insist that you share a cab with other passengers waiting in line at the airport. After dropping the other passengers off at various places around the city, the cab driver might then attempt to charge you the full price of the journey, despite the fact that the other passengers paid for their sections. You certainly won't save any money sharing a cab if this happens, and your journey will be a long one. I find it's often better to wait until you can get your own cab or catch an airport bus to the city center (and then take a taxi from there to your hotel, if necessary). If you are first in line in the taxi rank, the law states you can refuse to share the cab with anyone else.

By Train **Central Station** (☎ **13 15 00** for information) is the main city and interstate train station. It's at the top of George Street in downtown Sydney. All interstate trains depart from here, and it's a major CityRail hub. Many buses leave from here for Town Hall and Circular Quay. All buses departing from the main bus station on George Street (locals also call the top of George Street "Broadway") outside the main exit (follow the signs for "Countrytrains") go to Circular Quay or Town Hall. Buses departing from the side exit (Eddy Avenue) go to the eastern suburbs (such as Balmain and Glebe).

By Bus The **Greyhound-Pioneer Australia** terminal is on the corner of Oxford and Riley streets in Darlinghurst (☎ **13 20 30** in Australia or 02/9283 5977). The **Sydney Coach Terminal** (☎ **02/9281 9366**) is on the corner of Eddy Avenue and Pitt Street, near Central Station.

By Cruise Ship Cruise ships dock at the Overseas Passenger Terminal in The Rocks, just opposite the Sydney Opera House, or in Darling Harbour if The Rocks facility is already occupied by another vessel.

By Car Drivers coming into Sydney from the north enter the city on the Pacific Highway, those approaching from the south on the Hume and Princes highways, and those from the west on the Great Western Highway.

VISITOR INFORMATION The **Sydney Visitor Centre,** 106 George St., The Rocks (☎ **02/9255 1788**), is a good place for maps, brochures, and general tourist information and has two floors of excellent displays on The Rocks. The office is open daily from 6am to 6pm. Also in The Rocks is the **National Parks & Wildlife Centre** (☎ **02/9247 8861**), in Cadmans Cottage, 110 George St. If you are in Circular Quay, the **CityRail Host Centre** (no phone), opposite no. 5 jetty, has a wide range of brochures and a staff member on hand to help with general inquiries. It's open daily from 9am to 5pm. Elsewhere, the **Sydney Convention and Visitors Bureau** (☎ **02/9235 2424**) operates an information kiosk in Martin Place, near Castlereagh Street, Monday to Friday from 9am to 5pm. The **Manly Visitors Information Bureau** (☎ **02/9977 1088**), right opposite Manly beach near the Corso, offers general information but specializes in Manly and the northern beaches.

Electronic information on cinema, theater, exhibitions, and other events can be accessed through **Talking Guides** (☎ **13 16 20**).

Sydney at a Glance

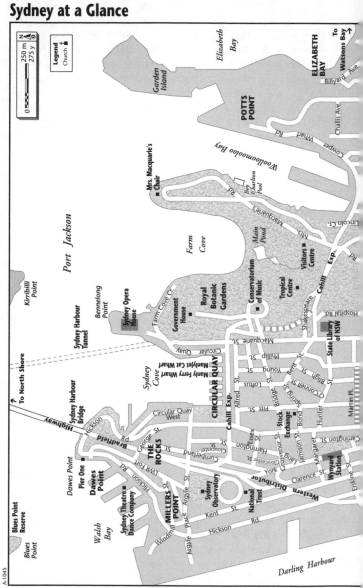

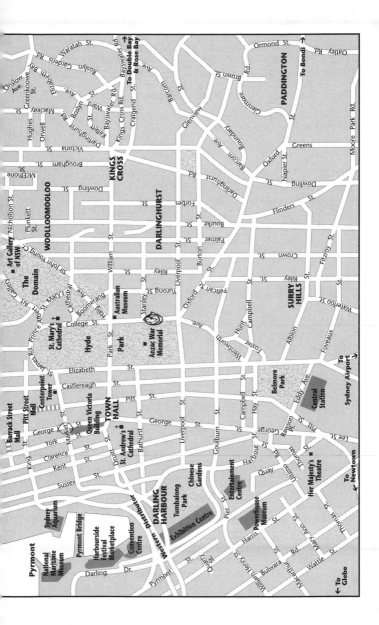

You'll need a code number for each topic, which you can find on page 3 of the A-K section of the *Sydney Yellow Pages* phone directory. The service costs the same as a local call.

CITY LAYOUT   Sydney is one of the largest cities in the world by area, covering more than 1,730 square kilometers (668 sq. miles) from the sea to the foothills of the Blue Mountains. The jewel in Sydney's crown is its harbor, which empties into the South Pacific Ocean through the headlands known simply as North Head and South Head. On the southern side of the harbor are the high rises of the city center; the Sydney Opera House; a string of beaches, including Bondi; and the inner-city suburbs. The Sydney Harbour Bridge and a tunnel take you northwards past the high rises of the North Sydney business district to the affluent northern suburbs and a series of beautiful ocean beaches, including the oceanfront resort suburb of Manly.

Main Arteries & Streets   The city's main thoroughfare, **George Street,** runs up from Circular Quay (pronounced "key"), past Town Hall and on past Central Station. A whole host of streets bisects the city parallel to George, including Pitt, Elizabeth, and Macquarie streets. **Macquarie Street** runs from the Sydney Opera House, past the Royal Botanic Gardens, colonial architecture, and Hyde Park. **Martin Place** is a long pedestrian thoroughfare that stretches from Macquarie to George streets. It's about halfway between Circular Quay and Town Hall—in the heart of the city center. The easy-to-spot **Centerpoint Tower,** facing onto the pedestrian-only Pitt Street Mall, is the main city-center landmark. Next to Circular Quay and across from the Opera House is **The Rocks,** a cluster of small streets that were once city slums but are now a tourist attraction. From Town Hall, roads converge on Kings Cross in one direction and Darling Harbour in the other.

SYDNEY NEIGHBORHOODS IN BRIEF

SOUTH OF THE HARBOR

Circular Quay   This transport hub for ferries, buses, and trains also has terrific views over the Harbour Bridge and the Sydney Opera House, both of which are just a few minutes' walk away. The quay is a good spot for a stroll, and its outdoor eateries and buskers (street musicians/performers) are very popular. The Rocks, the Royal Botanic Gardens, and the start of the main shopping area are all nearby. To reach the area via public transportation, take a CityRail train, a ferry, or a city-bound bus to Circular Quay.

The Rocks This historic area, just a short stroll west of Circular Quay, is closely packed with colonial stone buildings, intriguing back streets, boutiques, popular pubs, tourist stores, and top-notch restaurants and hotels. On weekends it's the home of The Rocks Market, with its many street stalls. To reach the area via public transportation, take any bus bound for Circular Quay or The Rocks (via George Street) or a CityRail train or ferry to Circular Quay.

Town Hall Right in the heart of the city, this area houses all the main department stores and is home to two Sydney landmarks, the Town Hall and the Queen Victoria Building (QVB), and is close to Centerpoint Tower. Farther up George Street are major cinema complexes, the entrance to the Spanish area (around Liverpool Street), and the city's large Chinatown. To reach the area via public transportation, take any bus from Circular Quay or The Rocks via George Street, or take a CityRail train to the Town Hall stop.

Darling Harbour Designed from scratch as a tourist precinct, Darling Harbour now features Sydney's main convention, exhibition, and entertainment centers; a huge waterfront promenade; the Sydney Aquarium; the giant screen IMAX Theatre; the Sega World theme park; the Australian Maritime Museum; the Powerhouse Museum; a major food court; and plenty of shops. Star City, Sydney's casino and theater complex, opened in late 1997. To reach the area via public transportation, take a ferry from Circular Quay (Wharf 5) or a monorail or light rail from city center.

Kings Cross & the Suburbs Beyond "The Cross," as it's known, is famous as the city's red-light district—though it's also home to some of the city's best-known nightclubs and restaurants. Beyond the strip clubs and glitter, attractive suburbs—Elizabeth Bay, Double Bay, Rose Bay, and Watsons Bay—hug the waterfront. To reach the area via public transportation, take bus no. 324, 325, or 327 from Circular Quay, or no. 311 from Railway Square, Central Station; take a CityRail train to Kings Cross station.

Paddington/Oxford Street This inner-city suburb, centered on trendy Oxford Street, is crammed with expensive terrace houses, off-the-wall boutiques, bookshops, popular restaurants, pubs, and nightclubs. It's also the heart of Sydney's gay community. To reach the area via public transportation, take bus no. 380 or 382 from Circular Quay (via Elizabeth Street) or no. 378 from Railway Square, Central Station.

Darlinghurst   Wedged between downmarket Kings Cross and upmarket Oxford Street, this extroverted and grimy terraced suburb is home to some of Sydney's finest cafes. Take a CityRail train to the Kings Cross stop.

Newtown   This popular student area is focused on busy King Street, with its many alternative shops, bookshops, and cheap ethnic restaurants. It's a major hub for food buffs in the know. Take bus no. 422, 423, 426, or 428 from Circular Quay (via Castlereagh Street and City Road), or take a CityRail train to the Newtown stop.

Glebe   A mecca for young professionals and students, Glebe is popular for its cafes, restaurants, pubs, and shops. Take bus no. 431, 433, or 434 from Millers Point, The Rocks (via George Street and Railway Square, Central Station).

Bondi & Other Southern Beaches   Some of Sydney's most glamorous surf beaches—Bondi, Bronte, and Coogee—can be found basking along the South Pacific Ocean coastline southeast of the city center. To reach the areas via public transportation, take bus no. 380, 382, or 389 to Bondi Beach from Circular Quay or a CityRail train to Bondi Junction to connect with the same buses; bus no. 378 to Bronte from Railway Square, Central Station (via Oxford Street); or bus no. 373 or 374 to Coogee from Circular Quay.

Watsons Bay   Watsons Bay is known for the Gap—a section of dramatic sea cliffs—as well as for several good restaurants, such as Doyles on the Beach, and the popular Watsons Bay Hotel beer garden. Take bus no. 324 or 325 from Circular Quay, or a ferry from Circular Quay (Wharf 2) on Saturday and Sunday.

NORTH OF THE HARBOR

North Sydney   Just across the Harbour Bridge, the high rises of North Sydney attest to its prominence as a major business area. Take a CityRail train to the North Sydney stop.

North Shore   Ferries and buses provide good access to these wealthy neighborhoods across the Harbour Bridge. Balmoral Beach, Taronga Zoo, and upmarket boutiques are the main attractions in Mosman, while Chatswood is a good bet for more-general shopping. Take bus no. 250 from North Sydney to Taronga Zoo, or a ferry from Circular Quay (Wharf 4). Take a CityRail train from Central or Wynyard stations to Chatswood.

Manly & the Northern Beaches   Half an hour away by ferry, or just 15 minutes by the faster JetCat, Manly is famous for its beautiful ocean beach and scores of cheap-food outlets. Farther north are more magnificent beaches popular with surfers. At the end of the line, Palm Beach has both magnificent surf and lagoon beaches, nice walks, and a scenic golf course. To reach the area via public transportation, take the ferry or JetCat from Circular Quay (Wharves 2 and 3) to Manly. Change at Manly interchange for various northern-beach buses. You can also take bus no. 190 from Wynyard Station.

WEST OF THE CITY CENTER

Balmain   Located west of the city center, a short ferry ride from Circular Quay, Balmain was once Sydney's main shipbuilding area. In the last few decades the area has become trendy and expensive. The suburb has a village feel about it and is filled with restaurants and pubs and hosts a popular Saturday market. Take bus no. 441, 442, or 432 from Town Hall or George Street, or a ferry from Circular Quay (Wharf 5).

Homebush Bay   This will be one of the major sites of the Sydney 2000 Olympic Games. Here you'll find the Olympic Stadium, the Aquatic Center, and the Homebush Bay Information Center, as well as parklands and a waterbird reserve. To reach the area via public transportation, take a CityRail train to Strathfield and connect with a shuttle bus.

2 Getting Around

BY PUBLIC TRANSPORTATION

State Transit operates the city's buses and the ferry network, CityRail runs the urban and suburban trains, and Sydney Ferries runs the public passenger ferries. Some private bus lines operate buses in the outer suburbs. For timetable information on buses, ferries, and trains, call the **InfoLine** at ☎ **13 15 00** (daily 6am to 10pm). In addition, a monorail connects the city center to Darling Harbour and a light-rail line runs between Central Station and Wentworth Park in Pyrmont. Pick up a *Sydney Transport Map* (a guide to train, bus, and ferry services) at any rail, bus, or ferry information office.

MONEY-SAVING PASSES   Several passes are available for visitors who will be using public transportation frequently—all are much cheaper than buying individual tickets. The **SydneyPass** is a great buy if you plan to do a lot of sightseeing. It allows 3, 5, or 7 days' unlimited travel on buses and ferries, including the high-speed

Sydney Transportation Systems

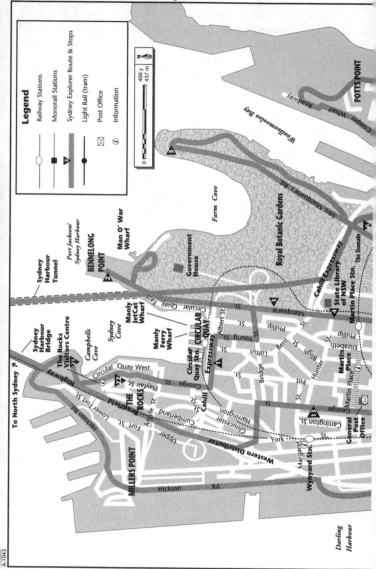

Legend

Railway Stations
Monorail Stations
Sydney Explorer Route & Stops
Light Rail (tram)
Post Office
Information

0   400 y
     437 m

POTTS POINT

Cowper Wharf

Woolloomooloo Bay

Cowper Wharf Roadway

Royal Botanic Gardens

Mrs Macquarie's Rd.

The Domain

Cahill Expressway

State Library of NSW

Martin Place Stn.

Farm Cove

Government House

Port Jackson/ Sydney Harbour

Man O' War Wharf

BENNELONG POINT

Sydney Harbour Tunnel

Macquarie St.

Phillip St.

Young St.

Albert St.

Bent St.

Bligh St.

Hunter St.

Elizabeth St.

Phillip St.

Martin Place

Martin Place

General Post Office

George St.

Circular Quay East

Manly JetCat Wharf

Manly Ferry Wharf

CIRCULAR QUAY

Circular Quay Stn.

Cahill Expressway

Sydney Cove

Loftus St.

Pitt St.

Bridge St.

Harrington St.

Carrington St.

York St.

Margaret St.

Wynyard Stn.

Western Distributor

Hickson   Rd.

To North Sydney

Sydney Harbour Bridge

The Rocks Visitors Centre

Campbells Cove

Circular Quay West

Bradfield Highway

Lower Fort St.

Hickson Rd.

Upper Fort St.

Fort St.

Argyle St.

Cumberland St.

Gloucester St.

Playfair St.

George St.

THE ROCKS

MILLERS POINT

Darling Harbour

A-1043

42

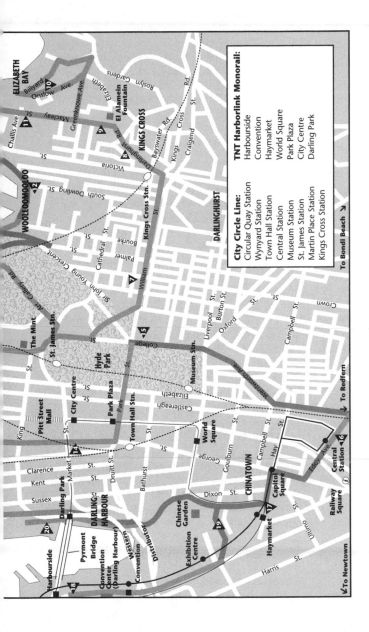

TNT Harborlink Monorail:

Harbourside
Convention
Haymarket
World Square
Park Plaza
City Centre
Darling Park

City Circle Line:

Circular Quay Station
Wynyard Station
Town Hall Station
Central Station
Museum Station
St. James Station
Martin Place Station
Kings Cross Station

To Bondi Beach ↗

↓ To Redfern

↙ To Newtown

43

JetCat services to Manly, the Red Sydney Explorer bus (see below), the Blue Bondi and Bay Explorer bus, the Airport Express bus, and all harbor cruises operated by State Transit. A 3-day pass costs A$70 (U.S.$49) for adults, A$60 (U.S.$42) for children under 16, and A$200 (U.S.$140) for a family; a 5-day pass runs A$95 (U.S.$66.50) for adults, A$80 (U.S.$56) for children, and A$270 (U.S.$189) for a family; a 7-day pass costs A$110 (U.S.$77) for adults, A$95 (U.S.$66.50) for children, and A$315 (U.S.$220.50) for a family. (State Transit defines a "family" as two adults and any number of children from the same family.) Buy tickets at the airport (proof of overseas residence required), Countrylink offices, Public Transport ticket offices, Circular Quay ferry ticket offices, and anywhere else a SydneyPass logo is displayed.

A **Weekly Travel Pass** allows unlimited travel on buses, trains, and ferries. There are six different color passes depending on the distance you need to travel. The passes most commonly used by visitors are the Red Pass and the Green Pass. The Red Pass costs A$23 (U.S.$16.10) and covers all transport within the city center and surrounding area (so this pass will get you aboard inner-harbor ferries, for example). The Green Pass, which costs A$29 (U.S.$20.30), will take you to more far-flung destinations, including the Manly Ferry (but not the JetCat). I recommend purchasing the Green Pass, just to be safe. You can buy either pass at newsagents or bus, train, and ferry ticket outlets.

The **Day Rover** gives you unlimited bus, train, and ferry travel for 1 day. Tickets cost A$20 (U.S.$14) for adults and A$10 (U.S.$7) for children for travel in peak hours, and A$16 (U.S.$11.20) for adults and A$8 (U.S.$5.60) for children for travel in off-peak hours. The pass is available at all bus, train, and ferry ticket offices.

A **Travelten** ticket offers 10 bus or ferry rides for a discounted price. A blue Travelten covers two sections on the bus route and costs A$8.60 (U.S.$6) for adults and A$4.40 (U.S.$3.10) for children; a red Travelten covers up to nine sections and costs A$17.60 (U.S.$12.30) for adults and A$8.80 (U.S.$6.15) for children. The Travelten ferry ticket costs A$17 (U.S.$11.90) for trips within the inner harbor (this excludes Manly). Buy Travelten tickets at newsagents, bus depots, or at the Circular Quay ferry terminal. If you will be traveling short distances mostly by bus, purchase a blue Travelten. *Note:* These tickets are transferable, so if two or more people are traveling together, you can each put the same ticket in the machine on the bus.

For a full day's unlimited travel by bus, you can't go wrong with the **Bus Tripper.** It costs A$7.80 (U.S.$5.45) for adults and A$3.90 (U.S.$2.75) for children 4 to 15, and can be bought from newsagents and at bus depots. An unlimited 1-day bus/ferry tripper costs A$12 (U.S.$8.40) for adults and A$6 (U.S.$4.20) for children.

BY PUBLIC BUS   Buses are frequent and reliable and cover a wide area of metropolitan Sydney—though you might find the system a little difficult to navigate if you're visiting some of the outer suburbs. The minimum fare (which covers most short hops within the city) is A$1.20 (U.S.85¢) for a 4-kilometer (2.5-mile) "section." The farther you go, the cheaper each section is. For example, the 44-kilometer (27-mile) trip to beautiful Palm Beach, way past Manly, costs just A$4.40 (U.S.$3.10). Sections are marked on bus-stand signs (though most Sydneysiders are as confused about them as you might be). Buses bound for the suburbs leave the main terminals of Circular Quay; Railway Square, next to Central Station; and York Street, behind Wynyard train station. Call ☎ **13 15 00** for timetable and fare information, or ask the staff at the **bus information kiosk** on the corner of Alfred and Loftus streets, just behind the Circular Quay railway station (☎ **02/9219 1680**). The kiosk is open Monday to Saturday from 8am to 8pm and Sunday from 8am to 6pm. Buses run from 4am to around midnight during the week, less frequently on weekends and public holidays. Some night buses to outer suburbs run after midnight and throughout the night. You can purchase single tickets onboard from the driver; exact change is not required.

BY RED SYDNEY EXPLORER BUS   These bright red buses travel a 35-kilometer (22-mile) circuit with 22 stops at top sightseeing attractions throughout the city. Passengers can get on and off anytime they like. Buses run every 20 minutes between 9am and 3pm. One-day tickets cost A$25 (U.S.$17.50) for adults, A$18 (U.S.$12.60) for children under 16, and A$60 (U.S.$42) for a family of two adults with two or more children. Tickets are sold onboard and are valid only on the day of purchase—so start early. Bus stops are marked with red-and-green SYDNEY EXPLORER signs. The same ticket gives free travel on any State Transit bus within the boundaries of the Explorer circuit until midnight on the day of purchase.

BY BLUE BONDI & BAY EXPLORER BUS   This bus operates on the same principle as the Red Sydney Explorer bus, but visits

Sydney's famous Bondi Beach and the scenic harbor suburbs of Double Bay, Rose Bay, and Watsons Bay. The bus covers a route of 45 kilometers (28 miles) in all and stops at 20 locations, including Circular Quay, the oceanfront suburbs of Bronte and Clovelly, the Royal Randwick Racecourse, and the Sydney Cricket Ground. Buses leave every 30 minutes between 9am and 6pm. The fare is A$25 (U.S.$17.50) for adults, A$18 (U.S.$12.60) for children under 16, and A$68 (U.S.$47.60) for a family.

BY FERRY & JETCAT   The best way to get a taste of a city that revolves around its harbor is to jump aboard a ferry. The main ferry terminal is at Circular Quay. Tickets can be purchased at machines at each wharf (there are also change machines) or at the main Circular Quay ticket offices. For ferry information call ☎ **13 15 00,** or visit the ferry information office opposite Wharf 4. Timetables are available for all routes.

Journeys within the inner harbor (virtually everywhere except Manly and Parramatta) cost A$3.20 (U.S.$2.25) for adults one-way and A$1.60 (U.S.$1.10) for children. The frequency of services varies. The ferry to Manly takes 30 minutes and costs A$4 (U.S.$2.80) for adults and A$2 (U.S.$1.40) for children. It leaves from Wharf 3. The rapid JetCat service to Manly takes 15 minutes and costs A$5.20 (U.S.$3.65) for adults and children alike. After 7:15pm all trips to and from Manly are by JetCat at ferry prices.

You can also a take a ferry to Taronga Zoo, just across the harbor. At the Taronga Zoo wharf, a bus will take you to the upper zoo entrance for A$1.20 (U.S.85¢), or you can take a cable car to the top for A$2.50 (U.S.$1.75). The lower entrance is 2 minutes up the hill. A combined ferry, bus, aerial safari, and zoo admission ticket costs A$21 (U.S.$14.70) for adults and A$10.50 (U.S.$7.35) for children.

Other places that can be reached by ferry include Darling Harbour, the Star City casino, Neutral Bay, Watsons Bay, Kirribilli, Cremorne, Balmain, Greenwich, Cockatoo Island, Hunters Hill, Meadowbank, and Parramatta. Ferries run from 6am to midnight.

Sydney Ferries also operates a special "Summer Harbor Beaches" service between Manly, Watsons Bay, and Balmoral on weekends only. This "loop" service allows you to get on and off when you want and rejoin a later ferry. Tickets, valid for 1 day, cost A$10 (U.S.$7) for adults and A$5 (U.S.$3.50) for children and include the return fare to Circular Quay. Timetables are available from the ferry information office opposite Wharf 4.

Sydney Ferries

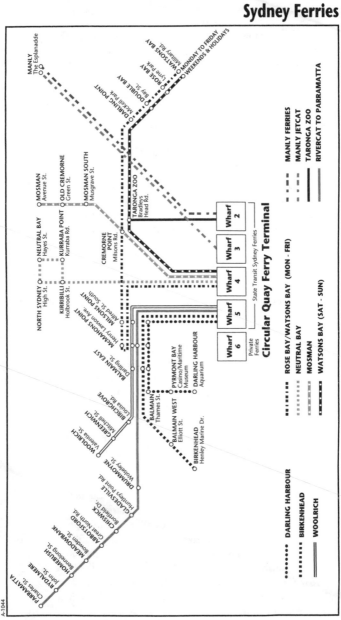

Circular Quay Ferry Terminal

| Wharf 2 | Wharf 3 | Wharf 4 | Wharf 5 | Wharf 6 |

State Transit Sydney Ferries

Private Ferries

MANLY The Esplanadde

MANLY
WATSONS BAY Military Rd.
MONDAY TO FRIDAY
WEEKENDS & HOLIDAYS
ROSE BAY Lyne Park
DOUBLE BAY Bay St.
DARLING POINT McKell Park
TO WATSONS BAY

MOSMAN Avenue St.
OLD CREMORNE Green St.
MOSMAN SOUTH Musgrave St.
TARONGA ZOO Bradleys Head Rd.

NEUTRAL BAY Hayes St.
KURRABA POINT Kurraba Rd.
CREMORNE POINT Milsons Rd.

NORTH SYDNEY High St.
KIRRIBILLI Hollbrook St.
MILSONS POINT Alfred St. South

McMAHONS POINT Henry Lawson Ave.

BALMAIN EAST Darling St.

PYRMONT BAY Casino/Maritime Museum
DARLING HARBOUR Aquarium

BALMAIN Thames St.
BALMAIN WEST Elliott St.
BIRKENHEAD Henley Marine Dr.

BIRCHGROVE Louisa Rd.
GREENWICH Mitchell St.
WOOLRICH Valetta St.
DRUMMOYNE Wolseley St.

CHISWICK Bortfield Dr.
CABARSVILLE Punters Point Rd.
ABBOTSFORD Great North Rd.
MEADOWBANK Bowden St.
HOMEBUSH Benming St.
RYDALMERE John St.
PARRAMATTA Charles St.

Legend:

- - - - **MANLY FERRIES**
- - - - **MANLY JETCAT**
────── **TARONGA ZOO**
────── **RIVERCAT TO PARRAMATTA**

▪▪▪▪ **ROSE BAY/WATSONS BAY (MON - FRI)**
░░░░ **NEUTRAL BAY**
░░░░ **MOSMAN**
▬▬▬ **WATSONS BAY (SAT - SUN)**

●●●● **DARLING HARBOUR**
■■■■ **BIRKENHEAD**
────── **WOOLRICH**

A-1044

47

At the time this book went to press, tours of **Homebush Bay,** the site of the new Olympic Park, were also available, including transport to the site on a Rivercat ferry up the Parramatta River. Tours depart Circular Quay Monday to Friday at 10am, 11am, noon, 1pm, and 1:30pm, and Saturday and Sunday at 10:35am and 12:25pm. Weekday tours cost A$15 (U.S.$10.50) per person; weekend tours cost A$22 (U.S.$15.40) per person and include an extra tour of the Aquatic Center, built specifically for the Sydney Olympic Games. Buy tickets at Wharf 5 before departure. Contact **State Transit** at ☎ **02/9207 3170** for more details.

BY HARBOUR EXPRESS   **Matilda Cruises** (☎ **02/9264 7377**) operates the high-speed Matilda Rocket that runs between Darling Harbour and Circular Quay daily from 9:30am to 4:30pm. The Rocket leaves Darling Harbour Aquarium Wharf on the half hour and Circular Quay Commissioner Steps (a small wharf opposite the Museum of Contemporary Art) at a quarter to the hour. The boat stops off at the Opera House and Darling Harbour Harbourside Shopping Center and includes commentary along the way. You get on and off when you want. The fare is A$16 (U.S.$11.20) for adults and A$8 (U.S.$5.60) for children 5 to 12; children under 5 are free. Buy tickets on the boat.

BY TRAIN   Sydney's **CityRail** train system is a cheap and relatively efficient way to see the city without experiencing the congestion on the roads in a bus or car. The system is limited, though, with many tourist areas—including Manly—not connected to the railway network. The CityRail system is somewhat antiquated and trains have a reputation of "running late and out of timetable order," so the best plan is just to show up—something will come along, eventually. All train stations have automatic ticket machines and most have ticket offices.

In the central region, the **City Circle** train line runs underground and stops at Central Station, Town Hall, Wynyard Station, Circular Quay, St. James Station, and Museum Station.

Off-peak return (round-trip) fares, which must be purchased after 9am, are the least expensive at A$2.20 (U.S.$1.55). Two single tickets work out to be more expensive than a round-trip. Information is available from **InfoLine** (☎ **13 15 00**) and at the **CityRail Host Centers** opposite Wharf 4 at Circular Quay (☎ **02/9224 2649**) and at **Central Station** (☎ **02/9219 1977**), both open daily from 9am to 5pm.

At the time this book went to press, a new train link from Bondi Junction to Bondi beach was being seriously discussed. If built, the privately financed train line is expected to cost A$5 (U.S.$3.50) round-trip and take around 10 minutes.

Countrylink trains are comfortable and efficient and operate out of Central Station to the far suburbs and beyond. For reservations call ☎ **13 22 32** between 6:30am and 10pm, or visit the **Countrylink Travel Center,** 11-31 York St. (☎ **02/9379 3111**), open Monday to Friday from 8:30am to 5pm, or the Countrylink Travel Center at Circular Quay, open Monday to Friday from 9am to 5:30pm and Saturday from 8am to 3pm.

BY MONORAIL   The monorail, with its single overhead line, is seen by many as a blight on the city and by others as a futuristic addition. The monorail connects the central business district to Darling Harbour. The system operates Monday to Wednesday from 7am to 10pm, Thursday and Friday from 7am to midnight, Saturday from 8am to midnight, and Sunday from 9am to 8pm. Tickets are A$2.50 (U.S.$1.75); children under 5 ride free. An all-day monorail pass is a good value at A$6 (U.S.$4.20). The trip from the city center to Darling Harbour takes around 12 minutes. Look out for the gray overhead line and the plastic tubelike structures that are the stations. I think this is the best way to get to Darling Harbour, particularly if you are shopping around Town Hall. Call **TNT Harbourlink** (☎ **02/9552 2288**) for more information.

BY SYDNEY LIGHT RAIL   A new system of "trams" opened in late 1997 with a route that traverses a 3.6-kilometer (2.2-mile) track between Central Railway Station and Wentworth Park in Pyrmont. The system provides good access to Chinatown, Paddy's Markets, Darling Harbour, Star City casino, and the Fish Markets. The trams run every 5 minutes in peak period and every 11 minutes off-peak. One-way fare is A$3.20 (U.S.$2.25) for adults and A$1.80 (U.S.$1.25) for children 4 to 15. Round-trip fare is A$4.40 (U.S.$3.10) for adults and A$2.60 (U.S.$1.80) for children.

BY TAXI   The city center and suburbs are serviced by several taxi companies. All journeys are metered. Extra charges apply if you call for a cab (A$1/U.S.70¢). You must also pay extra for waiting time, luggage weighing over 25 kilograms (55 lb.), and if you cross either way on the Harbour Bridge or through the harbor tunnel (A$2/ U.S.$1.40).

Taxis line up at ranks in the city, such as opposite Circular Quay and at Central Station, and are frequently hanging around hotels. A small yellow light on top of the cab means it's vacant. Cabs can be particularly hard to get on Friday and Saturday nights and between 2 and 3pm every day, when tired cabbies are changing shift after 12 hours on the road. Tipping is not necessary, but appreciated. It is compulsory for passengers to wear seat belts. The **Taxi Complaints Hot Line** (☎ **02/9270 6100**) deals with problem taxi drivers.

The main cab companies are **Taxis Combined Services** (☎ 02/9332 8888), **RSL Taxis** (☎ 02/9581 1111), **Legion Cabs** (☎ 131 451), and **Premier** (☎ 131 017). Call **Premier Limousines** (☎ 02/9451 5901) for your own chauffeur and limo.

BY WATER TAXI   Harbor Taxis, as they are called, operate 24 hours a day and are a quick and convenient way to get to waterfront restaurants, harbor attractions, and some suburbs. They can also be hired for private cruises of the harbor. A journey from Circular Quay to Watsons Bay, for example, would cost A$40 (U.S.$28) for two. An hour's sightseeing excursion around the harbor costs A$150 (U.S.$105) for two. There are two main operators, **Taxis Afloat** (☎ **02/9955 3222**) and **Water Taxis Combined** (☎ **02/9810 5010**).

BY CAR   Traffic restrictions, parking problems, and congestion can make getting around the city center by car a frustrating experience, but if you plan to visit some of the outer suburbs or take excursions elsewhere in New South Wales, then renting a car will give you more flexibility. The **NRMA**'s (National Roads and Motorists' Association—the New South Wales auto club) emergency breakdown service can be contacted at ☎ **13 11 11.**

Car-rental agencies in Sydney include **Avis,** 214 William St. (☎ 02/9357 2000); **Budget,** 93 William St. (☎ 13 28 48 or 02/9339 8888); **Dollar,** Domain Car Park, Sir John Young Car Park (☎ 02/9223 1444); **Hertz,** Corner of William and Riley streets (☎ 02/9360 6621); and **Thrifty,** 75 William St. (☎ 02/9380 5399). Avis, Budget, Hertz, and Thrifty also have desks at the airport. Rental rates average about A$30 (U.S.$21) per day for weekly rentals and A$90 (U.S.$63) for single-day rentals.

If you plan to leave the city and head to the bush for a few days, you can rent a campervan from **NQ Australia Rentals** (☎ **02/9316 8663;** fax 02/9666 5340). Vans cost from A$60 (U.S.$42) a day.

FAST FACTS: Sydney

American Express   The main AMEX office is at 92 Pitt St. (☎ **02/9239 0666**). It's open Monday to Friday from 8:30am to 5:30pm and Saturday from 9am to noon.

Baby-Sitters   **Dial an Angel** (☎ **02/9416 7511** or 02/9362 4225) offers a well-regarded baby-sitting service. Charges for one or two children are as follows: daytime, A$48 (U.S.$33.60) for the first 3 hours, then A$11 (U.S.$7.70) for each hour thereafter; evening, A$45 (U.S.$31.50) for the first 3 hours, then A$10 (U.S.$7) for each hour thereafter. Extra charges apply after midnight and on Sundays.

Business Hours   General office and banking hours are 9am to 5pm Monday to Friday. Shopping hours are usually 8:30am to 5:30pm daily, though most stores stay open until 9pm on Thursday. Stores outside main areas are either closed or open for limited periods on Sundays.

Car Rentals   See "Getting Around," earlier in this chapter.

Currency Exchange   Most major bank branches offer currency exchange services. Small foreign-currency exchange offices are clustered at the airport and around Circular Quay and Kings Cross. **Thomas Cook** foreign exchange offices can be found at the airport; at 210 George St. (☎ **02/9251 9063**); in Kingsgate Shopping Center, Kings Cross (☎ **02/9356 221**); and on the lower ground floor of the Queen Victoria Building, Town Hall (☎ **02/9264 1133**).

Dentist   For dental problems after hours call **Dental Emergency Information** (☎ **02/9369 7050**).

Doctor   Respected city doctors include **Peter Brook General Practice,** 3rd floor, The Dymocks Building, 428 George St. (☎ **02/9223 4706**), open Monday to Friday from 9am to 5pm; and **Macquarie Health Centers,** 822 George St. (☎ **02/9212 2733**), open daily from 7am to 10pm. **The Park Medical Centre,** Shop 4, 27 Park St. (☎ **02/9264 4488**), in the city center near Town Hall, is open Monday to Friday from 8am to 6pm; consultations cost $A35 (U.S.$24.50) for 15 minutes.

Drugstores   Most suburbs have pharmacies that are open late. For after-hours referral, contact the **Emergency Prescription Service** (☎ **02/9235 0333**).

Embassies/Consulates   All foreign embassies are based in Canberra. You'll find the following consulates in Sydney: **United Kingdom,** Level 16, Gateway Building, 1 Macquarie Place, Circular Quay (☎ **02/9247 7521**); **New Zealand,** 1 Alfred St., Circular Quay (☎ **02/9247 1999**); **United States,** 19-29 Martin Place (☎ **02/9373 9200**). There is no Canadian consulate in Sydney; the **Canadian High Commission** is in Canberra at Commonwealth Ave., Yarralumla (☎ **02/6273 3844**).

Emergencies   Dial ☎ **000** to call police, the fire service, or an ambulance. Call the **Emergency Prescription Service** (☎ **02/9235 0333**) for emergency drug prescriptions, and the **NRMA** for car breakdowns (☎ **13 11 11**).

Eyeglass Repair   **Perfect Vision,** Shop C22A, in the Centerpoint Tower, 100 Market St. (☎ **02/9221 1010**), is open Monday to Friday from 9am to 6pm (Thurs to 9pm) and Saturday from 9am to 5pm.

Holidays   See "When to Go" in chapter 1. New South Wales also observes Labour Day on the 1st Monday in October.

Hospitals   Make your way to **Sydney Hospital,** on Macquarie Street, at the top end of Martin Place (☎ **02/9382 7111** for emergencies). You'll find **St. Vincents Hospital** on Victoria and Burton streets in Darlinghurst (near Kings Cross) (☎ **02/9339 1111**).

Hot Lines   Contact the **Poisons Information Center** at ☎ 13 11 26; the **Gay and Lesbian Counseling Line** (4pm to midnight) at ☎ 02/9207 2800; the **Rape Crisis Center** at ☎ 02/9819 6565; and the **Crisis Center** at ☎ 02/9358 6577 for problems with suicide or abuse.

Library   The **State Library of New South Wales** is on Macquarie Street, near Martin Place (☎ **02/9230 1414**).

Lost Property   There is no general lost property bureau in Sydney. Contact the nearest police station if you think you've lost something. For items lost on trains, buses, and ferries, contact the **Lost Property office,** 490 Pitt St., near Central Railway Station (☎ **02/9211 4535** or 02/9211 1176). The office is open Monday to Friday from 8:30am to 4:30pm. For items left behind on planes or lost at the airport, go to the **Federal Airport Corporation**'s administration office on the top floor of the International Terminal (☎ **02/9667 9583**).

Luggage Storage   You can leave your bags at the **International Terminal** at the airport. A locker here costs A$4 (U.S.$2.80) per day, or you can put them in the storage room for A$6 (U.S.$4.20) per day per piece. The storage room is open from 4:30am to the last flight of the day. Call ☎ **02/9667 9848** for information. Otherwise, leave luggage at the **Cloakroom at Central Railway Station,** near the front of the main building off George Street in the Country Trains section (☎ **02/9219 4395**). Storage at the rail station costs A$1.50 (U.S.$1.05) per article until 10:30pm the following evening and A$4.50 (U.S.$3.15) per article every day thereafter.

Newspapers   The *Sydney Morning Herald* is considered one of the world's best newspapers and is available throughout metropolitan Sydney. The equally prestigious *Australian* is available nationwide. The metropolitan *Telegraph Mirror* is a more casual read. The *International Herald Tribune, USA Today,* the *British Guardian Weekly,* and other newspapers can be found at Circular Quay newspaper stands and most newsagents.

Photographic Needs   **Fletchers Fotographics,** 317 Pitt St., near Town Hall (☎ **02/9267 6146**), is a quality photographic store selling cameras, films, and accessories. **Paxton's,** 285 George St., (☎ **02/9299 2999**) is also good. The **Camera Service Centre,** 1st Floor, 203 Castlereagh St. (☎ **02/9264 7091**), is a tiny place up a flight of stairs not far from the Town Hall station. It repairs all kinds of cameras on the spot, or within a couple of days if parts are needed.

Police   In an emergency dial ☎ **000.**

Post Office   You'll find the General Post Office (GPO) at 130 Pitt St. (☎ **13 13 17**). It's open Monday to Friday from 8:30am to 5:30pm and Saturday from 8am to noon. Letters can be collected c/o Poste Restante, GPO, Sydney, 2000, Australia. For directions to the nearest local post office, call ☎ **1800/043 300.**

Rest Rooms   Public rest rooms can be found in the Queen Victoria Building (second floor), most department stores, at Central Station and Circular Quay, and in the Harbourside marketplace in Darling Harbour.

Safety   Be wary in Kings Cross and Redfern at all hours. If traveling by train at night, travel in the carriages next to the guard's van, marked with a blue light on the outside.

Taxes   As yet, there is no GST in Australia. A 10% state government "Bed Tax" was introduced for hotels in September 1998.

Taxis   See "Getting Around," earlier in this chapter.

Telephone & Fax   Local calls cost A40¢ from a public telephone, or A25¢ from a private phone in someone's home or office. Newsagents and some tourist information booths sell phone cards containing a prepaid allotment of call time in A$5 (U.S.$3.50), A$10 (U.S.$7), A$20 (U.S.$14), or A$50 (U.S.$35) denominations; not all public telephones take these cards yet.

Local phone calls made from hotels are never free in Australia; you'll usually pay a surcharge of as much as A75¢ (U.S.53¢). Australians get around this by using their mobile phones (probably more expensive in the end, but it's satisfying to outwit the charges), ringing from a pay phone with change or a phone card, or calling collect. Another way to get around hotel phone surcharges is to carry a calling card that bills calls back to your home phone account.

To make a collect or "reverse charges" call within Australia, dial the operator at ☎ **12550.**

To make a calling-card call or an international collect call, dial one of the following access codes: **AT&T Direct** ☎ 1800/881 011, **Sprint** ☎ 1800/881 877, **MCI** ☎ 1800/881 100, **Worldcom** ☎ 1800/881 212, or **Bell Atlantic** ☎ 1800/881 152 in the United States; **BT** ☎ 1800/881 441 or **Mercury** ☎ 1800/881 417 in the United Kingdom; or ☎ 1800/881 640 in New Zealand.

Australian phone numbers starting with 1800 are **toll-free;** numbers starting with 13 or 1300 are charged at the local fee of 25¢ from anywhere in Australia; 0055 or 1900 means the line is pay-for-service at a set rate per minute (like 900 numbers in the U.S.), which can be more than A$1 (U.S.70¢) a minute. None of these numbers requires an area code.

To find out a telephone number anywhere in Australia, ring **Directory Assistance** at ☎ **013.** This number is due to change soon to 1223. To locate a number overseas, ring **International Directory Assistance** on ☎ **1225.** General Post Offices (GPOs) in each state capital keep a copy of every telephone directory in the country for the public to use.

Cellular or "mobile" telephones are hugely popular in Australia, and you can rent them by the day in major cities. If your telephone provider has a reciprocal agreement with Telstra, Optus, or Australia's third mobile network, Vodafone, you will be able to use your phone Down Under. You may need to arrange this before you leave, however, so check the conditions, cost, and requirements with your carrier. You will probably incur a registration fee, a daily charge of a few dollars, plus airtime. Remember, overseas mobile calls can be made only on the digital, not the analogue, network. Australia currently uses both networks, but will be all-digital by 2000. Mobile numbers in Australia start with 014, 015, 018, 0412 or 0419, followed by six digits.

To call Australia from the United States, dial the international access code 011; then **Australia's country code (61);** then the area code, but always drop the first zero of the area code; then the number you want to call. For example, to ring the Sydney Opera House (☎ 02/9250 7111) to book a guided tour from the United States, dial ☎ 011 61 2 9250 7111.

To call the United States from Australia, dial the international access code 0011 (note it has two zeros, not one like the international access code from the U.S.); then the country code for the United States (1); then the area code; then the number you want to call.

To make a long-distance call within Australia, dial the area code including the initial zero, followed by the number you are calling. Australia's area codes are in the process of being switched from a plethora of two- and three-digit codes to a uniform two-digit code in each state, followed by an eight-digit number. The new codes are: New South Wales and the A.C.T. (02); Victoria and Tasmania (03); Queensland (07); and South Australia, Western Australia, and the Northern Territory (08). To reach the operator to help you make a call within Australia or an international call, dial ☎ **1234.**

To send a fax internationally, long-distance, or locally, all the same rules apply as for phone calls. You can use 0011 or 0015 as the international access code for a fax. You can send and receive local and international faxes at most Australia Post Offices. Some newsagents also have a fax and photocopy service.

The cheapest time to make international calls and send faxes is after 6pm and before 9am Monday to Friday and anytime on weekends. The cheapest time to make long-distance calls within Australia is before 7am and after 7pm Monday to Friday and anytime on weekends.

Television   There are five TV stations in Sydney: three commercial networks, one semicommercial, and one publicly owned. ABC (Australian Broadcasting Corporation) is the equivalent of PBS in the United States; SBS concentrates on ethnic programming, including international films, and has excellent news programs (at 6:30pm and 9pm daily); channels 7, 9, and 10 offer a variety of commercial programming, including many U.S. and British imports (in between enormous amounts of advertising!). For TV program information, buy the *Sydney Morning Herald* on Monday or the *Sun Herald* on Sunday.

Time   Australia crosses three time zones. When it is noon in New South Wales, the A.C.T., Victoria, Queensland, and Tasmania, it is 11:30am in South Australia and the Northern Territory and 10am in Western Australia. All states except Queensland and Western Australia observe daylight saving time from around the last Sunday in October (the 1st Sun in Oct in Tasmania's case) to around the last Sunday in March. Just to confuse things, not all states switch over to daylight saving time the same day or even the same week; Queensland sometimes does, sometimes doesn't, observe daylight saving, depending on its mood. At the time of this writing, Queensland does not observe daylight saving time.

When it is noon (standard time) on Australia's east coast, it is 3am in London that morning, and 7pm in Los Angeles and 10pm in New York the previous night. Allow 2 more hours difference when Australia's east coast begins daylight saving time and the Northern Hemisphere goes back to standard time; in that case, when it's noon in Sydney it's 1am in London that morning, and 5pm in Los Angeles, and 8pm in New York the previous night. New Zealand is 2 hours ahead of the Australian east coast.

Tipping   Tipping was once almost unheard of in Australia. However, these days it is customary to tip 10% for a substantial meal in capital-city restaurants. Country folk don't expect it, nor do city staff who serve you a simple coffee and a sandwich. Some passengers round up to the nearest dollar in a cab, but it's OK to insist on every last 5¢ piece of change back from the driver if you want. No one tips bar staff, barbers, or hairdressers.

Transit Information   Call the **InfoLine** at ☎ **13 15 00** (daily 6am to 10pm).

Useful Telephone Numbers   For news, dial ☎ **1199;** for the time, ☎ **1194;** for Sydney entertainment, ☎ **11 688;** for phone directory/assistance, ☎ **013** (local numbers), ☎ **0175** (interstate numbers), or ☎ **0103** (international numbers); for Travellers Aid Society, ☎ **02/9211 2469.**

Weather   For the local forecast call ☎ **1196.**

Accommodations

S ydney's success in winning the 2000 Olympic Games and the increased media exposure the city has received as a result have led to more visitors and more hotels to cater to them. Although it's unlikely you'll find the city's hotels completely booked if you simply turn up looking for a bed for the night, I always recommend reserving in advance. Most hotel rooms are also much cheaper if bought as part as a package deal before leaving home. (See "Booking a Package Tour" in chapter 2.)

WHERE TO STAY   Hotels are generally clustered around the main tourist spots, with the more expensive ones generally occupying the prime positions. Those in The Rocks and around Circular Quay are just a short stroll from the Sydney Opera House, the Harbour Bridge, the Royal Botanic Gardens, the ferry terminals, and the train station, and are close to main shopping areas.

Hotels around Darling Harbour offer good access to the local facilities, including museums, the Sydney Aquarium, the Star City casino, the IMAX Theatre, and Sega World. Most Darling Harbour hotels are a 15-minute walk, or a short monorail or light-rail trip, from Town Hall and the central shopping district in and around Centerpoint Tower and Pitt Street Mall.

More hotels are grouped around Kings Cross, Sydney's seedy red-light district. While some of the hotels found here are among the city's best, in this area you'll also find a range of cheaper lodgings, including several backpacker hostels. Kings Cross can be unnerving at any time, but especially so on Friday and Saturday nights when the area's strip joints and nightclubs are doing their best business. Staying here does have it's advantages, though: you get a real inner-city feel and its close to some excellent restaurants and cafes centered around the Kings Cross/Darlinghurst and Oxford Street areas.

If you want to stay near the beach, check out the options in Manly and Bondi.

HOW TO GET THE MOST FOR YOUR MONEY   Many hotels, especially the more expensive ones, drop their room rates significantly on weekends (when business travelers, the bread-and-

Central Sydney Accommodations

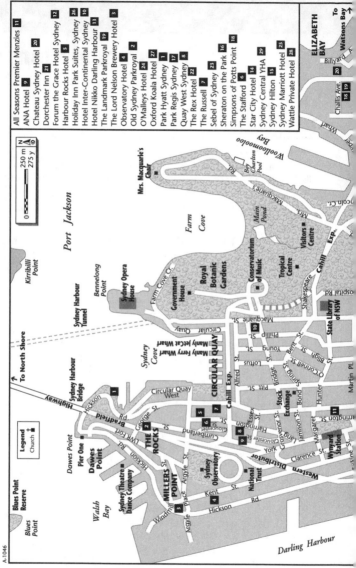

All Seasons Premier Menzies 11
ANA Hotel 9
Chateau Sydney Hotel 20
Dorchester Inn 21
Forum the Grace Hotel Sydney 12
Harbour Rocks Hotel 5
Holiday Inn Park Suites, Sydney 26
Hotel Inter-Continental Sydney 10
Hotel Nikko Darling Harbour 13
The Landmark Parkroyal 19
The Lord Nelson Brewery Hotel 3
Observatory Hotel 4
Old Sydney Parkroyal 2
O'Malleys Hotel 27
Oxford Koala Hotel 24
Park Hyatt Sydney 1
Park Regis Sydney 17
Quay West Sydney 8
The Rex Hotel 22
The Russell 7
Sebel of Sydney 23
Sheraton on the Park 16
Simpsons of Potts Point 18
The Stafford 6
Star City Hotel 14
Sydney Central YHA 29
Sydney Hilton 15
Sydney Marriott Hotel 25
Wattle Private Hotel 28

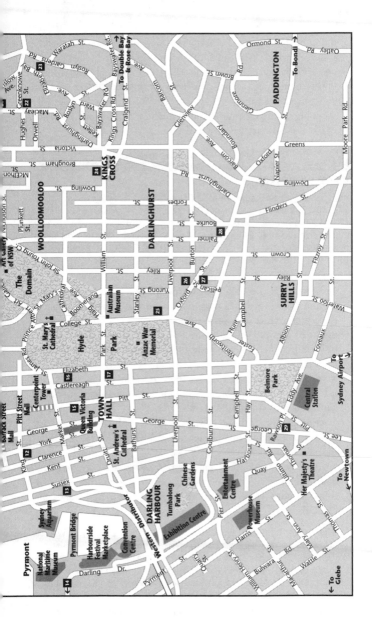

butter of so many hotels, clear out). Some hotels also offer special packages, which might include a room upgrade or a free meal or bottle of champagne on arrival. Many top hotels are also open to limited bargaining—simply ask them for their best offer.

Serviced apartments are well worth considering because they mean big savings on meals—and you can eat exactly what you want. Many also have free laundry facilities.

1 Near Circular Quay

VERY EXPENSIVE

All Seasons Premier Menzies. 14 Carrington St., Sydney, NSW 2000. ☎ **1300 363 600** in Australia or 02/9299 1000. 454 units. A/C MINIBAR TV TEL. A$300–$325 (U.S.$210–$227.50) double; A$480 (U.S.$336) suite. Additional person A$40 (U.S.$28) extra. Children under 12 stay free in parents' room. Ask about special packages. AE, BC, DC, MC, V. Parking A$22 (U.S.$15.40). CityRail: Wynyard.

A fair bit of recent sprucing-up helped this four-star hotel win a 1997 NSW Excellence in Tourism award. The 14-story Menzies was built in 1963 as Sydney's first premier hotel. It's positioned right in the center of town and sports one of the city's few public clocks on top of its impressive facade. Rooms are spacious and newly refurbished, decorated with colonial furniture and outfitted with a fax machine and all mod cons (modern conveniences). Deluxe rooms, as you'd expect, are slightly larger and a touch more upscale. Though it took A$14 million (U.S.$9.8 million) to modernize it, this hotel has retained its Grand Old Dame appeal.

Dining: The Carrington Restaurant serves high-class à la carte meals and fabulous lunch and dinner buffets. A brasserie offers snacks, lunch, and afternoon tea in a very elegant atmosphere.

Amenities: Indoor pool, sauna, spa, massage, gym, concierge, 24-hour room service, free daily newspapers, nightly turndown, shoeshine, laundry, valet, business services, gift shop, newsstand, currency exchange.

✪ **Hotel Inter-Continental Sydney.** 117 Macquarie St., Sydney, NSW 2000. ☎ **1800/221 828** in Australia (outside New South Wales) or 02/9230 0200. Fax 02/9240 1240. 498 units. A/C MINIBAR TV TEL. A$375–$495 (U.S.$262.50–$346.50) double; from A$765 (U.S.$535.50) suite. Additional person A$30 (U.S.$21) extra. Children under 18 stay free in parents' room. Parking A$20 (U.S.$14). CityRail, bus, or ferry: Circular Quay.

In a city with so many excellent hotels, the Hotel Inter-Continental Sydney is one of my firm favorites. As you walk up Macquarie Street from Circular Quay, you can't fail to notice the blue carpet across the sidewalk and the top-hatted doorman under the hotel's awning. From there on in, it's unadulterated luxury. In a class with the world's best hotels, the Hotel Inter-Continental is wonderfully positioned opposite the Royal Botanic Gardens and is just a stroll away from many other main attractions. The hotel is situated in the former Treasury building (later the VD clinic) and was built between 1849 and 1917. All rooms have been elegantly refurbished to unite 19th-century classicism with the best of the 20th century. Half of the rooms have a harbor view and all come complete with everything you'd expect, and some features, like a toaster, that might surprise you. Special rooms for business travelers are slightly larger (and more expensive) and come with dedicated business facilities such as modem lines, printer, scanner, and fax machine.

Dining/Diversions: Afternoon tea, lunch, and cocktails are taken in the white marbled Cortile, the building's architectural focal point. The Cortile features live classical music Wednesday to Sunday. The Treasury is the hotel's fine-dining venue. The 30-Something Lounge on the 31st floor has panoramic views over Sydney Harbor and the Royal Botanic Gardens and good pizzas and pasta. Sketches Bar & Bistro serves freshly made pasta (see chapter 4, "Dining"). Café Opera is an informal buffet specializing in sushi and wok-prepared foods.

Amenities: Indoor pool, sauna, spa, gym, power-walking classes, massage therapists, concierge, 24-hour room service, free daily newspapers, nightly turndown, shoe-shine, laundry, valet, baby-sitting, business center, hair/beauty salon, gift shop, newsstand, early-arrivals/late-departure lounge, currency exchange.

2 In The Rocks

VERY EXPENSIVE

ANA Hotel. 176 Cumberland St., The Rocks, Sydney, NSW 2000. ☎ **1800/ 801 088** in Australia or 02/9250 6000. Fax 02/9250 6044. 570 units. MINIBAR TV TEL. A$340–$435 (U.S.$238–$304.50) double depending on view; from A$590 (U.S.$413) and way up for suites. Additional person $40 (U.S.$28) extra. Children stay free in parents' room. AE, BC, DC, JCB, MC, V. Parking A$17 (U.S.$11.90). CityRail or ferry: Circular Quay.

For a room with a view, you're not going to do better than this ultramodern landmark hotel. All rooms look out onto either Darling Harbour, or across the Opera House and Harbour Bridge. Try to book a room on the 20th floor or above, because from here Sydney is laid out at your feet, with the ferries buzzing around below you like wind-up bathtub toys. If you really want to splurge, book a corner suite for an extraordinary vista. Rooms are comfortably furnished and decorated to blend with sky, city, and sea. The hotel is popular with tour groups, particularly from Japan.

Dining/Diversions: The Lilyvale restaurant, which sits next door in a heritage-listed structure built in 1845, serves delicious modern Australian dishes. The Rocks Teppanyaki is the hotel's popular Japanese food outlet, whereas the Lobby Lounge serves up cocktails and a view of the landscaped gardens, though it can get noisy when tour groups arrive.

Amenities: Indoor pool, spa and sauna, fitness center, massage, concierge, 24-hour room service, free daily newspapers, nightly turndown, shoe-shine, laundry, valet, baby-sitting, business center, meeting facilities, hair/beauty salon, sundry/gift shop, currency exchange, early arrivals/late departures lounge.

Observatory Hotel. 89-113 Kent St., Sydney, NSW 2000. ☎ **1800/806 245** in Australia or 02/9256 2222. Fax 02/9256 2233. 100 units. A/C MINIBAR TV TEL. A$350–$425 (U.S.$245–$297.50) double; from A$595 (U.S.$416.50) suite. Additional person A$60 (U.S.$42) extra. Children under 14 stay free in parents' room. AE, BC, DC, JCB, MC, V. Parking A$18 (U.S.$12.60). Bus: 339, 431, or 433 to Millers Point.

This exclusive hotel, a 10-minute walk uphill from The Rocks and George Street, is a turn-of-the-century beauty competing for top-hotel-in-Sydney honors. It's fitted out with antiques, objets d'art, and the finest carpets, wallpapers, and draperies, and is renowned for its personalized service. Rooms are plush, quiet, and come with all modern amenities, including a CD player and a VCR. Some have city views while others have good views over the harbor. If you don't fancy the walk into town, then take advantage of the hotel's free BMW limo service, which delivers guests to the central business district on weekdays. The pool here is one of the best in Sydney: note the Southern Hemisphere constellations on the roof. The health club offers everything from massage and beauty therapies to a free float in the flotation tank for early arrivals coming in from overseas.

Dining/Diversions: The Galileo Restaurant offers very good food in an elegant candlelit atmosphere with silk wallpaper, polished walnut furniture, and original Venetian etchings and Australian impressionist works of art. The Globe Bar feels like an old-world colonial English club.

Amenities: Chemical-free indoor pool, sauna, steam room, flotation tank, health club, tennis courts, concierge, 24-hour room service, newspaper delivery, nightly turndown, twice-daily maid service, dry cleaning/laundry, business center.

Old Sydney Parkroyal. 55 George St., The Rocks, Sydney, NSW 2000. ☎ **02/9252 0524.** Fax 02/9251 2093. 174 units. A/C TV TEL. A$350 (U.S.$245) double. Additional person A$25 (U.S.$17.50) extra. Children under 15 stay free in parents' room. AE, BC, DC, MC, V. Parking A$16 (U.S.$11.20). CityRail, bus, or ferry: Circular Quay.

Though very conveniently placed in the heart of The Rocks, I found the Old Sydney Parkroyal quite disappointing when I stayed there recently. Though the foyer, restaurant, and bar area are handsome enough, the standard room I experienced was cramped and uninspiring, with an ugly brown carpet and a small window. Rooms come with a tub/shower, simple robes, and an iron and ironing board. On the roof there is a tiny pool, and a separate spa and sauna. For the price, you'd be much better staying at the Stafford, or taking the best suite at the Russell (see below for both).

Dining: The Playfair Terrace restaurant is nicely positioned in the center of the hotel and serves dinner and a buffet breakfast.

Amenities: Rooftop pool, sauna, spa, massage, concierge, 24-hour room service, free daily newspaper, nightly turndown, shoe-shine, laundry, valet, baby-sitting, gift shop.

✪ **Park Hyatt Sydney.** 7 Hickson Rd., The Rocks, Sydney, NSW 2000. ☎ **131 1234** in Australia, 800/835-7742 in the U.S. and Canada, or 02/9241 1234. Fax 02/9256 1995. 158 units. A/C MINIBAR TV TEL. A$550–$610 (U.S.$385–$427) double depending on view; A$710–$810 (U.S.$497–$567) executive studio; from A$1,000 (U.S.$700) suite. Additional person A$30 (U.S.$21) extra. Children under 18 stay free in parents' room. Ask about lower weekend rates and packages. AE, BC, DC, JCB, MC, V. Parking A$20 (U.S.$14). CityRail, bus, or ferry: Circular Quay.

This artistically curving property on The Rocks foreshore is without doubt the best positioned hotel in Sydney. It's literally right on the water, with some rooms having fantastic views directly across the harbor to Sydney Opera House. Its location and general appeal mean it's consistently fully occupied and has to frequently turn guests away. The building itself is a pleasure to look at, and from a ferry on the harbor it looks like a wonderful addition to the toy town feel of The Rocks. The lobby is marbled and elegant, and every possible luxury has been incorporated into the rooms. Room rates here really depend on views; the least expensive have only glimpses of the harbor. Each of the 33 executive suites has two balconies with a telescope.

Dining/Diversions: Verandah on the Park offers good buffet food either indoors or in a fabulous location on the edge of the harbor. No. 7 at the Park is more formal and has excellent harbor views. The bar, which has a fireplace, resembles an English club.

Amenities: Outdoor pool, health club, gym, steam room, sauna, spa, massage, concierge, butler, 24-hour room service, nightly turn-down, free newspaper, laundry, shoe-shine, valet, baby-sitting, business center, lobby shop.

EXPENSIVE

Harbor Rocks Hotel. 34-52 Harrington St., The Rocks, Sydney, NSW 2000. ☎ **1800/251 210** in Australia or 02/9251 8944. Fax 02/9251 8900. 55 units. MINIBAR TV TEL. A$210–$240 (U.S.$147–$168) double. Penthouse suite A$400 (U.S.$280). Additional person A$30 (U.S.$21) extra. Children under 16 stay free in parents' room. AE, BC, DC, MC, V. Parking A$15 (U.S.$10.50) across the road. CityRail or ferry: Circular Quay.

This four-story, heritage-listed boutique hotel is right in the heart of Sydney's historical Rocks district. Rooms are clean and well appointed with free videos thrown in, but there is no elevator, so guests have to climb the stairs. Rooms vary in size, with some being quite large and others much smaller; bathrooms also vary in size, and none (except the penthouse suite) has a tub. There's one room equipped for travelers with disabilities on the ground floor. In my experience, service here can be offhand.

Dining/Diversions: The beautiful Harbor Rocks Café overlooks a leafy balcony perfect for those sultry summer evenings. Live local jazz bands play in the bar area on Friday nights and Sunday afternoon.

Amenities: Limited room service, laundry service and coin-operated laundry, baby-sitting.

A BED & BREAKFAST INN

✪ **The Russell.** 143A George St., The Rocks, Sydney, NSW 2000. ☎ **02/ 9241 3543.** Fax 02/9252 1652. 29 units, 19 with bathroom. TV TEL. A$110–$200 (U.S.$77–$140) double; A$230 (U.S.$161) suite. Additional person A$15 (U.S.$10.50) extra. Rates include continental breakfast. AE, BC, DC, MC, V. Parking not available. CityRail or ferry: Circular Quay.

If I were going to recommend the coziest place to stay in The Rocks, and perhaps in the whole of Sydney, it would have to be The Russell. It's more than 100 years old, and it shows its age wonderfully in the creak of floorboards and the ramshackle feel of its brightly painted corridors. Every room is totally different in style, size, and shape; all come with queen-size beds, cable TV, and bathrobes, and most have adjoining bathrooms. All have immense character, including a series of rooms added on above the Fortune of War Hotel next door in 1990. There are no harbor views, but from some rooms you can see the tops of the ferry terminals at

Circular Quay. Guests have the use of a comfortable sitting room, a living room scattered with magazines and books, and a rooftop garden. Boulders restaurant serves good food on the ground floor.

PUB LODGING

The Lord Nelson Brewery Hotel. At the corner of Kent and Argyle sts., The Rocks, Sydney, NSW 2000. ☎ **02/9251 4044.** Fax 02/9251 1532. 10 units, 6 with bathroom. TV TEL. A$90 (U.S.$63) double without bathroom; A$110 (U.S.$77) double with bathroom. Additional person A$15 (U.S.$10.50) extra. Rates include continental breakfast. AE, BC, DC, MC, V. Parking not available. CityRail or ferry: Circular Quay.

Sydney's oldest pub was established in 1841 after serving as a private residence since its construction in 1836. It's an attractive, three-floor sandstone building with a busy pub on the ground floor, a good brasserie on the second, and hotel accommodations on the third. The "small" rooms are true to their name, with room for not much more than a bed and a small TV. For the extra A$20 (U.S.$14) you get far more space to stretch out. From its creaky floorboards and bedroom walls made from convict-hewn sandstone blocks to the narrow corridors and the wood fire and homemade beer down in the bar, the Lord Nelson positively wallows in atmosphere.

SERVICED APARTMENTS

Quay West Sydney. 98 Gloucester St. (Corner of Essex St.), The Rocks, Sydney, NSW 2000. ☎ **1800/805 031** in Australia, 0800/444 300 in New Zealand, or 02/9240 6000. 132 apts. A/C MINIBAR TV TEL. A$320–$415 (U.S.$224–$290.50) 1-bedroom apt depending on view; A$530 (U.S.$371) 2-bedroom apt. Additional person A$30 (U.S.$21) extra. Ask about long-stay rates and weekend packages. AE, BC, DC, JCB, MC, V. Parking A$15 (U.S.$10.50). CityRail, bus, or ferry: Circular Quay or Wynyard.

The very best serviced-apartment complexes, like this one, can even better superior five-star hotels. Quay West, which faces onto the back of the ANA Hotel (visible from Circular Quay), is a hard-hitting competitor to its rivals in and around The Rocks area, having everything they've got and more. After walking through the plush and hotel-like lobby and taking the elevators up, you'll arrive at very spacious rooms, each with, among other things, a fully-equipped kitchen, a laundry, CD player, a fold-out sofa in the living room as well as a queen-size bed in a separate bedroom, a dining table seating six, and a balcony. Bathrooms are large and feature a separate tub and shower. Some rooms have fantastic views over the Harbour Bridge and the harbor—but you pay through the nose for them. The 28-floor apartment building has a spa, sauna, a gym, a

---

👪 Family-Friendly Accommodations

Manly Lodge *(see page 79)*   This ramshackle old place near the beach has great family rooms as well as table tennis and an Olympic-size trampoline. In-line skates and body boards are rented on the beachfront.

Ravesi's on Bondi Beach *(see page 76)*   The family rooms here are spacious and have views of famous Bondi Beach. The hotel is close to a whole range of budget restaurants and take-out joints suitable for the kids.

---

beautiful indoor Roman-style swimming pool with great views, and the high-quality Carrington Restaurant.

It's all very luxurious, and much appreciated by the famous personalities who have stayed here since its opening in 1992 (Michael Hutchence, the lead singer of the famous Aussie band INXS was supposed to stay here the night he committed suicide over at the Ritz-Carlton Double Bay).

The Stafford. 5 Harrington St., The Rocks, Sydney, NSW 2000. ☎ **02/9251 6711.** Fax 02/9251 3458. 61 apts. A/C TV TEL. A$210–$245 (U.S.$147– $171.50) studio double; A$250 (U.S.$175) 1-bedroom apt; A$280 (U.S.$196) executive 1-bedroom apt; A$265 (U.S.$185.50) terrace house; A$335 (U.S.$234.50) 1-bedroom penthouse. Additional person A$15 (U.S.$10.50) extra. Children under 16 stay free in parents' room. Ask about lower weekly and weekend rates. AE, BC, DC, MC, V. Parking A$15 (U.S.$10.50). CityRail or ferry: Circular Quay.

Along with Quay West Sydney (see above), The Stafford offers the best positioned serviced apartments in Sydney, being right in the heart of The Rocks, very close to the harbor and Circular Quay, and a short stroll from the central business district. The property consists of modern apartments in a six-story building (the best units, for their harbor and Opera House views, are on the top three floors) and seven two-story terrace houses dating from 1870 to 1895. While the overall bearing of the place isn't as exclusive as Quay West, it is still highly recommended for its location, spacious rooms, and fully equipped kitchens. There's an outdoor pool, gym, spa and sauna, and complimentary self-service laundry.

3 Near Town Hall

VERY EXPENSIVE

Sheraton on the Park. 161 Elizabeth St., Sydney, NSW 2000. ☎ **1800/80 2782** in Australia or 02/9286 6000. Fax 02/9286 6686. 559 units. A/C MINIBAR

TV TEL. A$370–$410 (U.S.$259–$287) double; from A$650 (U.S.$455) suite. Children under 12 stay free in parents' room. Ask about lower weekend rates and packages. AE, BC, DC, MC, V. Parking A$18 (U.S.$12.60). CityRail: St. James. Monorail: City Centre.

The Sheraton on the Park is one of Sydney's most sophisticated hotels and a great place to escape the rush of the city. The lobby, with its three-story-high black marble columns, polished wood paneling, and curving staircases is an impressive foretaste of what's to come. The long upstairs hallways lead to classically furnished rooms complete with marble bathrooms, three phones each, fax machines, and in-room safes. Two-thirds of the standard rooms have views over the city or Hyde Park. The swimming pool on the 22nd floor also has panoramic views.

Dining/Diversions: The Conservatory has a lovely aspect with its own lily pond and high arched windows overlooking Hyde Park. Afternoon tea is served from 2pm and snacks and cocktails are available throughout the day. The Gekko is a contemporary eatery.

Amenities: Indoor pool, large health club, spa, sauna, steam room, massage, concierge, 24-hour room service, free daily newspapers, nightly turndown, laundry, valet, shoe-shine, baby-sitting, secretarial services, currency exchange.

Sydney Hilton. 259 Pitt St., Sydney, NSW 2000. ☎ **1800/222 255** in Australia or 02/9266 2000. Fax 02/9265 6065. 585 units. A/C MINIBAR TV TEL. A$290–$390 (U.S.$203–$273) double; A$500–$1,320 (U.S.$350–$924) suite. Additional person A$40 (U.S.$28) extra. Children under 18 stay free in parents' room. AE, BC, DC, JCB, MC, V. Parking $24 (U.S.$16.80). CityRail: Town Hall.

Right in the middle of town and close to all major shops, the Sydney Hilton is a 1970s conglomerate with a decidedly ugly facade rearing onto both Pitt and George streets. The lackluster gold lobby— if you can find it (the main entrance is hidden away in a warren of concrete)—is dimly lit and houses a popular cafe and boutique shops. The rooms are all nicely refurbished and many, especially from the 32nd floor up, have panoramic views of Sydney Tower (Centerpoint), the Harbour Bridge, and neighboring skyscrapers.

Dining/Diversions: Some of Sydney's best bars are in the Sydney Hilton, including the stunning Marble Bar, with its extravagant central-European feel, and the popular English-style Henry the Ninth Bar. The Hilton has two restaurants, an à la carte restaurant open for lunch and dinner and a fine-dining grill open for lunch on weekdays and dinner on Saturday.

Amenities: Outdoor pool, sauna, spa, gym, massage, concierge, 24-hour room service, free daily newspaper, nightly turndown, shoe-shine, laundry, valet, baby-sitting, business center, tour desk, gift shop, newsstand, currency exchange.

Sydney Marriott Hotel. 36 College St., Sydney, NSW 2010. ☎ **1800/025 419** in Australia or 02/9361 8400. Fax 02/9361 8599. 241 units. A/C MINIBAR TV TEL. A$360 (U.S.$252) double; A$595 (U.S.$416.50) junior suite; A$735 (U.S.$514.50) premier suite. Additional person A$25 (U.S.$17.50) extra. Children under 12 stay free in parents' room. Ask about lower weekend rates and discount packages. AE, BC, DC, JCB, MC, V. Free parking. CityRail: Museum.

Accommodations in this centrally located property seem more like serviced apartments than standard hotel rooms. All rooms are spacious and come with plates, cutlery, toasters, and microwaves, while one-third of the rooms also have hot plates. Everything else you need for a pleasant stay is also available. All rooms have impressive triangular bathtubs, and either look out over Hyde Park or eastern Sydney. Many readers have recommended the Marriott.

Dining/Diversions: Windows on the Park offers à la carte meals with nice views over Hyde Park. There's also a coffee shop and a cocktail bar.

Amenities: Heated outdoor pool and sundeck with good views, health club, small gym, steam room, sauna, spa, concierge, room service.

EXPENSIVE

Forum the Grace Hotel Sydney. 77 York St., Sydney, NSW 2000. ☎ **1800/ 682 692** in Australia or 02/9299 8777. Fax 02/9299 8189. 412 units. A/C MINIBAR TV TEL. A$290–$315 (U.S.$203–$220.50) double; A$460 (U.S.$322) suite. Additional person A$40 (U.S.$28) extra. Children under 17 stay free in parents' room. AE, BC, CB, DC, MC, V. Parking A$10 (U.S.$7) for 2 hours; A$15 (U.S.$10.50) flat rate after 6pm. CityRail: Wynyard.

Situated within the historic Grace Building, a replica of the Tribune Building in Chicago and one of Australia's finest examples of commercial Gothic architecture, the Forum is the city's newest centrally located hotel. The 11-story hotel's L-shaped lobby has heritage marble flagstones, stained-glass windows, a lace ironwork balcony, art-deco furniture and light fittings, and high ceilings supported by marble columns. Guest rooms vary in size, with either king-size beds or a pair of doubles, and are fronted by almost surreally wide corridors. Each room has three telephones, computer connections, and an in-room safe.

Dining: A cafe on the lobby level serves snacks and beverages in a relaxed, informal atmosphere. Breakfast, lunch, and à la carte evening meals are served in the second-floor brasserie.

Amenities: Heated outdoor swimming pool, sauna, gym, massage, concierge, 24-hour room service, free daily newspaper, nightly turndown on request, shoe-shine, laundry, valet, baby-sitting, postal and business services, tour desk, express checkout, currency exchange.

MODERATE

Park Regis Sydney. 27 Park St. (at Castlereagh St.), Sydney, NSW 2000. ☎ **1800/221 138** in Australia or 02/9267 6511. Fax 02/9264 2252. 120 units. A/C TV TEL. A$160 (U.S.$112) double; A$190 (U.S.$133) suite. Additional person A$15 (U.S.$10.50) extra. Children under 14 stay free in parents' room. Ask about lower rates available through Aussie auto clubs. AE, BC, DC, MC, V. Free parking. Monorail: Park Plaza. CityRail: Town Hall.

This hotel occupies the top 15 floors of a 45-story building and is well placed in the central business district, just 2 blocks from Hyde Park and Town Hall. There's nothing spectacular about this place; the lobby is plain and functional and the rooms light, modern, and equally practical. The bathrooms have a shower and no tub. Many of its occupants are business travelers, which gives the hotel a corporate feel. Nevertheless, it's a relatively good value considering the location. Rooms at the front have views over the city and park. There's a rooftop pool.

INEXPENSIVE

Sydney Central YHA. 11 Rawson Place, Sydney, NSW 2000. ☎ **02/9261 1111.** Fax 02/9265 6065. 151 units. A$18–$22 (U.S.$12.60–$15.40) in dorm; A$56 (U.S.$39.20) single; A$62 (U.S.$43.40) double. Non-YHA members pay A$3 (U.S.$2.10) extra. BC, JCB, MC, V. On-street parking. CityRail: Central. It's located on the corner of Pitt St., right outside Central Station.

This youth hostel is considered one of the biggest and busiest in the world. With a 98% year-round occupancy rate, you'll have to book early to be assured of a place. Opened in 1987 in a historic nine-story building, it offers far more than standard basic accommodations. In the basement is the Scu Bar, a very popular drinking hole with pool tables and occasional entertainment. There's also a bistro selling cheap meals, a convenience store, two fully equipped kitchens, an entertainment room with more pool tables and e-mail facilities, TV rooms on every floor, and an audiovisual room showing movies. If you want more, try the heated swimming pool and the sauna! Rooms are clean and basic, with the single and double rooms just a touch classier. The YHA is completely accessible to travelers with disabilities.

SERVICED APARTMENTS

Holiday Inn Park Suites, Sydney. 16-32 Oxford St., Sydney, NSW, 2010.
☎ **1800/553 888** in Australia or 02/9331 7728 (☎ 800/HOLIDAY in the U.S.
and Canada). Fax 02/9360 6649. 135 apts. A/C MINIBAR TV TEL. A$222
(U.S.$155.40) 1-bedroom apt; A$242 (U.S.$169.40) 2-bedroom apt. Additional
person A$25 (U.S.$17.50) extra. Children under 15 stay free in parents' room.
Ask about special rates. AE, BC, DC, MC, V. Parking A$5 (U.S.$3.50). CityRail:
Museum.

These serviced apartments give Quay West Sydney (see above) a run
for its money in terms of luxuriousness, but in my opinion Quay
West wins on views and its slightly superior location. Each of the
one- and two-bedroom apartments is plush, with a full kitchen, a
balcony, and all extras. Laundry service is available for a charge.
Guests have use of an outdoor pool, a sauna, and a health club. The
Holiday Inn's restaurant is popular with locals, who come for the
specialty smoked sardine fillets with olives and the Muscovy duck
breast with red and yellow beetroot and lettuce.

4 At Darling Harbour

VERY EXPENSIVE

Star City Hotel. 80 Pyrmont St., Pyrmont, Sydney, NSW 2009. ☎ **1800/700
700** in Australia or 02/9777 9000. Fax 02/9657 8344. 352 units. A/C MINIBAR
TV TEL. A$340–$360 (U.S.$238–$252) standard double, depending on view;
from A$450 (U.S.$315) and way up for suites. Additional person A$40 (U.S.$28)
extra. Ask about special packages. AE, BC, DC, JCB, MC, V. Parking A$15
(U.S.$10.50). Ferry: Piermont Bay. Monorail: Harbourside. Light rail: Star City.
Free commuter buses from central business district. The hotel also runs a free
shuttle bus to the city.

Opened at the end of 1997, this A$900 million (U.S.$630 million)
gambling and entertainment complex includes Sydney's newest five-
star hotel with rooms overlooking both Darling Harbour and
Pyrmont Bridge. Although the four split-level Royal Suites
(A$1,500/U.S.$1,050) are quite spectacular, each with three televi-
sions, a giant spa, a full kitchen, two bathrooms, its own sauna, and
the services of the former butler to the governor of Queensland, the
standard rooms, on the other hand, are somewhat sterile. If you
aren't attracted to the glamour of this place, or the gambling, you
can find nicer rooms for the price elsewhere. If you do stay here, pay
the extra money for a room with truly spectacular views over
Darling Harbour.

Dining/Diversions: The Astral restaurant is the top-flight dining choice here. It's reached by an external glass elevator and offers
top-rated cuisine and the best service I've come across in Sydney.

Other major restaurants are Al Porto, serving Italian, and the Lotus Pond, serving Chinese; there are also a couple of bistro-style places. The gaming rooms are sectioned into four areas; there are also two theaters, the 2,000-seat Lyric Theatre (the largest in Sydney) and the 900-seat Showroom, which presents Las Vegas–style productions.

Amenities: Nice heated outdoor pool, sauna, spa, massage, concierge, 24-hour room service, free daily newspaper, nightly turndown, shoe-shine, laundry, valet, business center, tour desk, shopping arcade, newsstand, beauty salon, currency exchange.

EXPENSIVE

Hotel Nikko Darling Harbour. 161 Sussex St. (at Market St.), Sydney, NSW 2000. ☎ **800/NIK-KOUS** in the U.S. and Canada, or 02/9299 1231. Fax 02/9299 3340. 645 units. A/C MINIBAR TV TEL. A$290–$310 (U.S.$203–$217) double, depending on view; from A$470 (U.S.$329) and way up for suites. Add a A$25 (U.S.$17.50) per-person supplement for Nikko-floor rooms. Extra bed A$30 (U.S.$21). Ask about special packages. AE, BC, DC, JCB, MC, V. Parking A$16 (U.S.$11.20). CityRail: Town Hall. Ferry: Darling Harbour.

The Hotel Nikko is Sydney's largest hotel and has some enviable views over Darling Harbour from its front-facing rooms. It's made up of the Corn Exchange Building, built by Sydney's City Council in 1887; the Dundee Arms hotel; and two sandstone warehouses dating from the 1850s. The interior has a nautical theme to complement the 15-story hotel's waterside position. Rooms are compact, some have balconies, and all have full polished granite bathrooms with tubs. The hotel is well placed for all the Darling Harbour entertainment facilities and museums, and is a pleasant 10- to 15-minute walk from Chinatown and the central shopping area around Town Hall. It's about a 5-minute stroll from the ferry, which stops at the far side of Sydney Aquarium. The Hotel Nikko is very popular with guests from Japan.

Dining/Diversions: Japanese give the thumbs up to the Kamogawa Japanese Restaurant. There's also the Dundee Arms Tavern, a disco on the ground floor, a lobby bar, and the Corn Exchange Brasserie offering casual dining.

Amenities: Concierge, 24-hour room service, laundry valet, business center, early-arrival lounge, roof garden, tour desk, duty-free shops.

5 In Kings Cross & the Suburbs Beyond

VERY EXPENSIVE

Ritz-Carlton Double Bay. 33 Cross St., Double Bay, NSW 2028. ☎ **1300/361 180** in Australia, 800/241-3333 from the U.S. and Canada, 0800/443 030 from New Zealand, 0800/234 000 from the U.K., or 02/9362 4455. Fax 02/ 9362 4744. 149 units. A/C MINIBAR TV TEL. A$349–$409 (U.S.$244.30– $286.30) double; from A$499 (U.S.$349.30) and up for suites. A$399–$449 (U.S.$279.30–$314.30) Club floor. AE, BC, DC, JCB, MC, V. Parking A$15 (U.S.$10.50). Ferry: Double Bay. CityRail: Edgecliff, then 1km (half a mile) walk. Bus: 325 or 324 from Circular Quay.

Madonna, Princess Diana, Tom Jones, George Bush, Neil Diamond—they've all stayed in this five-star darling of the establishment, situated about 4 kilometers (2.5 miles) from the city center in Sydney's poshest harborside suburb. The grand lobby is decked out in a maritime theme, the corridors are somberly lit, and antiques and Persian rugs are scattered tastefully here and there. The large guest rooms are done in Regency style and are almost unnervingly quiet—you could literally hear a pin drop on the bathroom's marble floor. Everything you would expect at the best in town is here, from the enormous TV and the fluffy robes down to designer bathtub salts and a perfect, single rose. Most rooms have balconies with water views. Most notable hotel's have their tragic stories—this was where Michael Hutchence, the lead singer of the Australian rock group INXS, hanged himself in November 1997.

Dining/Diversions: The Saltwater Grill has good continental cuisine served in an intimate, elegant environment; the Bar is plush and popular for cigars and brandy; and the Lobby Lounge is wonderfully civilized for breakfast and a favorite lunch and afternoon-tea spot for the local social set.

Amenities: Heated rooftop pool, fitness center, concierge, 24-hour room service, nightly turndown, twice-daily maid service, valet, baby-sitting, separate kosher kitchen, business center, meeting facilities, sundry/gift shop, currency exchange.

Sebel of Sydney. 23 Elizabeth Bay Rd., Elizabeth Bay, NSW 2011. ☎ **1800/ 222 266** in Australia or 02/9358 3244. Fax 02/9357 1926. 189 units. A/C MINIBAR TV TEL. A$125 (U.S.$87.50) standard double; A$285 (U.S.$199.50) superior double; from A$319 (U.S.$U.S.$223.30) suite. Additional person A$25 (U.S.$17.50) extra. Children under 12 stay free in parents' room. Rates include breakfast. Ask about much cheaper weekend and off-season rates. AE, BC, DC, JCB, MC, V. Free parking. CityRail: Kings Cross.

Just a block away from the bright lights and sleazy sights of Kings Cross, the Sebel is an upmarket boutique hotel known for its personal service and "theatrical" theme. It's long been hotel of choice for such international celebs as Elton John, Richard Harris, Cliff Richard, Phil Collins, Rex Harrison, Lauren Bacall, and Rod Stewart, and it remains a place to see and be seen. To make guests feel at home, they're called by name, and the restaurant and bar only close when the last person has left. Rooms are a great value for the price and come with either queen- or king-size beds and traditional furniture. Half the rooms look out over the picturesque marina at Rushcutters Bay. Suites have VCRs and CD players, as well as kitchenettes.

Dining/Diversions: The Encore Restaurant offers semifine dining, serving up everything from steaks to stir-fries. The cocktail bar is a favorite with local actors and performers.

Amenities: Rooftop outdoor pool, gym, sauna, concierge, 24-hour room service, free daily newspaper, nightly turndown, shoe-shine, laundry, valet, baby-sitting, business center, gift shop.

EXPENSIVE

The Landmark Parkroyal. 81 Macleay St., Potts Point, NSW 2011. ☎ **02/9368 3000.** Fax 02/9358 6631. 463 units. A/C MINIBAR TV TEL. A$300–$330 (U.S.$210–$231) double; A$750 (U.S.$525) suite. Extra bed A$25 (U.S.$17.50). Children under 19 stay free in parents' room. Ask about weekend and excellent money-saving packages. AE, BC, DC, MC, V. Parking A$9 (U.S.$6.30). CityRail: Kings Cross, about 1km (half a mile) away. Bus: 311 from Circular Quay.

This top-flight, four-star hotel is where airline pilots stay when they're stopping off in Sydney. Though not slap bang in the city center, it's just a 5-minute walk from Kings Cross station and very close to some of the city's best restaurants. The lobby is big and grand and leads off into the restaurant, which serves an interesting buffet. The recently refurbished guest rooms are a good size and have large windows that open. Some rooms have spectacular views over the inner harbor, the Heads, and parts of the city; others have good skyline views; while still others look over the Sydney Opera House and Harbour Bridge. Depending on the room, it will have either one or two queen-size beds, or a single king-size bed. Bathrooms are small, but come with a tub/shower combination. Guests on the two more-expensive "Parkroyal floors" (the 16th and 17th) receive complimentary breakfast and drinks every evening.

Dining: The hotel's Macleay Restaurant serves an interesting seafood buffet and Asian gourmet foods.

Amenities: Small outdoor pool, free access to Bayswater Gym just up the road, concierge, 24-hour room service, free daily newspaper, nightly turndown, shoe-shine, laundry, valet, baby-sitting, gift shop.

MODERATE

Chateau Sydney Hotel. 14 Macleay St., Potts Point, NSW 2011. ☎ **1800/221 412** in Australia or 02/9358 2500 (☎ 800/624-3524 in the U.S. and Canada). Fax 02/9358 1959. 96 units. MINIBAR TV TEL. A$180–$200 (U.S.$126–$140) double, depending on view; A$350 (U.S.$245) suite.

Additional person A$20 (U.S.$14) extra. Children under 12 stay free in parents' room. Ask about lower weekend rates and packages. AE, BC, DC, JCB, MC, V. Free parking. CityRail: Kings Cross, about 1km (half a mile) away. Bus: 311 from Circular Quay.

This boutique hotel is a sister to the Sebel of Sydney (see above) and in direct competition with the Rex Hotel and the Landmark Parkroyal (see below and above, respectively), all three of which I prefer to this older-style property. Rooms here are light and look out either across the city or onto the sailboats in Elizabeth Bay. There's a lot of 1970s wood grain around, and rooms have queen-size beds, pay-per-view movies, irons and ironing boards, and the like. Along with the views, the one thing this place does have in its favor is the superb service. The Terrace is a comfortable restaurant serving pastas, steaks, and seafood. Amenities include an outdoor heated pool, concierge, 24-hour room service, free daily newspapers, laundry, valet, and baby-sitting.

The Rex Hotel. 50-58 Macleay St., Potts Point, NSW 2011. ☎ **02/9383 7788.** Fax 02/9383 7777. 255 units. A/C MINIBAR TV TEL. A$220 (U.S.$154) double; A$280–$420 (U.S.$196–$294) suite. Additional person A$20 (U.S.$14) extra. Child under 14 stay free in parents' room. AE, BC, DC, JCB, MC, V. Parking A$5 (U.S.$3.50). CityRail: Kings Cross.

The Rex, a modern, pristine establishment with all the modern conveniences you'd expect, was opened in mid-1997. Guest rooms are quite large and comfortable, with extras such as Asian-style noodles in the minibar. Some standard rooms and all suites have good views across the Sydney Opera House and Harbour Bridge, and all suites have private terraces. There's a large pool, a spa, a gym, a laundry service, baby-sitting, a concierge, and 24-hour room service. The Compass Bar overlooks busy MacLeay Street, and Fitzroys restaurant serves Modern Australian food.

INEXPENSIVE

O'Malleys Hotel. 228 William St., on the corner of Brougham St. (P.O. Box 468), Kings Cross, NSW 2011. ☎ **02/9357 2211.** Fax 02/9357 2656. 15 units. A/C TV TEL. A$82.50–$93.50 (U.S.$57.75–$65.45) double. Rates include continental breakfast. AE, BC, MC, V. On-street parking. CityRail: Kings Cross.

If you don't mind a short stagger up the stairs from the popular "backpackers" Irish Pub below, then you'll enjoy this place. It's just a 2-minute stroll from the main Kings Cross drag and has standard-size three-star rooms. The rooms on the first floor are cheaper, because they are right above the bar—and the cheery hum of drinkers below could keep you awake (the bar's open from 11am to 3am Mon to Sat, and noon to midnight on Sun). Rooms on the second floor are much quieter and a good value. All rooms are furnished country-style, with natural wood trim, and have private bathrooms (although bathrooms for rooms on the first floor are across the corridor).

A BED & BREAKFAST INN

Simpsons of Potts Point. 8 Challis Ave., Potts Point, NSW 2011. ☎ **02/ 9356 2199.** Fax 02/9356 4476. 14 units. A/C MINIBAR TV TEL. A$160 (U.S.$112) double; A$175 (U.S.$122.50) queen room; A$245 (U.S.$171.50) Cloud Suite (includes private spa). Rates include breakfast. BC, MC, V. Free parking. CityRail: Kings Cross, about 1km (half a mile) away. Bus: 311 from Circular Quay. Children under 12 not allowed.

Though this B&B is quite a bit away from the main shopping areas and tourist attractions (though a subway CityRail from Kings Cross will get you to Town Hall in about 5 minutes), this drawback is offset by the old-world charm you'd be hard-pressed to find for the price anywhere nearer the city center. This National Trust–listed property was built in 1892 and retains the charm of the period in its stained-glass windows, period antiques, and cedar staircase. Rooms are large; some have a tub/shower combination, while others have just a shower. All are warmed in winter by open fires, and cooled in summer by ceiling fans (or air-conditioning). The breakfast room is particularly nice—it's a restored, high-beamed glass conservatory overlooking trees and shrubs in the garden. There's a laundry on the premises.

SERVICED APARTMENTS

Dorchester Inn. 38 Macleay St., Potts Point, NSW 2011. ☎ **02/9358 2400.** Fax 02/9357 7579. 14 apts. A/C TV TEL. A$98 (U.S.$68.60) studio double; A$160 (U.S.$112) executive studio or 1-bedroom apt; A$210 (U.S.$147) 2-bedroom apt. Additional person A$15 (U.S.$10.50) extra. AE, BC, DC, MC, V. Parking A$8 (U.S.$5.60). CityRail: Kings Cross. Bus: 311 from Circular Quay.

This Victorian mansion, in the same block as the Chateau Sydney Hotel (see above), boasts that 70% of its guests have stayed there before. It's a favorite with people from overseas, particularly North Americans, who use it as a home base to discover Sydney and the rest of the country, and who prefer the personalized service offered by the small staff rather than the anonymity of larger hotels. The reception desk takes up most of the foyer in this colonial relic. Each apartment is spacious and bright, and furnished with reproduction antiques. All have kitchenettes with conventional ovens as well as microwaves, queen-size or double beds, and free in-house movies. There's a good Japanese steak house and a coffee shop on the premises, plus an upscale Thai restaurant next door.

6   In Darlinghurst

Oxford Koala Hotel. Corner of Oxford and Pelican sts. (P.O. Box 535), Darlinghurst, NSW 2010. ☎ **1800/222 144** in Australia or 02/9269 0645. Fax 02/9283 2741. 330 units (including 78 apts). A/C TV TEL. A$120–$140 (U.S.$84–$98) double; A$160 (U.S.$112) 1-bedroom apt. Additional person A$25 (U.S.$17.50) extra. Children under 14 stay free in parents' room. AE, BC, DC, JCB, MC, V. Free parking. Bus: 380 or any bus traveling via Taylor Sq.

You won't find many three-star hotels that offer as much value for your dollar as the Oxford Koala. A very popular tourist hotel, it is well placed just off trendy Oxford Street, a 5- to 10-minute bus trip from the city center and Circular Quay. There are 13 floors of rooms in this tower block; rooms on the top floor have reasonable views over the city. Superior rooms (A$140/U.S.$98) are very comfortable and more spacious than standard rooms and have better-quality furniture. All come with a shower/tub combination or just a shower. Apartments are good-sized, come with a full kitchen and are serviced daily. On the premises are a swimming pool, a restaurant, and a cocktail bar.

A BED & BREAKFAST INN

Wattle Private Hotel. 108 Oxford St. (at Palmer St.), Darlinghurst, NSW 2010. ☎ **02/9332 4118.** Fax 02/9331 2074. 12 units. MINIBAR TV TEL. A$88 (U.S.$61.60) double. Additional person A$10 (U.S.$7) extra. Rates include continental breakfast. BC, MC, V. Parking not available. Bus: Taylor Sq.

This attractive Edwardian-style house, built between 1900 and 1910, offers homey accommodation in the increasingly fashionable inner-city suburb of Darlinghurst, known for its great cafes, nightlife, and restaurants. Rooms are found on four stories, but there's no elevator (lift), so if you don't fancy too many stairs, try to get a room on the lower floor. Rooms are smallish, but are opened up by large windows. Twin rooms have better bathrooms, with tubs. The decor is a jumble of Chinese vases, ceiling fans, and contemporary bedspreads. Laundry facilities are on the premises.

7   In Bondi

Ravesi's on Bondi Beach. Corner of Hall St. and Campbell Parade, Bondi Beach (NSW P.O. Box 198, Bondi Junction 2022). ☎ **02/9365 4422.** Fax 02/9365 1481. 16 units. A/C TV TEL. A$99 (U.S.$69.30) standard double; A$135–$145 (U.S.$94.50–$101.50) double with side view; A$165 (U.S.$115.50) 1-bedroom suite; A$190 (U.S.$133) split-level 1-bedroom; A$165–$190 (U.S.$115.50–$133) ocean view. Additional person A$20 (U.S.$14) extra. 2 children under 14 stay free in parents' room. AE, DC, MC, V. Free parking. CityRail: to Bondi Junction then bus 380. Bus: 380 from Circular Quay.

Right on Australia's most famous golden sands, this art-deco boutique property offers Mediterranean-influenced rooms with a beachy decor. Standard doubles are spacious, quite basic, and don't have air-conditioning—though you'd hardly need it with the ocean breeze. The one-bedroom suite is good for families, having two sofa beds in the living room. The split-level room has a bedroom upstairs and a single sofa bed in the living area. Rooms 5 and 6 and the split-level suite have the best views of the ocean. All rooms have Juliet balconies, and the split-level suite has its own terrace. It's best to request a room on the top floor because the popular Ravesi's Restaurant can cook up quite a bit of noise on busy nights.

8 On the North Shore

Duxton Hotel. 88 Alfred St., Milsons Point, NSW 2061. ☎ **02/9955 1111.** Fax 02/9955 3522. 165 units. A/C MINIBAR TV TEL. A$255 (U.S.$178.50) double; A$335 (U.S.$234.50) suite. Additional person $20 (U.S.$14) extra. AE, BC, DC, MC, V. Free parking. CityRail: Milsons Point.

The newest hotel on the North Shore, the four-star Duxton Hotel is at the far end of the Harbour Bridge and right opposite Milsons Point train station, which in turn is just one stop from the city center. Some rooms and all suites have fabulous views of the yachts moored in Lavender Bay and across the water to the Harbour Bridge and Opera House. Rooms are light and comfortable, with satellite TV and pay-per-view movies. The hotel is especially popular with business travelers.

Dining: The hotel's restaurant has an extensive selection of finely prepared Modern Australian–style meals.

Amenities: Small pool and sauna, concierge, 24-hour room service, free daily newspaper, laundry, baby-sitting, business center.

9 In Manly

Manly is 30 minutes from Circular Quay by ferry, or 15 minutes by JetCat.

EXPENSIVE

✪ **Manly Pacific Parkroyal.** 55 North Steyne, Manly, NSW 2095. ☎ **800/ 835-7742** in the U.S. and Canada (☎ 02/9977 7666 in Australia). Fax 02/9977 7822. 169 units. A/C MINIBAR TV TEL. A$250–$290 (U.S.$175–$203) double, depending on view; A$400–$440 (U.S.$280–$308) suite. Additional person A$25 (U.S.$17.50) extra. AE, BC, DC, JCB, MC, V.

If you could bottle the views from this top-class hotel—across the sand and through the Norfolk Island Pines to the Pacific Ocean— you'd make a fortune. Standing on your private balcony in the evening with the sea breeze in your nostrils and the chirping of hundreds of lorikeets in the trees searching for a pine-tree roost is nothing short of heaven. The Manly Pacific is the only hotel of its class in this wonderful beachside suburb. There's nothing claustrophobic here, from the broad expanse of glittering foyer to the wide corridors and spacious rooms. Views over the ocean are really worth paying extra for, but in any case each standard room is light and modern with two double beds, a balcony, limited cable TV, and everything necessary from robes to an iron and ironing board. The hotel is a pleasant 10-minute walk (or a A$4/U.S.$2.80 taxi fare) from the Manly ferry.

Dining/Diversions: Gilbert's Restaurant has fine dining and views of the Pacific. Nells Brasserie & Cocktail Bar serves a buffet breakfast and dinner daily, with a menu ranging from complete meals to snacks. The Charlton Bar and Grill has live bands every evening from Wednesday to Sunday and attracts a young crowd.

Amenities: Rooftop spa, pool, gym, sauna, concierge, 24-hour room service, laundry.

MODERATE

Manly Paradise Motel and Beach Plaza Apartments. 54 North Steyne, Manly, NSW 2095. ☎ **1800/815 789** in Australia or 02/9977 5799. Fax 02/9977 6848. 20 units, 16 apts. A/C TV TEL. A$85–$115 (U.S.$59.50–$80.50) double motel unit; A$210 (U.S.$147) 2-bedroom apt. Additional person A$20 (U.S.$14) extra. Ask about lower long-stay rates. AE, BC, DC, MC, V. Parking free, with undercover security.

I walked into this place after taking a good look around the modern Manly Waterfront Apartment Hotel next door and immediately felt more at home here. The motel and the apartment complex are separate from each other, but share the same reception area. Though there is one motel room that goes for A$85 (U.S.$59.50), it's a bit small for my liking, but the rest of the irregularly shaped rooms are big yet cozy, and come with a shower (no tub) and a springy double bed. Though there is no restaurant, you can get breakfast in bed. My only concern is that the traffic outside can make it a little noisy during the day. Some rooms have sea glimpses. A swimming pool (with views) on the roof is shared with the apartment complex.

The apartments are magnificent—very roomy, with thick carpets—and are stocked with everything you need, including a private laundry, a full kitchen with dishwasher, and two bathrooms (one with a tub). The sea views from the main front balcony are heartstopping.

A GUEST HOUSE

Manly Lodge. 22 Victoria Parade, Manly, NSW 2095. ☎ **02/9977 8655.** Fax 02/9976 2090. 30 units. A/C TV. A$98–$120 (U.S.$68.60–$84) double, depending on season; A$120–$140 (U.S.$84–$98) deluxe room; A$110–$140 (U.S.$77–$98) family room; A$170–$240 (U.S.$119–$168) 2-bedroom family suite with spa. Rates include continental breakfast. Additional person A$28 (U.S.$19.60) extra. Children under 10 A$15 (U.S.$10.50) extra when they stay in parents' room. Ask about weekly rates; management will also negotiate off-season prices. AE, BC, MC, V. Free parking.

At first sight, this ramshackle building halfway between the main beach and the harbor doesn't look like much—especially the cramped youth-hostel foyer bristling with tourist brochures. But don't let the taint of tattiness put you off. Some of the rooms here are really lovely, and the whole place has a nice atmosphere about it and plenty of character. Double rooms are not exceptional, and come with a double bed, stone or carpet floors, a TV and VCR, a small kitchen area, and either a spa or tub-and-shower combination. Each family room has a set of bunk beds and a double in one room, and a shower. Family suites are very classy, come with a small kitchen area, one double and three singles in the bedroom, and two sofa beds in the living area. The lodge also has a communal spa, sauna, gym, laundry, table tennis, and even an Olympic-size trampoline.

10 At the Airport

The three airport hotels listed below also accommodate guests for short-term stays between flights. Sample costs for the Sheraton are A$60 (U.S.$42) for two hours and A$70 (U.S.$49) for four hours.

Sheraton Sydney Airport Hotel. Corner of O'Riordan and Robey sts., (P.O. Box 353), Mascot, Sydney, NSW 2020. ☎ **1800/073 535** in Australia, 800/325-3535 in the U.S. and Canada, 0800/353 535 in the UK, 0800/443535 in New Zealand, or 02/9317 2200. Fax 02/9669 1116. 314 units. A/C MINIBAR TV TEL. A$240–$265 double (U.S.$168–$185.50); A$390 (U.S.$273) suite; A$900 (U.S.$630) Governor and Royal suites. Additional person A$25 (U.S.$17.50) extra. Children under 17 free in parents' room. Ask about discount packages and weekend rates. AE, BC, DC, JCB, MC, V. Free parking.

Of the three airport hotels, this is by far the best. Opened in 1992, it has the largest rooms complete with a king size bed or two twins, in-house movies, access to airport information, and a good-sized bathroom with tub. It's close to the airport, too, with the free pick-up service taking only around seven minutes to do the dash to and from the airport. It's also got a fine gym and a good outdoor swimming pool.

Dining/Diversions: The two restaurants here serve buffet and à la carte meals. There's also a lounge bar.

Amenities: Concierge, 24-hour room service, laundry, valet, free daily newspapers, nightly turndown, pool, spa and sauna, fitness center, business center, meeting facilities, currency exchange.

Sydney Airport Parkroyal. Corner of O'Riordan St. and Bourke Rd., Mascot, NSW 2020. ☎ **1800/621 859** in Australia, or 02/9330 0600. Fax 02/9667 4517. 244 units. A/C MINIBAR TV TEL. A$270 (U.S.$189) double; A$390 (U.S.$273) suite. Additional person A$25 (U.S.$17.50) extra. Children under 15 free in parents' room. Ask about packages. AE, BC, DC, JCB, MC, V. Free parking.

Ranking number two in my opinion, the Parkroyal is a modern '90s hotel with all the facilities you'd expect except a swimming pool. Rooms are moderately large with either king size or queen beds, in-house movies, and facilities to access the airport arrival and departure information. Free shuttle buses take five minutes to and from the airport. The Parkroyal's service can be variable.

Dining/Diversions: Amelia's Brasserie and the Biggles Bar and Cafe both serve up food. There's also a comfortable bar.

Amenities: Concierge, 24-hour room service, laundry, free daily newspapers, nightly turndown on request, fitness center, hotel gift shop, business and meeting facilities, currency exchange. There are a newsstand and takeaway food shop belonging to an office complex below.

Hilton Sydney Airport. 20 Levey St., Arncliffe, NSW 2205. ☎ **02/9518 2000.** Fax 02/9518 2002. 266 units. A/C MINIBAR TV TEL. A$230–$290 (U.S.$161–$203) double. Additional person A$50 extra. Children under 16 free in parents' room. Ask about weekend and special packages. AE, BC, DC, JCB, MC, V. Free parking.

Trying to gather basic information for this guide from the Hilton's administrative staff was like trying to squeeze blood from a stone. It's the oldest of the three hotels, built in 1981 and showing its age. Rooms are nothing to write home about. The indoor pool is nice, though, and there's a BBQ area. The biggest advantage of staying here is its proximity to Kogarah Golf Course just over the road. It takes around seven minutes to get to/from the airport on the free hotel shuttle service.

Dining/Diversions: Seasons restaurant offers all meals. There's also a cocktail bar.

Amenities: Concierge, 24-hour room service, laundry, free daily newspapers, pool, spa and sauna, fitness center, business center, meeting facilities, currency exchange, lobby gift shop.

4

Dining

Sydney is a gourmet paradise, with an abundance of fresh seafood, a vast range of vegetables and fruit always in season, prime meats at inexpensive prices, and top-quality chefs making an international name for themselves. You'll find that Asian cooking has had a major influence on Australian cooking, with spices and herbs finding their way into most dishes. Immigration has brought with it almost every type of cuisine you could imagine, from African to Tibetan, from Russian to Vietnamese, with whole areas of the city dedicated to one type of food, while other areas are a true melting pot of styles. Most moderate and inexpensive restaurants in Sydney are BYO, as in "bring your own" bottle, though some may also have extensive wine and beer lists of their own. Watch out for "corkage" fees, marked on the menu, which could mean you pay anywhere from A$1 to $4 (U.S.70¢ to $2.80) per person for the privilege of the waiter opening your bottle of wine. You can "bring your own bottle" to more expensive restaurants, but they generally turn up their noses at customers who do so, pointing out that their wine list is hand-picked by experts, so bringing your own is an insult. (Plus, they'll whack you with a hefty corkage fee, so it's usually more economical to order off the wine list.)

1 Restaurants by Cuisine

AFRICAN

Le Kilimanjaro (Newtown, *I*)

BARBECUE

Phillip's Foote (The Rocks, *M*)

BAVARIAN

The Löwenbräu Keller (The Rocks, *M*)

INDIAN

Ashiana (Manly, *I*)

INTERNATIONAL

Bourbon & Beefsteak Bar (Kings Cross & Beyond, *M*)

Level Two Revolving Restaurant (Near Town Hall, *E*)

Key to abbreviations: *VE* = Very Expensive, *E* = Expensive, *M* = Moderate, *I* = Inexpensive

ITALIAN

City Extra (Near Circular
   Quay, *I*)
No Names (Darlinghurst, *I*)
Rossini (Near Circular
   Quay, *I*)

JAPANESE

Shiki (The Rocks, *M*)

MEDITERRANEAN

Botanic Gardens Restaurant
   (Near Circular Quay, *E*)
The Gumnut Tea Garden
   (The Rocks, *I*)

MODERN ASIAN

The Wokpool (Darling
   Harbour, *E*)

MODERN AUSTRALIAN

Bayswater Brasserie (*M*,
   Kings Cross & the
   Suburbs Beyond)
Bennelong Restaurant (Near
   Circular Quay, *VE*)
Forty One (Near Circular
   Quay, *VE*)
Merrony's (Near Circular
   Quay, *VE*)
Reds (The Rocks, *E*)
Rockpool (The Rocks, *VE*)

MODERN ITALIAN

bel mondo (The Rocks, *VE*)
Mezzaluna (Kings Cross &
   the Suburbs Beyond, *E*)

MODERN THAI

Darley Street Thai (Kings
   Cross & the Suburbs
   Beyond, *E*)

NORTHERN ITALIAN

L'Incontro Italian Restaurant
   (The North Shore, *E*)

PASTA

Sketches Bar and Bistro
   (Near Circular Quay, *I*)
Zia Pina (The Rocks, *I*)

PIZZA

Portobello Café (Near
   Circular Quay, *I*)
Zia Pina (The Rocks, *I*)

SEAFOOD

Bilson's (The Rocks, *VE*)
Doyles at the Quay (The
   Rocks, *E*)
Fishy Affair (Bondi, *M*)
MCA Café (Near Circular
   Quay, *M*)
Sydney Cove Oyster Bar
   (Near Circular Quay, *M*)
Waterfront Restaurant (The
   Rocks, *E*)

SPANISH

Captain Torres (Near Town
   Hall, *M*)

THAI

Nina's Ploy Thai Restaurant
   (Bondi, *I*)
Sailors Thai (The Rocks, *M*)

VEGETARIAN

Govindas (Kings Cross & the
   Suburbs Beyond, *I*)

VIETNAMESE

Old Saigon
   (Newtown, *I*)

2 Near Circular Quay

VERY EXPENSIVE

Forty One. Level 41, Chifley Tower, 2 Chifley Sq. ☎ **02/9221 2500.** Reservations essential. Main courses lunch Mon–Fri A$28 (U.S.$19.60); Sun lunch: 3 courses A$70 (U.S.$49), 4 courses A$80 (U.S.$56), 5 courses A$90 (U.S.$63). Mon–Sat dinner: 3 courses A$75 (U.S.$52.50), 4 courses A$85 (U.S.$59.50), 5 courses A$95 (U.S.$66.50). AE, BC, DC, MC, V. Sun–Fri noon–2:30pm; Mon–Sat 6:30pm–late. CityRail: Wynyard. MODERN AUSTRALIAN.

Powerful people, international celebrities, and average Sydneysiders out for a special celebration all come here to feel exclusive. The views over the city are terrific, the service is fun, the cutlery is the world's best, and Swiss-chef Dietmar Sawyere has given the food a wickedly good Asian slant. In all, it's a very glamorous place to experience the best of Australian cuisine. Try the specialty crown roast wild hare, with braised Belgian endives and chartreuse jus. The seared yellowfin tuna on sesame and miso English spinach is another favorite. If there are 6 to 10 people in your group, hire one of the three special private dining rooms.

Merrony's. 2 Albert St., Circular Quay. ☎ **02/9247 9323.** Reservations recommended for lunch any day and dinner Fri–Sat. Main courses A$28–$29.75 (U.S.$19.60–$20.85). AE, BC, DC, MC, V. Mon–Fri noon–3pm; Mon–Sat 5:45pm–late. Closed public holidays. CityRail, bus, or ferry: Circular Quay. MODERN AUSTRALIAN.

Come here for great views across Sydney Harbour towards the Harbour Bridge and the Luna Park fun fair and the wonderfully acclaimed bistro-style food from master chef Paul Merrony. The signature mains are the fillet of beef with mashed potatoes, witloof, and sautéed mushrooms; and the steamed John Dory with eggplant purée, crushed olives, and potato galette. Follow the locals by coming here before or after a show at the Opera House. The wine list is extensive. If you need to drive, the restaurant has a parking arrangement with the adjacent Ritz-Carlton hotel (it costs A$5/U.S.$3.50).

Bennelong Restaurant. In the Sydney Opera House, Bennelong Point. ☎ **02/9250 7548** or 02/9250 7578. Reservations recommended. Main courses A$30–$35 (U.S.$21–$24.50). AE, BC, DC, MC, V. Mon–Sat 7–10:30pm. CityRail, bus, or ferry: Circular Quay. MODERN AUSTRALIAN.

The Bennelong belongs up there in the must-do category. If you go to Bondi, you have to swim in the Pacific; if you see the Harbour

Central Sydney Dining

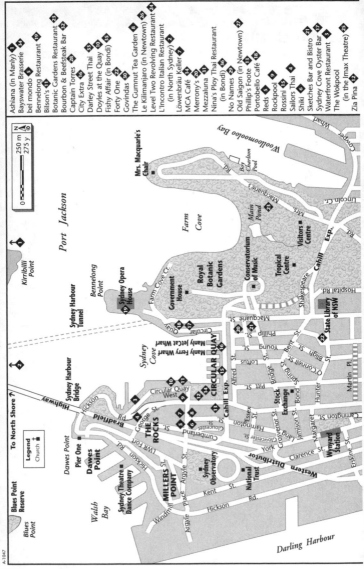

Ashiana (in Manly) 🔷
Bayswater Brasserie 🔷
bel mondo 🔷
Bennelong Restaurant 🔷
Bilson's 🔷
Botanic Gardens Restaurant 🔷
Bourbon & Beefsteak Bar 🔷
Captain Torres 🔷
City Extra 🔷
Darley Street Thai 🔷
Doyles at the Quay 🔷
Fishy Affair (in Bondi) 🔷
Forty One 🔷
Govindas 🔷
The Gumnut Tea Garden 🔷
Le Kilimanjaro (in Newtown) 🔷
Level Two Revolving Restaurant 🔷
L'Incontro Italian Restaurant
  (in North Sydney) 🔷
Löwenbräu Keller 🔷
MCA Café 🔷
Merrony's 🔷
Mezzaluna 🔷
Nina's Ploy Thai Restaurant
  (in Bondi) 🔷
No Names 🔷
Old Saigon (in Newtown) 🔷
Philip's Foote 🔷
Portobello Café 🔷
Reds 🔷
Rockpool 🔷
Rossini 🔷
Sailors Thai 🔷
Shiki 🔷
Sketches Bar and Bistro 🔷
Sydney Cove Oyster Bar 🔷
Waterfront Restaurant 🔷
The Wokpool
  (in the Imax Theatre) 🔷
Zia Pina 🔷

84

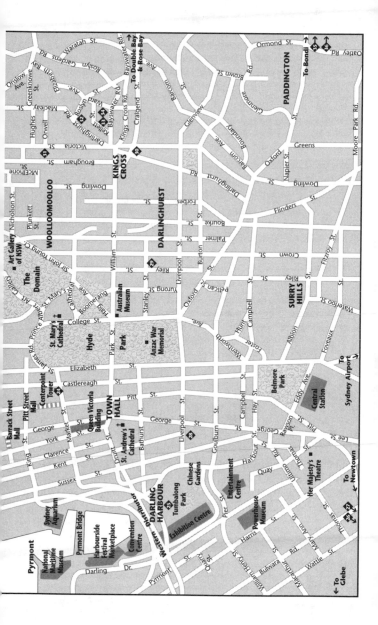

Bridge, you have to walk across it; if you visit the Opera House, you have to eat at the Bennelong. The restaurant is as uniquely designed as the building itself, with tall glass windows furrowing around in an arch and grabbing the harbor and Circular Quay by the throat. Diners munch on mains such as roasted tuna steak and roasted tomato with tomato-and-chili jam, or red emperor with sweet-and-sour eggplant baked in clay, and often eat through the first half of the opera they'd paid a fortune for because otherwise they'd miss out on dessert.

EXPENSIVE

Botanic Gardens Restaurant. Mrs. Macquarie's Rd., in the Royal Botanic Gardens. ☎ **02/9241 2419.** Reservations recommended. Main courses A$21–$28 (U.S.$14.70–$19.60). AE, BC, DC, MC, V. Daily noon–2:30pm. Bus or ferry: Circular Quay. MEDITERRANEAN.

You couldn't hope for a better walk to get to a restaurant than through the Royal Botanic Gardens, next to the Sydney Opera House. Enjoying lunch out on the wisteria-covered balcony right in the middle of Sydney's most beautiful park is a treat every visitor should enjoy. The food is somewhat pricey, but it's got a great reputation. The desserts (A$12.50/U.S.$8.75)—such as the fig, walnut, and mascarpone tart with rosewater granita—make my mouth water just writing about them.

MODERATE

MCA Café. Museum of Contemporary Art, Circular Quay West. ☎ **02/9241 4253.** Main courses A$19–$20 (U.S.$13.30–$14). 10% surcharge weekends and public holidays. AE, BC, MC, V. Daily noon–2:30pm. CityRail, bus, or ferry: Circular Quay. SEAFOOD.

If you find yourself having lunch at 1 of the 16 tables outside the old sandstone building to the west of Circular Quay, consider yourself fortunate. The views over the ferries and the Opera House are wonderful and you are far enough away from the crowds of Circular Quay to watch the action without feeling a spectacle yourself. Whether you dine outside or in, the food here is great. Eighty percent of the dishes are seafood, but there are some pasta and meat dishes, too. The signature dishes are the trevally (a sea fish) with a lemon, olive, and parsley salad, and the smoked salmon lasagna with eggplant caviar.

Sydney Cove Oyster Bar. No. 1 Eastern Esplanade, Circular Quay East. ☎ **02/9247 2937.** Main courses A$20–$23.50 (U.S.$14–$16.45). 10% surcharge weekends and public holidays. AE, BC, DC, MC, V. Mon–Sat 11am–11pm, Sun 11am–8pm. CityRail, ferry, or bus: Circular Quay. SEAFOOD.

Just before you reach the Sydney Opera House, you'll notice a couple of small shedlike buildings with tables and chairs set up to take in the stunning views of the harbor and the Harbour Bridge. The first of these is a Sydney institution, serving some of the best natural Sydney rock oysters in town. Light meals such as Asian-style octopus and seared tuna steak are also on the menu.

INEXPENSIVE

City Extra. Shop E4, Circular Quay. ☎ **02/9241 1422.** Main courses A$10.30–$17.65 (U.S.$7.20–$12.35). 10% surcharge midnight–6am, Sun, and public holidays. AE, BC, DC, MC, V. Daily 24 hours. CityRail, bus, or ferry: Circular Quay. ITALIAN.

Because this place stays open all day and all night, it's convenient if you get the munchies at a ridiculous hour. It's also nicely placed right next to the Manly ferry terminal. The plastic chairs and tables placed outside make it a pleasant spot to while away an inexpensive meal. A range of pastas is offered as well as salads, pies, steaks, ribs, fish, and Asian-influenced dishes. There's also a fat selection of deserts. That said, I agree with several friends of mine who believe the food's much nicer and a better value next door at Rossini.

Portobello Café. No.1 Eastern Esplanade, Circular Quay East. ☎ **02/9247 8548.** Main courses A$8 (U.S.$5.60). 10% surcharge Sun and public holidays. AE, BC, DC, JCB, MC, V. Credit-card minimum purchase A$30 (U.S.$21). Daily 8am–11:50pm. CityRail, bus, or ferry: Circular Quay. PIZZA/SANDWICHES.

Sharing the same address as the Sydney Cove Oyster Bar (and the same priceless views), the Portobello Café offers first-class gourmet sandwiches on Italian wood-fired bread, small but delicious gourmet pizzas, breakfast croissants, snacks, cakes, and hot and cold drinks. Walk off with sensational ice cream in a cone for around A$3 (U.S.$2.10).

✪ **Rossini.** Shop W5, Circular Quay. ☎ **02/9247 8026.** Main courses A$7–$14 (U.S.$4.90–$9.80). Cash only. Daily 7am–10:30pm. CityRail, bus, or ferry: Circular Quay. ITALIAN.

This cafeteria-style Italian restaurant opposite ferry wharf 5 at Circular Quay is wonderfully positioned for people-watching. The outside tables make it a perfect spot for breakfast or a quick bite before a show at the Opera House. Breakfast croissants, Italian donuts, muffins, and gorgeous Danish pastries cost just A$2 (U.S.$1.40) and bacon and eggs just A$8 (U.S.$5.60). Wait to be seated for dinner, make your choice, pay your money at the counter, take a ticket, and then pick up your food. Meals, including veal parmigiana, cannelloni, ravioli, chicken crepes, and octopus salad, are large and tasty. Coffee fanatics I know rate the Rossini brew as only average.

Sketches Bar and Bistro. In the Hotel Inter-Continental, 117 Macquarie St. (enter from Bridge St.). ☎ **02/9230 0200.** Reservations recommended. Pasta A$10.90–$12.90 (U.S.$7.65–$9); help-yourself salads A$4.10 (U.S.$2.85). Pastas and salads an extra A$2 (U.S.$1.40) each on weekends. AE, BC, DC, MC, V. Mon–Fri 5:30–9:30pm; Sat 5:30–10pm. CityRail, bus, or ferry: Circular Quay. PASTA.

Sketches is a favorite with people on their way to the Opera House and those who really know a good cheap meal when they taste one. After getting the barman's attention, point at one of three different-sized plates stuck to the bar itself, above your head—a small size is adequate if you're an average eater, a medium is good for filling up after a hard day of sightseeing (and no lunch), while I've yet to meet a man who can handle the large serving with its accompanying bread, pine nuts, and Parmesan cheese. Then, with ticket in hand, head towards the chefs in white hats and place your order. There are 12 pastas to choose from and several sauces, including carbonara, marinara, pesto, vegetarian, and some unusual ones such as south Indian curry. It's all cooked in seconds while you wait. Bring your own pasta if you suffer from wheat intolerance.

3 In The Rocks

VERY EXPENSIVE

bel mondo. 3rd floor in the Argyle Department Store, 12 Argyle St., The Rocks. ☎ **02/9241 3700.** Reservations recommended well in advance. Main courses A$33–$39 (U.S.$23.10–$27.30). 10% surcharge Sun and public holidays. AE, BC, DC, MC, V. Mon–Fri noon–2:30pm; Mon–Thurs 6:30–10:30pm; Fri–Sat 6:30–11pm; Sun 6:30–10pm. CityRail, bus, or ferry: Circular Quay. NORTHERN ITALIAN.

bel mondo has deservedly positioned itself alongside the very best of Sydney's upscale restaurants with its uncomplicated northern Italian cuisine. At this family-run affair, chef Stefano Manfredi is helped out in the kitchen by his mum Franca, a pasta diva in her own right. The restaurant is large and long with high ceilings. The energetic pace and the banging and clashing coming from the open kitchen give the place a New York brasserie feel. Standout appetizers include grilled sea scallops with soft polenta and pesto. Favorite mains include roast suckling-pig cutlets with beans and olives, and roast pigeon with Italian couscous and potato. The wine list is very extensive. bel mondo's Antibar is cheaper, more relaxed, has a good

---

👬 Family-Friendly Restaurants

Rossini *(see page 87)* This indoor/outdoor dining spot right next to the ferry terminals on Circular Quay offers authentic Italian food with small pizzas and half-portion pastas perfect for children.

Level Two Revolving Restaurant *(see page 93)* This rotating eagle's-nest restaurant is located atop the impossible-to-miss AMP Centerpoint Tower. Kids 3 to 12 can munch on discounted lunch and early dinner portions as they stare goggle-eyed at the views across the city.

The Gumnut Tea Garden *(see page 92)* Take a break from sightseeing around The Rocks at this delightful little cafe/restaurant. Cheap lunches appealing to both adults and children are served in a leafy courtyard atmosphere.

---

selection of antipasto and lighter meals, and features jazz on Friday evenings from 5:30 to 7:30pm.

Bilson's. On the upper level of the Overseas Passenger terminal, Circular Quay West, The Rocks. ☎ **02/9251 5600.** Reservations recommended well in advance. Main courses A$33–$42 (U.S.$23.10–$29.40). A$6 (U.S.$4.20) per person surcharge Sun and public holidays. AE, BC, DC, JCB, MC, V. Daily noon–9:30pm. CityRail, bus, or ferry: Circular Quay. SEAFOOD.

Without question, Bilson's is Sydney's best fish and seafood restaurant—and, with its enviable location on top of the cruise-ship terminal, it offers perhaps the loveliest view in Sydney, too. In good weather the sun sparkles off the expanse of water, and from the large glass windows the Opera House, the city skyline, the North Shore suburbs, and the Harbour Bridge all look magnificent. At night, when the lights from the city wash over the harbor and the bridge and the Opera House's sails are all lit up, it's even better—making dinner in this place a truly magical experience. Expensive, yet select, this restaurant has tempted all the big-name visitors to Sydney. Believe me, they tell all their friends.

Rockpool. 109 George St., The Rocks. ☎ **02/9252 1888.** Reservations required. Main courses A$38 (U.S.$26.60). AE, BC, DC, MC, V. Mon–Fri noon–2:30pm and 6:30–10pm; Sat 6:30–11pm. CityRail, bus, or ferry: Circular Quay. MODERN AUSTRALIAN.

The Rockpool is an institution in Sydney, known for its inventive food. It's approached by a steep ramp and opens up into two stories of ocean-green carpet, designer chairs, and stainless steel. Along with the bar, the kitchen—with its busy chefs and range of copper pots and pans—is very much at the center of things. Menus change regularly, but you can expect to find anything from a dozen fresh oysters and spanner crab with lemon ravioli to fish cooked with coconut milk and Indian garum marsala and served with snow peas and semolina noodles. On my last visit, the desserts were a letdown after the fabulous main courses.

EXPENSIVE

Doyles at the Quay. Overseas Passenger terminal, Circular Quay. ☎ **02/ 9252 3400.** Main courses A$20–33 (U.S.$14–$23.10). AE, BC, DC, JCB, MC, V. Daily 11:30am–2:45pm; Mon–Sat 5:30–9:30pm; Sun 5:30–9pm. CityRail, bus, or ferry: Circular Quay. SEAFOOD.

Just below Bilson's (see above) is Doyles, a name synonymous with seafood in Sydney. Most customers sit outside to enjoy the fabulous views across the harbor, though a set of thick green railings does interrupt the view of the Opera House somewhat. Businesspeople and tourists come here if they don't want to lay out the cash for Bilson's or if they fancy a more relaxed style. The most popular dish here is basically pricey fish-and-chips (choose between ocean trout, garfish, John Dory, swordfish, whiting, and salmon). You can also pick up a dozen oysters for A$20 (U.S.$14) or a lobster for A$65 (U.S.$45.50). A second Doyles, Doyles on the Beach (☎ 02/9337 2007), at Watsons Bay, serves fabulous food. Nearby is a third Doyles, Doyles Fisherman's Wharf (☎ 02/9337 1572), located on the ferry wharf; it used to be a takeaway joint but now has sit-down service.

Reds. In the Argyle Department Store, 12 Argyle St., The Rocks. ☎ **02/9247 1011.** Reservations recommended. Main courses A$24–$49.50 (U.S.$16.80–$34.65). AE, BC, DC, MC, V. Daily noon–3pm and 5–10:30pm. CityRail, bus, or ferry: Circular Quay. MODERN AUSTRALIAN.

Revamped from its days as a barbecue restaurant, Reds is located in an 1828 bond store and warehouse. The light and airy dining area has a beachy feel. Light jazz trickles over the lemon-and-tangerine carpets to a bar area heaving with wooden beams, where you can have a drink before your meal. Contemporary starters include Sydney rock oysters and scallops with angel hair pasta, while you'll find char-grilled kangaroo strip loin with sweet potato on the limited selection of mains. Native herbs, nuts and berries, and exotic dairy produce are also featured.

Waterfront Restaurant. In Campbell's Storehouse, 27 Circular Quay West, The Rocks. ☎ **02/9247 3666.** Reservations recommended. Main courses A$23.90–$42.50 (U.S.$16.75–$29.75). A$3 (U.S.$2.10) per person surcharge weekends and public holidays. AE, BC, DC, MC, V. Daily noon to late. CityRail, bus, or ferry: Circular Quay. SEAFOOD.

You can't help but notice the mast, rigging, and sails outside this restaurant. It's very popular at lunch, when businesspeople snap up the best seats outside in the sunshine, but at night, with the colors of the city washing over the harbor, it can be magical. Most main courses cost a hefty A$25 (U.S.$17.50) or so, and for that you get a choice of such things as steaks, mud crab, fish fillets, prawns, or a seafood platter. The food is nice and simple, with the markup added for the location and views.

In the same building you'll find the Waterfront's sister restaurants **Wolfie's Grill** (☎ **02/9247 5577**), which serves good char-grilled beef and seafood dishes, and **The Italian Village** (☎ **02/9247 6111**), which serves regional Italian cuisine. Both these restaurants are similarly priced and offer fantastic water views and outdoor dining.

MODERATE

The Löwenbräu Keller. 18 Argyle St., The Rocks. ☎ **02/9247 7785.** Reservations recommended. Main courses A$15–$21.50 (U.S.$10.50–$15.05). AE, BC, DC, JCB, MC, V. Daily 9:30am–2am (kitchen closes 11pm). CityRail, bus, or ferry: Circular Quay. BAVARIAN.

Renowned for celebrating Oktoberfest every day for the past 20 years, this is the place to come to watch Aussies let their hair down. You can come for lunch and munch a club sandwich or focaccia in the glassed-off atrium while watching the daytime action of The Rocks. For a livelier scene, head here on a Friday or Saturday night, when mass beer-sculling (chugging) and yodeling are accompanied by a brass band, and costumed waitresses ferry foaming beer steins about the atmospheric, cellarlike bowels. Hearty southern German and Austrian fare and no fewer than 17 varieties of German beers in bottles or on draught (tap), are served. There's a good wine list, and, surprisingly, vegetarians are well catered for, too.

Phillip's Foote. 101 George St., The Rocks. ☎ **02/9241 1485.** Main courses A$17.50 (U.S.$12.25). AE, BC, JCB, MC, V. Mon–Sat noon–midnight; Sun noon–10pm. CityRail, bus, or ferry: Circular Quay. BARBECUE.

Venture back into the courtyard behind this historic pub and you'll find a popular courtyard strung with tables and benches and large barbecues. Choose your own steak, lemon sole, trout, chicken, or pork and throw it on the "barbie." It's fun, it's filling, and you might even meet some new friends while your meal's a-sizzling.

Sailors Thai. 106 George St., The Rocks. ☎ **02/9251 2466.** Reservations required well in advance; not accepted in canteen. Main courses A$14–$26 (U.S.$9.80–$18.20) in restaurant, A$11–$16 (U.S.$7.70–$11.20) in canteen. AE, BC, DC, MC, V. Restaurant Mon–Fri noon–2pm; Mon–Sat 6–11pm. Canteen daily noon–8pm. CityRail, bus, or ferry: Circular Quay. THAI.

With a reputation as hot as the chilies in its jungle curry, Sailors Thai canteen attracts lunchtime crowds who come to eat noodles, clams, curries, and Thai salads at its single, stainless-steel table lined with more than 40 chairs. Four other tables overlook the cruise-ship terminal and the quay. Downstairs an à la carte restaurant serves simple and cutting-edge food, like a pineapple curry of mussels and a steamed duck soup with pickles.

Shiki. Clock Tower Sq., corner of Argyle and Harrington sts., The Rocks. ☎ **02/9252 2431.** Reservations recommended well in advance. Meals around A$30 (U.S.$21) per person. AE, BC, DC, JCB, MC, V. Mon–Fri noon–2:30pm; daily 6–10pm. TRADITIONAL JAPANESE.

Shiki is making a name for itself as a top-flight place for traditional Japanese. You can eat at Western-style tables, at the sushi bar, or in one of the five tatami rooms, where you sit on Japanese mats around a raised table. Either way you can enjoy some good views over The Rocks (it's especially appealing at night, when the ferry lights strung across the area's trees are lit up). There are plenty of sushi, sashimi, and sukiyaki dishes on the menu, but "pot-cooking" at the table is very popular. Of these, the tobanyaki, where customers simmer a combination of beef and seafood on their own burner, steals the show. Lunch menus cost between A$13.50 (U.S.$9.45) and A$20 (U.S.$14), with the sushi plate—seven pieces, with six pieces of tuna rolls, salad, and miso soup—priced at A$20 (U.S.$14).

INEXPENSIVE

The Gumnut Tea Garden. 28 Harrington St., The Rocks. ☎ **02/9247 9591.** Main courses A$9.50–$12.50 (U.S.$6.65–$8.75). AE, BC, DC, MC, V. Daily 8am–5pm. CityRail, bus, or ferry: Circular Quay. MODERN MEDITERRANEAN.

A hearty lunch in a courtyard heavily scented with flowering shrubs and shaded from the sun by giant cream umbrellas—ah, heaven. With a great location in the heart of The Rocks, this delightful restaurant also has an extensive indoor seating area, so it's a perfect place to take a break from all that sightseeing. Breakfast specials (A$7.50/U.S.$5.25) are very popular with guests from surrounding hotels, while at lunchtime it's always bustling with tourists and local office workers. Lunchtime specials costing A$10 (U.S.$7) are always on offer, while the ploughman's lunch, chicken-and-leak pies, and pasta and noodle dishes always go down well.

Zia Pina. 93 George St., The Rocks. ☎ **02/9247 2255.** Reservations recommended well in advance. Main courses A$7.80–$19 (U.S.$5.45–$13.30). AE, BC, DC, JCB, MC, V. Daily noon–3pm; Sun–Mon 5–9pm; Tues–Thurs 5–10pm; Fri–Sat 5–11:30pm. CityRail, bus, or ferry: Circular Quay. PIZZA/PASTA.

With 10 tables crammed downstairs and another 24 upstairs, there's not much room to breathe in this cramped traditional pizzeria and spaghetti house. But squeeze in between the close-fit bare-brick walls and wallow in the clashes and clangs coming from the hard-working chefs in the kitchen. Pizzas come in two sizes; the larger feeds two people. Delicious gelatos go for a cool A$4 (U.S.$2.80).

4 Near Town Hall

EXPENSIVE

Level Two Revolving Restaurant. In Centerpoint Tower, Market St. (between Pitt and Castlereagh sts.). ☎ **02/9233 3722.** Reservations recommended. Lunch Mon–Sat A$32.50 (U.S.$22.75); lunch Sun A$36 (U.S.$25.20); early dinner A$36 (U.S.$25.20); dinner A$39.50 (U.S.$27.65). A$15 (U.S.$10.50) for children 3–12 at lunch and early dinner. 10%–15% surcharge on drinks only weekends and public holidays. AE, BC, DC, MC, V. Daily 11:30am–2:15pm and 6:15–11:45pm. CityRail: St. James. Monorail: City Centre. INTERNATIONAL.

Not for those scared of heights, Level Two offers a self-service "all you can eat buffet," which is ideal for those who don't want to fork over the cash for the à la carte goodies at the more expensive Level One restaurant, one floor down. This place is very popular with tourists, who come here for the stupendous views right across Sydney and, on a clear day, beyond to the Blue Mountains. It takes about an hour for the dining area to make a full rotation, but even going that slowly I find the motion a bit off-putting—especially when you're some 250 meters (820 ft.) above the ground. You can heap up your plate with a selection of five appetizers and then choose from among 15 main courses, including steaks, roasts, pork knuckles, beef stroganoff, seafood, and Asian dishes. Dessert presents five more options. It's all pretty basic stuff, but I guess you come here to say you've done it. The classier Level One restaurant is one floor below and serves à la carte meals in an intimate candlelit environment.

MODERATE

✪ **Captain Torres.** 73 Liverpool St. (just past the cinema strip on George St., near Town Hall). ☎ **02/9264 5574.** Reservations recommended. Main courses A$16.50–$19 (U.S.$11.55–$13.30); tapas A$5–$9 (U.S.$3.50–6.30). Daily noon–3pm; Mon–Sat 6–11pm; Sun 6–10pm. AE, BC, DC, MC, V. CityRail: Town Hall. SPANISH.

Sydney's Spanish quarter, based on Liverpool Street (a 10-minute walk from Town Hall station and just past Sydney's main cinema strip), offers some great restaurants, of which Captain Torres is my favorite. Downstairs is a tapas bar with traditional stools, Spanish serving staff, and that dark-oak coloring that gives it authenticity. Upstairs on two floors is a fabulous restaurant with heavy wooden tables and chairs and an atmosphere thick with sangria and regional food. The garlic prawns are incredible, and the whole snapper a memorable experience. The tapas are better, however, at another Spanish restaurant nearby called Asturiana. *A warning:* Spanish waiters around here are known for their offhand service.

5 At Darling Harbour

The Wokpool. IMAX Theatre, Southern Promenade, Darling Harbour. ☎ **02/9211 9888.** Main courses upstairs A$22–$38 (U.S.$15.40–$26.60); noodle-bar dishes A$8–$16 (U.S.$5.60–$11.20). AE, BC, DC, JCB, MC, V. Daily noon–3pm; Sun–Fri 6–10pm; Sat 6–11pm. Ferry: Darling Harbour. Monorail: Convention Center. MODERN ASIAN.

The best restaurant with the best views in Darling Harbour, this adventuresome child of co-owners Neil Perry and chef Kylie Kwong has taken off big-time. Upstairs, the main dining room is light and spacious with glass walls opening up across the water. The essence up here is Chinese with a twist, and the Sichuan duck and stir-fried spanner-crab omelet are always on the menu. Other dishes to go for are whole steamed snapper with ginger and shallot, rock lobster, and mud crab. Downstairs, the noodle bar is always happening, with tourists, locals, and business types crunched up along the bar or around the tables munching on light meals, such as beef curry and seafood sausages with a pork-and-peanut relish.

6 In Kings Cross & the Suburbs Beyond

EXPENSIVE

✪ **Darley Street Thai.** 28-30 Bayswater Rd., Kings Cross. ☎ **02/9358 6530.** Reservations recommended. Main courses A$27 (U.S.$18.90). 8-course set meal A$66 (U.S.$46.20). AE, DC, MC, V. Corkage fee $10 (U.S.$7) per bottle. Daily 6:30–10:30pm. CityRail: Kings Cross. MODERN THAI.

So trendy it has its name only on a small plaque about knee height, this Thai-inspired restaurant offers a full-blown experience that highlights the dizzying heights cooking has reached in Australia. Though the place doesn't look like much—a rather pretentious, Spartan affair with simple wooden floor boards and noisy fans in summer—I guarantee you will have never tasted anything quite so exquisite. Flavors and textures are so delicate and perfectly matched that course after course your taste buds virtually leap out of your mouth. The menu changes regularly, but some of the dishes offered might include green jungle curry of quail and smoked sausage of trout. The desserts—especially the sticky rice pudding with mango—are out of this world. Next door is a cheaper but equally flavorful Darley Street Thai take-away and bar-stool eatery.

✪ **Mezzaluna.** 123 Victoria St., Potts Point. ☎ **02/9357 1988.** Reservations recommended. Main courses A$19.50–$31 (U.S.$13.65–$21.70). A$2.90 (U.S.$2.05) Sun surcharge. AE, BC, DC, MC, V. Tues–Sun noon–3pm; Tues–Sat 6–11pm; Sun 6–10pm. Closed public holidays. CityRail: Kings Cross. MODERN ITALIAN.

Exquisite food, flawless service, and an almost unbeatable view across the city's western skyline have all helped Mezzaluna position itself firmly among Sydney's top restaurants. A cozy, candlelit place with plain white walls and polished wooden floorboards, the main dining room opens up onto a huge, all-weather terrace kept warm in winter by giant, overhead fan heaters. The restaurant's owner, and well-known Sydney culinary icon, Beppi Polesi, provides an exceptional wine list to complement an extravagant menu that changes daily. You could indulge in an unbeatable salmon risotto to start, followed by fillets of fish with scampi, scallops, mussels, oysters, and Morton Bay bugs, or succulent roasted lamb with grilled eggplant and sheep's yogurt. Whatever you choose, you can't go wrong. Highly recommended.

MODERATE

Bayswater Brasserie. 32 Bayswater Rd., Kings Cross. ☎ **02/9357 2177.** Reservations not accepted. Main courses A$16–$25 (U.S.$11.20–$17.50). AE, BC, DC, JCB, MC, V. Mon–Sat noon–midnight. CityRail: Kings Cross. MODERN AUSTRALIAN.

This hugely popular brasserie seems to have been around forever. Just off the main Kings Cross beat, it's popular with a hip lunchtime crowd, film-industry types, and those out for an evening of revelry in the surrounding nightclubs and bars. The atmosphere is very casual, inviting locals and visitors alike to drop in for a quick pasta or a coffee on the terrace or a more substantial meal—such as the grilled aged beef rump or the barbecued cuttlefish.

Bourbon & Beefsteak Bar. 24 Darlinghurst Rd., Kings Cross. ☎ **02/9358 1144.** Reservations recommended Fri–Sun. Main courses A$10.95–$23.95 (U.S.$7.65–$16.75). A$2 (U.S.$1.40) surcharge weekends and public holidays. AE, BC, DC, MC, V. Daily 24 hours (happy hour 4–7pm). CityRail: Kings Cross. INTERNATIONAL.

The Bourbon & Beefsteak has been a popular Kings Cross institution for more than 30 years, and it still attracts a similar clientele, everyone from visiting U.S. sailors and tourists to businesspeople and ravers. The fact that it's open 24 hours means many people never seem to leave, and occasionally you'll find someone taking a nap in a toilet cubicle. The restaurant here is busy at all hours, churning out steaks, seafood, salads, Tex-Mex, and pasta. Every night there's live music in the Piano Bar from 5 to 9pm, followed by a mixture of jazz, Top 40, and rock 'n' roll until 5am. A disco downstairs starts at 11pm every night, and a larger one takes off in The Penthouse at the Bourbon bar on Friday and Saturday nights. If you want to watch the sleazy sideshow of Kings Cross act out as you dine, make sure you get a table by the window.

INEXPENSIVE

Govindas. 112 Darlinghurst Rd., Darlinghurst. ☎ **02/9380 5162.** Dinner A$13.90 (U.S.$9.75), including free movie. BC, MC, V. Daily 6–11pm. CityRail: Kings Cross. VEGETARIAN.

When I think of Govindas, I can't help smiling. Perhaps it's because I'm reliving the happy vibe from the Hare Krishna center it's based in, or maybe it's because the food is so cheap! Or maybe it's because they even throw in a decent movie with the meal. The food is simple (and sometimes bland) Indian-style vegetarian, eaten in a basic room off black lacquer tables. It's BYO and doctrine-free.

7 In Darlinghurst

✪ **No Names.** 2 Chapel St. (or 81 Stanley St.), Darlinghurst. ☎ **02/9360 4711.** Main courses A$6–$8.50 (U.S.$4.20–$5.95). Cash only. Daily noon–2:30pm and 6–10pm. CityRail: Kings Cross or Town Hall, then a 10-minute walk. ITALIAN.

I had to include this fabulous Italian cafeteria-style joint because it's the place to go in Sydney for a cheap and cheerful meal. Downstairs you can nibble on cakes or drink good coffee, but upstairs you have a choice between either spaghetti bolognese or Neapolitana, and several meat dishes, which usually include fish, beef, and veal. The servings are enormous and often far more than you can eat. You get free bread, and simple salads are cheap. Help yourself to water and cordials. There are similar eateries in Burwood and Bondi.

8 In Newtown

Newtown is three stops from Central Station on the CityRail. The area has a very inner-city feel about it and is clustered with cheap restaurants frequented by students from nearby Sydney University.

Le Kilimanjaro. 280 King St., Newtown. ☎ **02/9557 4565.** Reservations recommended. Main courses A$8.50–$9.50 (U.S.$5.95–$6.65). No credit cards. CityRail: Newtown. AFRICAN.

With so many excellent restaurants to choose from in Newtown— they close down or improve quickly enough if they're bad—I picked Kilimanjaro because it's the most unusual. It's a tiny place, with very limited seating on two floors. Basically, you enter, choose a dish off the blackboard menu (while standing), and then you are escorted to your seats by one of the waiters. On a recent visit I had couscous, some African bread (similar to an Indian chapati), and the Saussou-gor di guan—tuna in a rich sauce. Another favorite dish is the Yassa—chicken in a rich African sauce. All meals are served on traditional wooden plates. It's BYO.

Old Saigon. 107 King St., Newtown. ☎ **02/9519 5931.** Reservations recommended. Main courses A$10–$13 (U.S.$7–$9.10). AE, BC, DC, MC, V. Wed–Fri noon–3pm; Tues–Sun 6–11pm. BYO only. CityRail: Newtown. VIETNAMESE.

Another Newtown establishment bursting with atmosphere, the Old Saigon was owned until 1998 by a former American Vietnam War correspondent who loved Vietnam so much he ended up living there and marrying a local, before coming to Australia. Just to make sure you know about it, he's put up his own photos on the walls and strewn the place with homemade tin helicopters that hang over the diners' heads. His Vietnamese brother-in-law has taken over the show, but the food is still glorious, with the spicy squid dishes among my favorites. A popular pastime is grilling your own thin strips of venison, beef, wild boar, or crocodile over a burner at your table, then wrapping the meat up in rice paper with lettuce and mint, then dipping it in a chili sauce. Highly recommended for a cheap night out.

9 In Bondi

Fishy Affair. 152-162 Campbell Parade, Bondi Beach. ☎ **02/9300 0494.** Main courses A$14.40–$21 (U.S.$10.10–$14.70). AE, BC, JCB, MC, V. Mon–Sat noon–3pm; Mon–Thurs 6–10pm; Fri–Sat 6–10:30pm; Sunday noon–10pm. Bus: Bondi Beach. SEAFOOD.

Of the many good restaurants, cafes, and take-aways along Bondi Beach's main drag, the Fishy Affair is a standout. Sitting outside watching the beach bums saunter past while diving into great fish-and-chips is a delightful way to spend an hour or so. The herb-crusted Atlantic salmon steak and the smoked salmon salad are both truly delicious. It's a pity, though, that all Bondi Beach eateries have to put up with the eyesore of a road between them and the beach.

✪ **Nina's Ploy Thai Restaurant.** 132 Wairoa Ave. (at the corner of Warners Ave.), Bondi Beach. ☎ **02/9365 1118.** Main courses A$8–$12.50 (U.S.$5.60–$8.75). Cash only. Thurs–Tues noon–3pm and 6:30–10pm. Bus: 380 Bondi Beach. THAI.

On a side street at the end of the main Campbell Parade shops (to your left as you face the ocean), you'll find this unpretentious but superb Thai restaurant. Sit inside or outside at one of the sidewalk tables, but, whatever you do, eat here! This is genuine Bangkok cooking at its best. The spicy soups make a good starter to the main courses, which include an excellent prawn red curry and great satays. The staff is friendly and can help you out with any questions about what's on offer. The take-away menu is the same.

10   On the North Shore

L'Incontro Italian Restaurant. 196 Miller St. (at McLaren St.), North Sydney. ☎ **02/9957 2274.** Reservations recommended. Main courses A$21.50–$32.50 (U.S.$15.05–$22.75). AE, DC, MC, V. Mon–Fri noon–3pm; Mon–Sat 6–10pm. CityRail: North Sydney. NORTHERN ITALIAN.

Less than 10 minutes by train from the city center, plus a 5-minute stroll up Miller Street (turn right up the hill as you exit the train station and take the first right), this little beauty, easy to miss in its turn-of-the century house, revealed itself to me by chance after futile years searching for really good moderately priced Italian cuisine. Dishes are beautifully prepared and well served in a stylish restaurant as far removed from the modern yuppie bistro as you can get. More important, the food is exquisite. The courtyard, with its vines and ferns, is delightful in summer. The menu changes regularly, so pray for the baked rainbow trout cooked with almonds and red-wine butter—simply the best fish I have ever tasted.

11   In Manly

Manly is 30 minutes from Circular Quay by ferry, or 15 minutes by JetCat.

⭐ **Ashiana.** 2 Sydney Rd., Manly. ☎ **02/9977 3466.** Reservations recommended. Main courses A$9.90–$15.90 (U.S.$6.95–$11.15). AE, BC, MC, V. Sun–Thurs 5:30–10:30pm and Fri–Sat 5:30–11pm. Ferry: Manly. INDIAN.

You'll be hard pressed to find a better cheap Indian restaurant in Sydney. Tucked away up a staircase next to the Steyne Hotel (just off the Corso and near the main beach), Ashiana has won a few prizes for its traditional spicy cooking. Portions are large and filling and the service is very friendly. The butter chicken is magnificent, while the Malai Kofta is the best this side of Bombay. Beer is the best drink with everything. My only gripe is that it's hard to avoid cigarette smoke in such a cozy place, especially on Friday and Saturday nights when the place is heaving. Clear your lungs and work off the heavy load in your stomach with a beachside stroll afterwards.

5

Exploring Sydney

*T*he only problem with visiting Sydney is fitting in everything you want to do and see. A well-planned itinerary can easily be upset by countless other sights and experiences that suddenly become "must sees" and "must dos" once you arrive and everyone you speak to starts sharing their opinions on what you shouldn't miss out on. This chapter covers all the main sights and experiences, as well as some off-the-beaten-path gems, with tips to help you organize your time.

SIGHTSEEING SUGGESTIONS FOR FIRST-TIME VISITORS

If You Have 1 Day   In the morning, make your way down to **Circular Quay** to look around the Opera House and admire the Sydney Harbour Bridge. Then head over to **The Rocks,** stopping off at The Rocks Visitor Centre to pick up maps and extra information and check out the fascinating exhibits on the top two floors. Take lunch around Circular Quay or The Rocks. A guided walking tour around The Rocks should be at the top of your agenda for the early afternoon. You can either follow the self-guided walking tour described in chapter 6, or book ahead for one of The Rocks Walking Tours (see "Organized Tours," below). The rest of the afternoon I'd spend browsing around the stores. An option for the late afternoon, or dinner, is to take a harbor cruise.

If You Have 2 Days   On the second day, head down to Circular Quay again and take the ferry that travels beneath the Harbour Bridge and across to Darling Harbour. At Darling Harbour, visit **Sydney Aquarium,** for its giant sharks, seals, underwater ocean tunnels, and Barrier Reef displays. Then visit the **National Maritime Museum,** or one of the other attractions that dot this tourist precinct. Take the monorail to Town Hall in time for sunset at the top of the **AMP Centerpoint Tower.**

If You Have 3 Days   If the weather's fine, head to the beach on your 3rd day. Go to either **Bondi Beach,** where you can take the cliff walk to Bronte Beach and back, or take the ferry to **Manly** (see "Getting Around," in chapter 2). If you have time in the afternoon,

I highly recommend a visit to **Taronga Zoo** or **Featherdale Wild-life Park.** Have dinner at Circular Quay with a view of the harbor and the lights of the Opera House and the Harbour Bridge.

If You Have 4 Days or More   Head out to the **Blue Mountains** on a day trip, or spend the day wandering around the city center with your credit card in hand.

1 The Opera House & Sydney Harbour

Sydney Opera House. Bennelong Point. ☎ **02/9250 7111** for guided tours and inquiries or 02/9250 7777 for information and tours. Fax 02/9250 8072. For bookings, call ☎ 02/9250 7777. Fax 02/9251 3943. Box office open Mon–Sat 9am–8:30pm, Sun 2 hours before performance. Tour prices A$10 (U.S.$7) adults, A$7 (U.S.$4.90) children. Regular 1-hour tours Mon–Sat 9am–4pm. CityRail, bus, or ferry: Circular Quay. Sydney Explorer bus: Stop 2. Parking: day-time A$6 (U.S.$4.20) per hour, evening A$19 (U.S.$13.30) flat rate.

Only a handful of buildings around the world have an architectural and cultural significance as great as the Sydney Opera House. But the difference between, say, the Taj Mahal, the Eiffel Tower, and the Great Pyramids of Egypt, for example, is that this great, white-sailed construction caught midbillow over the waters of Sydney Cove is a working building, not just a monument. Most people are surprised to learn that it's not just an Opera House, but a full-scale performing-arts complex with five major performance spaces. The biggest and grandest of the lot is the 2,690-seat Concert Hall, which has just about the best acoustics of any man-made building of its type in the world. Come here to experience opera, of course, but also chamber music, symphonies, dance, choral performances, and on occasion even rock 'n' roll. The Opera Theatre is smaller, seating 1,547, and is home to operas, ballets, and dance. The Drama Theatre, seating 544, and the Playhouse, seating 398, specialize in plays and smaller-scale performances. In March 1999 a new theater, the Boardwalk, seating 300, is due to open on the site of the old library. It will be used for dance and experimental music.

The history of the building is as intriguing as the design. The New South Wales government raised the money needed to build it from a public lottery. Danish Architect Jørn Utzon won an international competition to design it. From the start, the project was controversial, with many Sydneysiders believing it was a monstrosity. Following a disagreement, Utzon returned home, without ever seeing his finished project. And the cost? Well, initially it was budgeted at a cool A$7 million (U.S.$4.9 million), but by the time it was finished in 1973 it had cost a staggering A$102 million

Central Sydney Attractions

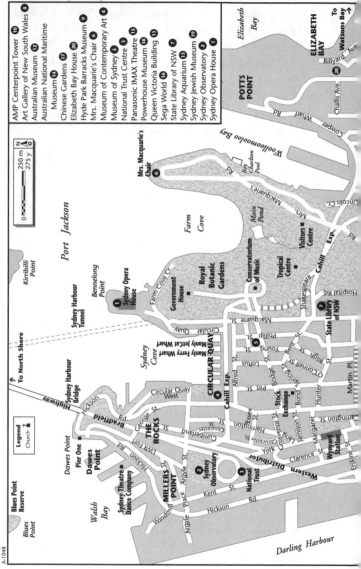

Legend
- Church ▪

AMP Centerpoint Tower ❿
Art Gallery of New South Wales ⑧
Australian Museum ⑫
Australian National Maritime Museum ⑭
Chinese Gardens ⑰
Elizabeth Bay House ⑳
Hyde Park Barracks Museum ⑨
Mrs. Macquarie's Chair ⑥
Museum of Contemporary Art ④
Museum of Sydney ⑤
National Trust Centre ③
Panasonic IMAX Theatre ⑮
Powerhouse Museum ⑯
Queen Victoria Building ⑪
Sega World ⑱
State Library of NSW ⑦
Sydney Aquarium ⑬
Sydney Jewish Museum ⑲
Sydney Observatory ②
Sydney Opera House ①

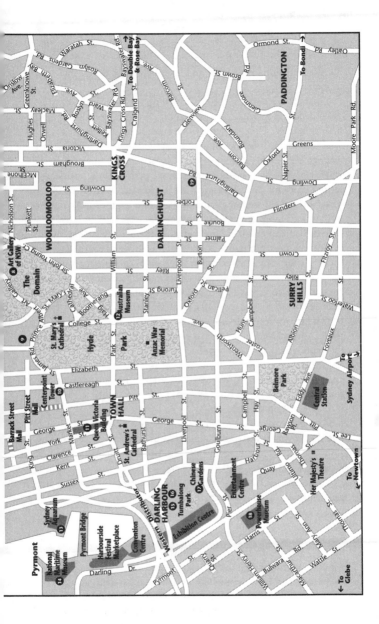

Waratah St.
Roslyn Gardens Rd.
Onslow Ave.
Greenknowe Ave.
Elizabeth Bay Rd.
Bayswater Rd.
→ To Double Bay & Rose Bay
Ormond St.
Oatley Rd.
→ To Bondi

PADDINGTON

Hughes St.
Orwell St.
MacLeay St.
Ward Ave.
Roslyn St.
Kellett St.
Kings Cross Rd.
Craigend St.

Victoria St.

KINGS CROSS

Brown St.
Glenmore Rd.

Greens

McElhone St.
Brougham St.
Nicholson St.
Dowling St.

WOOLLOOMOOLOO

Forbes St.

DARLINGHURST

Glenview
Barcom Ave.
Boundary
Oxford St.
Napier St.
Moore Park Rd.
Dowling

Darlinghurst Rd.

19

Flinders

Plunkett St.

Sir John Young C.

Art Gallery of NSW
8

The Domain

St. Mary's Ave.
St. Mary's Cathedral †
College St.
Boomerang
Prince Albert Rd.
Cathedral St.
William St.
Stanley St.
Riley St.
Palmer St.
Bourke St.
Burton St.
Forbes

Australian Museum
17

Crown St.
Riley St.
Fitzroy St.

SURRY HILLS

Waterloo St.

9

Prince Albert Rd.
St. James Rd.

St. Mary's Cathedral †

Hyde Park

Anzac War Memorial

Park St.

Pelican St.
Yurong St.
Liverpool St.
Oxford St.
Campbell St.
Hunt St.
Foster St.
Albion St.
Wentworth Ave.

To Sydney Airport →

Barrack Street Mall
11

Pitt Street Mall

Centrepoint Tower
10

Elizabeth St.
Castlereagh St.

Belmore Park

George St.
King St.
Market St.
York St.
Clarence St.
Kent St.
Sussex St.

Queen Victoria Building
11

TOWN HALL

St. Andrew's Cathedral †

Pitt St.
George St.
Liverpool St.
Bathurst St.
Goulburn St.
Hay St.
Campbell St.
Eddy Ave.

Central Station

Lee St.

To Newtown →

Sydney Aquarium
13

Pyrmont Bridge

DARLING HARBOUR

Convention Centre

Harbourside Festival Marketplace

National Maritime Museum
14

Pyrmont

Darling Dr.
Pyrmont St.

Western Distributor

Exhibition Centre

Chinese Gardens
15 16

Tumbalong Park

Entertainment Centre
17

Harbour St.
Quay St.
Pier St.
Thomas St.
Mary Ann St.

Her Majesty's Theatre

Powerhouse Museum
18

Harris St.
William Henry St.
Bulwara Rd.
Macarthur St.
Wattle St.

To Glebe →

103

(U.S.$71.4 million). Since then, continual refurbishment and the major task of replacing the asbestos-infected grouting between the hundreds of thousands of white tiles which make up its shell, has cost many millions more.

Tours & Tickets: Guided tours lasting about an hour are conducted daily between 9am and 4pm, except Good Friday and Christmas Day. Though guides try to take groups into the main theaters and around the foyers, if you can't get to see everything you want to see, it's because the Opera House is not a museum but a workplace, and there's almost always some performance, practice, or setting up to be done. Reservations are essential. Specialized tours, based around the building's architectural and engineering configurations, for example, can also be arranged.

The Tourism Services Department at the Sydney Opera House can book combination packages, including a dinner and show; a tour, dinner, and show; or a champagne interval performance. Prices vary depending on shows and restaurant venues. Visitors from overseas can buy tickets by credit card and then pick them up at the box office on arrival, or contact a local tour company specializing in Australia. Alternatively, contact the Sydney Opera House by e-mail at vso@soh.nsw.gov.au for information, and bookings@soh.nsw.gov.au to buy tickets. Tickets for performances vary from as little as A$9.50 (U.S.$6.65) for children's shows to A$150 (U.S.$105) for good seats at the opera. Plays cost between A$35 (U.S.$24.50) and A$45 (U.S.$31.50) on average.

Free performances are given outside on the Opera House boardwalks on Sunday afternoons and during festival times. The shows range from musicians and performance artists to school groups.

There are four restaurants on the premises—including the Bennelong Restaurant (see chapter 4)—and several bars.

Sydney Harbour. Officially called Port Jackson.

Sydney Harbour is the focal point of Sydney and one of the things—along with the beaches and the easy access to surrounding national parks—that make this city so special. It's entered through the Heads, two bush-topped outcrops (you'll see them should you take a ferry or JetCat to Manly), beyond which the harbor laps at some 240 kilometers (149 miles) of shoreline before stretching itself out into the Parramatta River. Visitors are often awestruck by its beauty, especially at night when the sails of the Opera House and

A Bridge to Cross, Mate

One thing so few tourists do, but which only takes an hour or so, is to walk right across the **Harbour Bridge.** The "Coat Hanger," as it's affectionately known, was finally completed in 1932. It's 1,150 meters (3,795 ft.) long and spans the 503-meter (1,650-ft.) distance from the south shore to the north, and accommodates pedestrian walkways, two railway lines, and an eight-lane road. The 30-minute stroll across offers some good views of the harbor. Once on the other side, you can take a CityRail train from Milsons Point train station back to the city (to Wynyard, Town Hall, or Central station).

As you walk across the bridge, you should stop off at the **Pylon Lookout** (☎ 02/9247 3408), located at the southeastern pylon. From the top of this bridge support, you are 89 meters (292 ft.) above the water and get excellent views of Sydney Harbour, the ferry terminals of Circular Quay, and beyond. An interesting museum here charts the building of the bridge. Approach the pylon by walking to the far end of George Street in The Rocks towards the Harbour Bridge. Just past the Mercantile Pub on your left you'll see some stone steps which bring you onto Cumberland Street. From there, it's a 2-minute walk to the steps underneath the bridge on your right. Climb four flights of stairs to reach the bridge's Western Footway, then walk along to the first pylon. *Note:* Climbing up inside the pylon involves 200 steps. Admission to the pylon is A$2 (U.S.$1.40) adults, and A$1 (U.S.70¢) children. It's open daily from 10am to 5pm (closed Christmas Day).

the girders of the Harbour Bridge are lit up, and the waters are swirling with the reflection of lights from the abutting high rises—reds, greens, blues, yellows, and oranges. During the day, it buzzes with green-and-yellow ferries pulling in and out of busy Circular Quay, sleek tourist craft, tall ships, giant container vessels making their way to and from the wharves of Darling Harbour, and hundreds of white-sailed yachts. The greenery along its edges is perhaps a surprising feature, and all thanks to the Sydney Harbour National Park, a haven for native trees and plants, and a feeding and breeding ground for lorikeets and nectar-eating bird life. In the center of the harbor is a series of islands, the most impressive being the tiny isle supporting Fort Denison, which once housed convicts and acted as part of the city's defense.

A Super Deal

Here's a good sightseeing deal for you: For A$29.90 (U.S.$20.95) for adults and A$19.90 (U.S.$13.95) for children 3 to 15, the Super Ticket gives you a ride on the monorail, entry to both the Sydney Aquarium and the Chinese Gardens, a 2-hour cruise on the Matilda Harbour Express, a meal at the Sydney Aquarium cafe, and discounts on a coach tour of the site of the Sydney 2000 Olympic Games at Homebush Bay. Tickets are available at monorail stations, the Sydney Aquarium, and Darling Harbour information booths.

The best way to see the harbor, of course, is from the water. Several companies operate tourist craft for fare-paying customers (see "Organized Tours," later in this chapter), and it's easy enough just to hop on a regular passenger ferry. Some of the best public passenger-ferry excursions you can take are over to the beachside suburb of Manly (come back after dusk to see the lights ablaze around The Rocks and Circular Quay); to Watsons Bay, where you can have lunch and a wander along the cliffs; to Darling Harbour, for all the area's entertainment, and the fact that you travel right under the Harbour Bridge; and to Mosman, just for the ride and to see the grand houses looking over exclusive harbor inlets.

2 What to See & Do at Darling Harbour

✪ **Australian National Maritime Museum.** Darling Harbour. ☎ **02/9552 7777.** Admission A$9 (U.S.$6.30) adults, A$4.50 (U.S.$3.15) children, A$19.50 (U.S.$13.65) families. Daily 9:30am–5pm (until 6pm in Jan). Ferry: Darling Harbour. Monorail: Harbourside. Sydney Explorer bus: Stop 18.

Modern Australia owes almost everything to the sea, therefore it's not surprising that there's a museum dedicated to the ships that overcame the tyranny of the waves, from Aboriginal vessels to submarines. Here you'll also find ships' logs, all sorts of things to pull and tug at, as well as the Americas Cup–winning vessel *Australia II*. Docked in the harbor outside you can also find an Australian Naval Destroyer, *The Vampire*, which you can clamber all over, and an Oberon Class submarine. Two fully-rigged tall ships are expected to be installed in 1999. Allow at least 2 hours to visit the museum.

Chinese Gardens. Darling Harbour (adjacent to the Entertainment Centre). ☎ **02/9281 6863.** A$3 (U.S.$2.10) adults, A$1.50 (U.S.$1.05) children, A$6 (U.S.$4.20) families. Daily 9:30am–dusk. Ferry: Darling Harbour. Monorail: Convention. Sydney Explorer bus: Stop 19.

The largest Chinese garden of its type outside China offers a pleasant escape from the city concrete. It was designed by expert gardeners from China's Guangdong Province to embody principals of garden design dating back to the 5th century.

Panasonic IMAX Theatre. Southern Promenade, Darling Harbour. ☎ **02/ 9281 3300.** Admission A$13.95 (U.S.$9.75) adults, A$9.95 (U.S.$6.95) children, A$42.95 (U.S.$30.05) families. Sun–Thurs 9:45am–10pm; Fri–Sat 9:45am– 11:30pm. Ferry: Darling Harbour. Monorail: Convention. Sydney Explorer bus: Stop 20.

There are usually four IMAX films showing on the gigantic eight-story-high screen, each lasting around 50 minutes or so. As you watch, your mind is tricked into feeling it's right in the heart of the action (that drop from the rooftop onto the street below looks realistically dangerous).

Powerhouse Museum. 500 Harris St., Ultimo (near Darling Harbour). ☎ **02/ 9217 0111.** Admission A$8 (U.S.$5.60) adults, A$2 (U.S.$1.40) children, A$18 (U.S.$12.60) families. Free admission first Sat of every month. Daily 10am–5pm. Ferry: Darling Harbour. Monorail: Harbourside. Sydney Explorer bus: Stop 17.

Sydney's most interactive museum is also one of the Southern Hemisphere's largest. Inside the postmodern industrial interior, you'll find all sorts of displays and gadgets relating to the sciences, transportation, human achievement, decorative art, and social history. The many hands-on exhibits make this fascinating museum worthy of a couple of hours of your time.

Sega World. Darling Harbour (between the IMAX Theatre and Chinese Gardens). ☎ **02/9273 9273.** Admission Mon–Fri A$20 (U.S.$14) adults, A$16 (U.S.$11.20) children; Sat–Sun A$25 (U.S.$17.50) adults, A$20 (U.S.$14) children. Entry includes all rides. Mon–Fri 11am–10pm; Sat–Sun 10am–10pm. Ferry: Darling Harbour. Monorail: Convention.

If you fancy a few hours' break from the kids, if you're just a big kid yourself, or if it's raining outside, then try out this indoor theme park. Simulators, 3-D rides, computer games, and the like are fun (but occasionally a little limp). It's good for a couple of hours. Avoid the huge queues on Friday nights and weekends.

✪ **Sydney Aquarium.** Aquarium Pier, Darling Harbour. ☎ **02/9262 2300.** Admission A$15.90 (U.S.$11.15) adults, A$8 (U.S.$5.60) children. The Aquarium Link ticket, available from CityRail train stations, is a combined rail and aquarium ticket that also includes a ferry ride on the harbor. It costs A$15.90 (U.S.$11.15) adults, A$8.20 (U.S.$5.75) children, and A$42 (U.S.$29.40) families. Daily 9:30am–10pm. Seal Sanctuary closes at 7pm in summer. CityRail: Town Hall. Ferry: Darling Harbour. Sydney Explorer bus: Stop 20.

This is one of the world's best aquariums and should be near the top of any Sydney itinerary. The main attractions are the underwater walkways, especially one containing giant rays and enormous gray nurse sharks. Other excellent exhibits include a walk into a giant clear Plexiglas room suspended inside a pool patrolled by rescued seals and good displays of fish from the Great Barrier Reef. Try to go during the week when it's less crowded.

3 Other Top Attractions: A Spectacular View, Sydney's Convict History & More

AMP Centerpoint Tower. Pitt and Market sts. ☎ **02/9229 7444.** Admission A$10 (U.S.$7) adults, A$4.50 (U.S.$3.15) children. Sun–Fri 9am–10:30pm; Sat 9am–11:30pm. CityRail: St. James or Town Hall. Sydney Explorer bus: Stop 14.

The tallest building in the Southern Hemisphere is not hard to miss—it resembles a giant steel pole skewering a golden marshmallow. Standing more than 300 meters (984 ft.) tall, it offers stupendous 360° views across Sydney and as far as the Blue Mountains. Fortunately, an elevator takes you to the indoor viewing platform. Don't be too concerned if you feel the building tremble slightly, especially in a stiff breeze—I'm told it's perfectly natural. Below the tower are three floors of stores and restaurants.

Hyde Park Barracks Museum. Queens Sq., Macquarie St. ☎ **02/9223 8922.** Admission A$6 (U.S.$4.20) adults, A$3 (U.S.$2.10) children, A$15 (U.S.$10.50) families. Daily 10am–5pm. CityRail: St. James or Martin Place. Sydney Explorer bus: Stop 4.

These Georgian-style barracks were designed in 1819 by the convict/ architect Francis Greenway. They were built by convicts and inhabited by fellow prisoners. These days they house relics from those early days in interesting, modern displays, including log books, early settlement artifacts, and a room full of ships' hammocks in which visitors can lie and listen to fragments of prisoner conversation. If you are interested in Sydney's early beginnings, then I highly recommend a visit. The courtyard cafe is excellent.

Museum of Contemporary Art (MCA). 140 George St., Circular Quay West. ☎ **02/9252 4033.** Admission A$9 (U.S.$6.30) adults, A$6 (U.S.$4.20) children, A$18 (U.S.$12.60) families. Daily 10am–6pm (until 5pm in winter). CityRail, bus, or ferry: Circular Quay. Sydney Explorer bus: Stop 1.

This imposing sandstone museum, set back from the water on The Rocks–side of Circular Quay, offers wacky, entertaining, inspiring, and befuddling displays of what's new (and dated) in modern art.

It houses the J. W. Power Collection of more than 4,000 pieces, including works by Andy Warhol, Christo, Marcel Duchamp, and Robert Rauschenberg, as well as temporary exhibits. Guided tours are offered Monday to Saturday at noon and 2pm, and Sunday at 2pm.

The Sydney International Aquatic and Athletic Centres. Sydney 2000 Olympic Site, Olympic Park, Homebush Bay. ☎ **02/9752 3666.** Tours A$14 (U.S.$9.80) adults, A$9 (U.S.$6.30) children, A$40 (U.S.$28) families. Tours Mon–Fri 10am, noon, and 2pm; Sat–Sun noon and 2pm. Train: Olympic Park.

A tour of the best Olympic swimming complex in the world, as well as the athletic center where the Olympic athletes will train, is fast becoming an essential thing to do for any visitor to Sydney. Tours last 90 minutes. If you fancy putting in a few laps afterwards, then be prepared to pay an additional A$4.50 (U.S.$3.15) for adults, and A$3.50 (U.S.$2.45) for children.

Gledswood Homestead. Camden Valley Way, Catherine Field. ☎ **02/9606 5111.** Fax 02/9606 5897. Farm activities A$12 (U.S.$8.40) adults, A$6 (U.S.$4.20) children, A$20 (U.S.$14) families. Homestead tour A$6 (U.S.$4.20) adults, A$4.50 (U.S.$3.15) children. Horseback riding A$16 (U.S.$11.20) for 30 minutes. Daily 10am–4pm. Several tour operators offer trips from Sydney. By car: Take the M5 to Camden Valley Way (Exit 89), an hour from Sydney. CityRail: Campbelltown station and then transfer to local Busways service 891 from outside station (20-minute trip).

If you have a day to spare, then you might consider the long trek to Gledswood, a sort of theme agricultural property set on 61.5 hectares (150 acres). You can try your hand at boomerang throwing, catch a sheep-shearing demonstration, learn how to crack a stockman's whip, watch working sheepdogs in action, and milk a cow. The homestead tour can be interesting if you're into colonial relics and architecture, and the gardens are nice (take a hat in summer). A hearty lunch and snacks are served by costumed staff in the restaurant. You can also sample billy tea and damper (bread made in the embers of a campfire). You'll come home feeling you've had a good taste of rural Australia.

Australia's Wonderland. Wallgrove Rd., Eastern Creek. ☎ **02/9830 9100.** Admission (includes all rides and entrance to the Australian Wildlife Park) A$37 (U.S.$25.90) adults, A$26 (U.S.$18.20) children, A$115 (U.S.$80.50) families. Daily 10am–5pm. CityRail: Rooty Hill (trip time: less than 1 hour); Australia's Wonderland buses leave from Rooty Hill station every half hour on weekends and at 8:55am, 9:32am, 10:10am, 10:25am, 11:35am, and 12:14 weekdays.

If you're used to big Disneyesque extravaganzas, then this theme park might be a bit of a disappointment—though I guarantee The

Demon roller coaster will more than satisfy in the terror department. Other big rides are Space Probe 7, which is basically a heart-stopping drop, and a cute and rattly wooden roller coaster called the Bush Beast. Live shows and bands round out the entertainment options. The entry ticket also includes a reasonable wildlife park, with all the old favorites—koalas, wombats, kangaroos, wallabies, and more.

4 Where to See 'Roos, Koalas & Other Aussie Wildlife

The world-class Sydney Aquarium is discussed above in section 2, "What to See & Do at Darling Harbour."

Taronga Zoo. Bradley's Head Rd., Mosman. ☎ **02/9969 2777.** Admission A$15 (U.S.$10.50) adults, A$9 (U.S.$6.30) seniors, A$7.50 (U.S.$5.25) children 4–15, A$38 (U.S.$26.60) families. Zoopass (includes entry, round-trip ferry from Circular Quay, and Aerial Safari cable-car ride from ferry terminal to upper entrance) A$21 (U.S.$14.70) adults, A$10.50 (U.S.$7.35) seniors and children. Daily 9am–5pm. Ferry: Circular Quay.

Taronga has the best view of any zoo in the world. Set on a hill, it looks out over Sydney Harbour, the Opera House, and the Harbour Bridge. The main attractions here are the fabulous chimpanzee exhibit and the Nocturnal Houses, where you can see some of Australia's many nighttime marsupials out and about, including the platypus and the cuter than cute bilby (the official Australian Easter bunny). There's an interesting reptile display, a couple of rather impressive Komodo dragons, a scattering of indigenous Australian beasties—including a few koalas, echidnas, kangaroos, dingoes, and wombats—and lots more. Animals are fed at various times. The zoo can get very crowded on summer weekends.

Featherdale Wildlife Park. 217 Kildare Rd., West Pennant Hills. ☎ **02/9622 1644.** Admission A$11.50 (U.S.$8.05) adults, A$6 (U.S.$4.20) children. Daily 9am–5pm. CityRail: Blacktown station, then take bus no. 725 to park (ask driver to tell you when to get off). By car: take the M4 motorway to Reservoir Rd. turn off, travel 4km (2.5 miles), then turn left at Kildare Rd.

If you only have time to visit one wildlife park in Sydney, make it this one. The selection of native Australian animals is excellent, and, most importantly, the animals are very well cared for. You could easily spend a couple of hours here despite the park's compact size. You'll have the chance to hand-feed plenty of friendly kangaroos and wallabies, and get a photo taken next to a koala (there are many here, both the New South Wales variety and the much larger Victorian type). The park offers twice-daily bus tours, which include hotel pickup and drop-off. Tours cost A$42 (U.S.$29.40) for adults, A$23.50 (U.S.$16.45) for children, and A$110 (U.S.$77) for a family of four; prices include park admission.

Koala Park. 84 Castle Hill Rd., West Pennant Hills. ☎ **02/9484 3141** or 02/9875 2777. Admission A$9.50 (U.S.$6.65) adults, A$5 (U.S.$3.50) children. Daily 9am–5pm. Closed Christmas Day. CityRail: Pennant Hills station via North Strathfield (45 minutes), then take to bus 651–655 to park.

Unless you want to go all the way to Kangaroo Island in South Australia, it's unlikely you're going to spot as many koalas in the trees as you can find here. In all, there are around 55 koalas roaming within the park's leafy boundaries. Koala cuddling sessions are free, and take place at 10:20am, 11:45am, 2pm, and 3pm daily. There are also wombats, dingoes, kangaroos, wallabies, emus, and native birds here. You can hire a private guide to take you around for A$70 (U.S.$49) for a 2-hour session, or hitch onto one of the free "hostess" guides who wander around like Pied Pipers.

Oceanworld. West Esplanade, Manly. ☎ **02/9949 2644.** Admission A$14.50 (U.S.$10.15) adults, A$7.50 (U.S.$5.25) children, A$39 (U.S.$27.30) families. Daily 10am–5:30pm. Ferry: Manly. JetCat: Manly.

Though not as impressive as the Sydney Aquarium, Oceanworld can be combined with the wonderful Manly beach for a nice day's outing. There's a pretty good display of Barrier Reef fish, a pool of giant saltwater turtles, and yet more giant sharks. For added thrills, you can swim with the seals and dive with the sharks. Seal swims run daily and cost A$65 (U.S.$45.50) for 20 minutes. Daily shark dives cost A$65 (U.S.$45.50) for a 45-minute dive for qualified divers (bring your own gear, or else rent it for A$30/U.S.$21), and A$115 (U.S.$80.50) for a 20-minute basic training dive for unqualified divers (price includes gear rental).

5 Historic Houses

Elizabeth Bay House. 7 Onslow Ave., Elizabeth Bay. ☎ **02/9356 3022.** Admission A$6 (U.S.$4.20) adults, A$3 (U.S.$2.10) children, A$15 (U.S.$10.50) families. Tues–Sun 10am–4:30pm. Closed Good Friday and Christmas. Bus: 311 from Circular Quay. Sydney Explorer bus: Stop 10.

This magnificent example of colonial architecture was built in 1835 and was described at the time as the "finest house in the colony." Visitors can tour the whole house and get a real feeling of the history of the fledgling settlement. The house is situated on a headland and has some of the best harbor views in Sydney.

Vaucluse House. Wentworth Rd., Vaucluse. ☎ **02/9337 1957.** Admission A$6 (U.S.$4.20) adults, A$3 (U.S.$2.10) children, A$15 (U.S.$10.50) families.

House Tues–Sun 10am–4:30pm. Grounds daily 7am–5pm. Free guided tours. Closed Good Friday and Christmas. Bus: 325 from Circular Quay.

Also looking over Sydney Harbour, this house includes lavish entertainment rooms and impressive stables and outbuildings. It was built in 1803 and was the home of Charles Wentworth, the architect of the Australian Constitution. It's set in 27 acres of gardens, bushland, and beach frontage—perfect for picnics.

6 Museums & Galleries

Art Gallery of New South Wales. Art Gallery Rd., The Domain. ☎ **02/9225 1744.** Free admission to most galleries. Special exhibitions vary, though expect around A$12 (U.S.$8.40) adults, A$7 (U.S.$4.90) children. Daily 10am–5pm. Tours of general exhibits Tues–Fri 11am, noon, 1pm, and 2pm. Call for weekend times. Tours of Aboriginal galleries Tues–Fri 11am. CityRail: St. James. Sydney Explorer bus: Stop 6.

The numerous galleries here present some of the best of Australian art and many fine examples by international artists, including good displays of Aboriginal and Asian art. You enter from the Domain parklands on the third floor of the museum. On the fourth is an expensive restaurant and a gallery often showing free photography displays. On the second floor is a wonderful cafe overlooking the wharves and warships of Wooloomooloo. Every January and February there is a fabulous display of the best work created by school kids throughout the state.

Australian Museum. 6 College St. ☎ **02/9320 6000.** Admission A$5 (U.S.$3.50) adults, A$2 (U.S.$1.40) children, A$12 (U.S.$8.40) families. Daily 9:30am–5pm. Closed Christmas Day. CityRail: Museum, St. James, or Town Hall. Sydney Explorer bus: Stop 15.

Though nowhere near as impressive as, say, the Natural History Museum in London, or similar museums in Washington or New York, Sydney's premier natural-history museum still ranks in the top five of its kind in the world. Displays are presented thematically, the best of them being the Aboriginal section with its traditional clothing, weapons, and everyday implements. There are some sorry examples of stuffed Australian wildlife, too. Temporary exhibits run from time to time.

Museum of Sydney. 37 Phillip St. ☎ **02/9251 5988.** Admission A$6 (U.S.$4.20) adults, A$3 (U.S.$2.10) children under 15, A$15 (U.S.$10.50) families. Daily 10am–5pm. CityRail, bus, or ferry: Circular Quay. Sydney Explorer bus: Stop 3.

You'll need your brain in full working order to make the best of the contents of this three-story postmodern building, which encompasses the remnants of Sydney's first Government House. This place is far from being a conventional showcase of history; instead, it's a rather minimalist collection of first-settler and Aboriginal objects and multimedia displays that invite the museum-goer to discover Sydney's past for him- or herself. By the way, that forest of poles filled with hair, oyster shells, and crab claws in the courtyard adjacent to the industrial-design cafe tables is called Edge of Trees. It's a metaphor for the first contact between Aborigines and the British.

Sydney Jewish Museum. 148 Darlinghurst Rd. (at Burton St.), Darlinghurst. ☎ **02/9360 7999.** Admission A$6 (U.S.$4.20) adults, A$4 (U.S.$2.80) children, A$15 (U.S.$10.50) families. Mon–Thurs 10am–4pm; Fri 10am–2pm. Closed Jewish holidays, Christmas Day, and Good Friday. CityRail: Kings Cross.

Harrowing exhibits here include documents and objects relating to the Holocaust and the Jewish culture, mixed with soundscapes, audiovisual displays, and interactive media. There's also a museum shop, a resource center, a theatrette, and a traditional kosher cafe. It's considered to be one of the best museums of its type in the world.

Sydney Observatory. Observatory Hill, Watson Rd., Millers Point. ☎ **02/9217 0485.** Free admission in daytime; A$6 (U.S.$4.20) for guided night tours (reservations essential). Mon–Fri 2–5pm; Sat and Sun 10am–5pm. CityRail, bus, or ferry: Circular Quay.

The city's only major museum of astronomy offers visitors a chance to see the southern skies through modern and historic telescopes. The best time to visit is during the night on a guided tour, when you can take a close-up look at some of the planets. A planetarium and a hands-on exhibition are also interesting.

State Library of NSW. Macquarie St., ☎ **02/9273 1414.** Free admission. Mon–Fri 9am–9pm; Sat, Sun, and selected holidays 11am–5pm. Closed New Year's Day, Good Friday, Christmas, and Boxing Day (Dec 26). CityRail: Martin Place. Sydney Explorer bus: Stop 4.

The state's main library is divided into two sections, located next door to one another. The newer reference-library complex has two floors of reference materials, local newspapers, and microfiche viewers. Leave your bags in free lockers downstairs. If you are over in this area of town at lunchtime, I highly recommend the library's leafy Glasshouse Café, in my opinion one of the best lunch spots in Sydney. The older building contains many older and more valuable books on the ground floor, and often hosts free art and photography displays in the upstairs galleries.

A small library section in the Sydney Town Hall building has international newspapers.

7 Parks & Gardens

IN SYDNEY

If you are going to spend time in one of Sydney's green spaces, then make it the **Royal Botanic Gardens** (☎ 02/9231 8111), next to the Sydney Opera House. The gardens were laid out in 1816 on the site of a farm dedicated to supplying food for the fledgling colony. The gardens are informal in appearance with a scattering of duck ponds and open spaces, though there are several areas dedicated to particular plant species, such as the rose garden, the cacti and succulent display, and the central palm and the rain-forest groves. Also interesting is the pyramidal Tropical Centre—admission is A$5 (U.S.$3.50) for adults, A$2 (U.S.$1.40) for children, and A$12 (U.S.$8.40) per family—and the fernery. Mrs. Macquarie's Chair, along the coast path, offers superb views of the Opera House and Harbour Bridge (it's a favorite stop for busloads of Japanese tourists). A popular walk takes you through the Royal Botanic Gardens to the Art Gallery of New South Wales. The gardens are open daily from 6:30am to dusk. Admission is free.

In the center of the city is **Hyde Park,** a favorite with lunching businesspeople. Of note here are the Anzac Memorial to Australian and New Zealand troops killed in the wars, and the Archibald Fountain, complete with spitting turtles and sculptures of Diana and Apollo. At night, avenues of trees are lit up with fairy lights giving the place a magical appearance.

Another Sydney favorite is the giant **Centennial Park** (☎ 02/9339 6699), usually accessed from the top of Oxford Street. It was opened in 1888 to celebrate the centenary of European settlement, and today encompasses huge areas of lawn, several lakes, picnic areas with outdoor grills, cycling and running paths, and a cafe. It's open from sunrise to sunset. To get there, take bus no. 373, 374, 377, 380, 396, or 398 from the city.

A hundred years later, **Bicentennial Park,** at Australia Avenue in Homebush Bay, came along. Forty percent of the park's total 100 hectares (247 acres) is general parkland reclaimed from a city rubbish tip; the rest is the largest remaining remnant of wetlands on the Parramatta River, and home to many species of both local and migratory wading birds, cormorants, and pelicans. At 1:30pm Monday to Friday, a tractor train takes visitors around the park on a

1- to 1¹/₂-hour guided trip. It costs A$6 (U.S.$4.20) per person. Follow park signs to the visitor information office (☎ 02/9763 1844), open Monday to Friday from 10am to 4pm, and Saturday and Sunday from 9:30am to 4:30pm. To reach the park, you can either take a CityRail train to Strathfield and then take bus no. 401 to Homebush Bay (ask the driver when to get off), or take a CityRail train to Concord West and walk in from there.

BEYOND SYDNEY

Forming a semicircle around the city are Sydney's biggest parks of all. To the west is the **Blue Mountains National Park** (see chapter 9, "Side Trips from Sydney"), to the northeast is **Ku-Ring-Gai Chase National Park,** and to the south is the magnificent **Royal National Park.** All three are home to marsupials such as echidnas and wallabies, numerous bird and reptile species, and a broad range of native plant life. Walking tracks, whether they stretch for half an hour or a few days, make each park accessible to the visitor. Skirting part of the harbor itself is **Sydney Harbour National Park,** a refuge for native species in the heart of the city. Bushwalking (hiking) in Australia can be a tough business, and you'll need to take plenty of water, a hat, and sunscreen. It's always wise to tell someone where you're going, too.

   Ku-Ring-Gai Chase National Park (☎ 02/9457 9322 or 02/9457 9310) is a great place to experience a bushwalk through gum trees and rain forest on the lookout for wildflowers, sandstone rock formations, and Aboriginal art. There are plenty of tracks throughout the park, but one of my favorites is a relatively easy 5.5-kilometer (3.5-mile) tramp to the Basin (Track 12). The well-graded dirt path takes you down to a popular estuary with a beach and passes some significant Aboriginal engravings. There are also some wonderful water views over Pittwater from the picnic areas at West Head. Pick up a free walking guide at the park entrance, or gather maps and information in Sydney at the **National Parks & Wildlife Service's center** at Cadman's Cottage, 110 George St., The Rocks (☎ 02/9247 8861). The park is open from sunrise to sunset, and admission is A$7.50 (U.S.$5.25) per car. You can either drive to the park or catch a regular ferry from Palm Beach to McMasters Beach or the Basin (both in the park). There is no train service to the park.

   While in the area you could visit the **Ku-Ring-Gai Wildflower Garden,** 420 Mona Vale Rd., St. Ives, which is essentially a huge area of natural bushland and a center for urban bushland education. There are plenty of bushwalking tracks, self-guided walks, and a number of nature-based activities. It's open daily from 8am to 4pm. Admission is A\$2.50 (U.S.\$1.75) for adults, A\$1 (U.S.70¢) for children, and A\$6 (U.S.\$4.20) for families.

To the south of Sydney is the remarkable **Royal National Park,** Farrell Avenue, Sutherland (☎ **02/9542 0648**). It's the world's oldest national park, having been gazetted as such in 1879 (the main competitor to the title is Yellowstone in the U.S., which was established in 1872 but not designated as a National Park until 1883). Severe bushfires almost totally destroyed the whole lot in early 1994, but the trees and bush plants have recovered remarkably. There's no visitor center, but you can pick up park information at park entrances, where you'll have to pay an A\$8 (U.S.\$5.60) per car entry fee.

There are several ways to access the park, but my favorites are the little-known access points from Bundeena and Otford. To get to Bundeena, take a CityRail train from Central Station to Cronulla. From there, hop on the delightful little ferry to Bundeena. After you get off the ferry, the first turn on your left just up the hill will take you to Bundeena Beach. It's another 5 kilometers (3 miles) or so to the wonderfully remote Little Marley Beach (with its dangerous surf), via Marley Beach.

An alternative way to reach the park is take the train from Central Station (or drive) to Otford, then climb the hill up to the sea cliffs. The entrance to the national park is a little tricky to find, so you may have to ask directions. The walk takes you 2 hours down to Burning Palms beach, through beautiful and varying bush land and a palm forest. The walk back up is steep, so only attempt this trek if you're reasonably fit. Trains to the area are irregular and the last one departs around 4pm, so give yourself at least $2^1/2$ hours for the return trip back to the station to make sure you don't get stranded. It's possible to walk from Otford to Bundeena, or vice versa, in 2 days (take all your food, water, and camping gear).

The best walk through the **Sydney Harbour National Park** is the **Manly-to-Spit-Bridge Scenic Walkway** (☎ **02/9977 6522**). This 10-kilometer (6.2-mile) track winds its way from Manly (it starts near Manly Oceanworld), via Dobroyd Head to Spit Bridge (where you can catch a bus back to the city). The walk takes between 3 and 4 hours, and the views across busy Sydney Harbour are fabulous. Maps are available from the **Manly Visitors Information Bureau,** right opposite the main beach (☎ **02/9977 1088**).

8 Fun in the Sun (& Sand)

One of the big bonuses of visiting Sydney in the summer months (Dec, Jan, and Feb) is that you get to experience the **beaches** in their full glory. All major beaches are patrolled by trained surf lifesavers, and you'll see red and yellow flags at various intervals to mark safe swimming spots (crossed flagpoles or a red flag mean the beach is closed due to extremely dangerous swimming conditions; a yellow flag means conditions are dangerous and swimming is not advised). One of the first things visitors wonder when they hit the water is, "Are there sharks?" The answer is yes, but fortunately they are rarely spotted inshore. In reality, they have more reason to be scared of us than we of them, as most of them end up as the fish portion in your average packet of fish-and-chips (you might see shark fillets sold as "flake"). Though some beaches, such as the small beach next to the Manly ferry wharf in Manly and a section of Balmoral Beach, have permanent shark nets, most rely on portable nets that are moved from beach to beach periodically.

SOUTH OF SYDNEY HARBOUR   Sydney's most famous beach is **Bondi.** In many ways it's similar to a typical California beach, with plenty of tanned skin and in-line skaters. Though the beach is nice, it's often crowded; and it's cut off from the cafe-and-restaurant strip by an almost treeless wasteland and a big ugly road that pedestrians have to funnel across in order to reach the sand. If you follow the water along to your right, you'll come across a very scenic cliff-top track that takes you to **Bronte Beach** (a 20-minute walk), via gorgeous little Tamarama, a boutique beach known for its dangerous rips. Bronte has better swimming. **Clovelly Beach,** farther along the coast, is blessed with a large rock pool carved into a rock platform and sheltered from the force of the Tasman Sea. This beach is accessible for visitors in wheelchairs, via a series of ramps.

NORTH OF SYDNEY HARBOUR   On the north shore you'll find Manly, a long curve of golden sand edged with Norfolk Island Pines (don't be fooled by the small beaches alongside the ferry terminal—some people have been!). Follow the beachfront along to your right, and it will lead you to the small and sheltered **Shelley Beach,** one of Sydney's best. Above the beach and carpark, a path cuts into the Sydney Harbour National Park, where there are some spectacular coastal views.

Farther along the north coast are a string of ocean beaches, which end at ✪ **Palm Beach,** a very long and beautiful strip of sand, cut from the calmer waters of Pittwater by sand dunes and a golf course. Here you'll also find the Barrenjoey Lighthouse, which also offers fine views along the coast (see the "Sydney & Environs" map in chapter 9 for a map of this area).

INSIDE SYDNEY HARBOUR   The best harbor beach can be found at **Balmoral,** a wealthy North Shore hangout complete with its own little island and some excellent cafes and restaurants. If getting an all-over tan is your scene, then head for the nudist beaches of **Lady Jane Bay,** a short walk from Camp Cove beach (accessed from Cliff Street, Watsons Bay). Be prepared for a largely male-orientated scene—as well as the odd boatload of beer-swigging peeping toms.

9 Kid Stuff

There are plenty of places kids can have fun in Sydney, but the recommendations below are particularly suitable for youngsters (all of the places are reviewed in full above).

Taronga Zoo (see p. 110) is an all-time favorite with kids, where the barnyard animals, surprisingly, get as much attention as the koalas. If your kids want hands-on contact with the animals, though, then you'd better head to **Featherdale Wildlife Park** (see p. 110), where they can get their photo taken next to a koala, and hand-feed and stroke kangaroos and wallabies.

Sega World (see p. 107) in Darling Harbour will no doubt entertain them for a few hours, but the trouble is, adults can't resist the rides either. Just as interactive are the hands-on exhibits just crying out to be touched and bashed at the **Powerhouse Museum** (see p. 107).

The sharks at **Oceanworld** (see p. 111) in Manly and at the **Sydney Aquarium** (see p. 107) in Darling Harbour are a big lure for kids, too, and the thrill of walking through a long Plexiglas tunnel as giant manta rays perch over their heads will lead to more squeals of excitement.

Another fascinating outing for both adults and children is to crawl around inside a navy destroyer at the **National Maritime Museum** (see p. 106)—if you're lucky there may even be a submarine to explore, too.

And, of course, what kid wouldn't enjoy a day at the beach, and Sydney's got plenty to choose from, like Bondi or Manly (see above).

10 Organized Tours

For details on the Red Sydney Explorer bus, see "Getting Around" in chapter 2.

WALKING TOURS

The center of Sydney is surprisingly compact, and you'll find you can see a lot in a day on foot. If you want to learn more about Sydney's early history, then you should really book a guided tour with **The Rocks Walking Tour** (☎ **02/9247 6678**), based at The Rocks Visitor Centre, 106 George St. Excellent walking tours leave Monday to Friday at 10:30am, 12:30pm, and 2:30pm, and Saturday and Sunday at 11:30am and 2pm, The 1¹/₂-hour tour costs A$11 (U.S.$7.70) for adults and A$7.50 (U.S.$5.25) for children 10 to 16. Accompanied children under 10 are free.

For other historical walks, contact **Sydney Guided Tours** (☎ **02/9660 7157;** fax 02/9660 0805). The company's owner, Maureen Fry, has been in the business for over 12 years and employs trained guides qualified in specific disciplines, such as history, architecture, and botany. She offers a range of tours including an introductory tour of Sydney, a tour of historical Macquarie Street, and many others. Walking tours cost A$13 (U.S.$9.10) for 2 hours as part of a group (call in advance to find out what's available), or A$130 (U.S.$91) for a 2-hour personalized tour.

A walking tour with a difference is **Unseen Sydney's History, Convicts, and Murder Most Foul** (☎ **02/9555 2700**). The tour is fascinating and fun, with the guide dressed up in old-time gear and theatrical storytellers spinning yarns about Sydney's mysteries and intrigue. The 1¹/₂-hour tour leaves at 6:30pm sharp from Circular Quay Tuesday and Thursday to Sunday. It costs A$15 (U.S.$10.50) for adults and A$10 (U.S.$7) for children.

MOTORCYCLE TOURS

Blue Thunder Motorcycle Tours (☎ **02/9977 7721;** fax 02 4578 5033) runs chauffeured Harley-Davidson tours of Sydney, the Blue Mountains, and other places around the state. A 1-hour bike ride (you sit on the back of the bike) around the city costs A$70 (U.S.$49); a half-day trip including lunch to the northern beaches or down the south coast through the Royal National Park costs A$210 (U.S.$147). Full-day trips cost A$300 (U.S.$210), including lunch and snacks, and go to either the Hunter Valley, the south coast, west to Bathurst, the Blue Mountains, or even include a 20-minute micro-light flight and a wine tour around Maitland.

Another Harley-Davidson tour specialist is **Dream Legends Motorcycle Tours** (☎ 02/9584 2451). One-hour city trips cost A$60 (U.S.$42), half-day jaunts go for A$180 (U.S.$126), and a full-day excursion "wherever you want to go" costs A$300 (U.S.$210).

A third mean-machine operator is **Eastcoast Motorcycle Tours** (☎ 02/9247 5151). One-hour city tours cost A$80 (U.S.$56), and 4-hour trips to the south coast, Ku-Ring-Gai Chase National Park, or Wisemans Ferry, cost A$240 (U.S.$168).

CRUISES

The best thing about Sydney is the harbor, so you shouldn't leave without taking a harbor cruise. **Sydney Ferries** (☎ 13 15 00) offers a 1-hour morning harbor cruise with commentary, departing Circular Quay, Wharf 4, daily at 10am and 11:15am. It costs A$12 (U.S.$8.40) for adults, A$8 (U.S.$5.60) for children under 16, and A$32 (U.S.$22.40) for a family (any number of children under 16). A $2^{1}/_{2}$-hour afternoon cruise explores more of the harbor and leaves from Wharf 4 at 1pm on weekdays and 1:30pm on weekends and public holidays. This tour costs A$17.50 (U.S.$12.25) for adults, A$12 (U.S.$8.40) for children, and A$47 (U.S.$32.90) for a family. The highly recommended $1^{1}/_{2}$-hour evening harbor tour, which takes in the city lights as far east as Double Bay and west to Goat Island, leaves Monday to Saturday at 8pm from Wharf 5. The cost for adults is A$15 (U.S.$10.50), children A$10 (U.S.$7), and a family A$40 (U.S.$28).

Other options include a trip on the paddle steamer *Sydney Showboat* (☎ 02/9552 2722; fax 02/9552 1934), which departs from Campbells Cove in The Rocks. Buy tickets at the no. 2 jetty in Circular Quay.

The best cruise in my opinion is aboard the fully rigged replica of Captain Bligh's *Bounty* (☎ 02/9247 1789). The boat was built for the movie *Mutiny on the Bounty,* which starred Mel Gibson, Anthony Hopkins, Daniel Day Lewis, and Liam Neeson. In today's prices, the vessel cost around U.S.$15 million to construct. Standard 2-hour lunch cruises run Monday to Friday and cost A$52 (U.S.$36.40) for adults. Two-and-a-half–hour dinner cruises depart daily and cost A$80 (U.S.$56). On Saturday and Sunday, there are

---

A Travel Tip

The one-stop shop for tickets and information on all harbor cruises is the **Australian Travel Specialists** (☎ 02/9247 5151). Find outlets at jetties no. 2 and no. 6 at Circular Quay, at Manly Wharf in Manly, and inside the Oxford Koala Hotel on Oxford Street.

3¹/₂-hour buffet-lunch sails costing A$75 (U.S.$52.50) and 1¹/₂-hour predinner sails costing A$45 (U.S.$31.50).

Cruise like a millionaire aboard **MV *Oceanos*** (☎ **02/9555 2701**), a 72-foot luxury motor cruiser. A 2¹/₂-hour cruise, which leaves the Eastern Pontoon at Circular Quay at 1pm daily, costs A$69 (U.S.$48.30) a head and includes a quality seafood lunch.

Sail Venture Cruises (☎ **02/9262 3595**) also has a range of cruises aboard their catamarans.

Captain Cook Cruises. Departing jetty no. 6, Circular Quay. ☎ **02/9206 1111.** Fax 02/9251 1281.

This major cruise company offers several harbor excursions on its sleek vessels, with commentary along the way. Morning and afternoon Coffee Cruises, lasting 2 hours and 20 minutes, leave at 10am and 2:15pm daily and cost A$32 (U.S.$22.40) for adults and A$19 (U.S.$13.30) for children.

The **Harbour Highlights** cruise runs at 9:30am, 11am, 12:30pm, 2:30pm, and 4pm daily and take in most of the main points of interest in 1¹/₂ hours. It costs A$17 (U.S.$11.90) for adults and A$12 (U.S.$8.40) for children. The 1¹/₂-hour **Sundowner** cruise takes in the last of the sun's rays starting out at 5:30pm daily; it costs the same as the Harbour Highlights cruise.

The **Sydney Harbour Explorer** leaves at 9:30am, 11:30am, 1:30pm, and 3:30pm, and combines visits to five major Sydney attractions with a 2-hour cruise. Get off where you want and join the boat again later. Tickets cost A$20 (U.S.$14) for adults and A$12 (U.S.$8.40) for children. An Aquarium Cruise, costing A$29 (U.S.$20.30) for adults and A$16 (U.S.$11.20) for children, includes the Sydney Harbour Explorer cruise with aquarium entry.

The company also offers a 1¹/₂-hour **Luncheon Cruise,** which leaves daily at 12:30pm. It costs A$45 (U.S.$31.50) for adults and A$33 (U.S.$23.10) for children. A **Showtime Dinner Cruise** leaves nightly at 7:30pm and includes a cabaret and dinner; it costs A$85 (U.S.$59.50) for adults and A$48 (U.S.$33.60) for children.

Superior meals are served aboard the John Cadman Cruising Restaurant boat. A nightly $1^{1}/_{2}$-hour **Sunset Dinner** cruise departs at 5:15pm and costs A$59 (U.S.$41.30) for adults and A$30 (U.S.$21) for children, which includes a two-course meal and drinks. A second dinner cruise leaves at 7:30pm nightly and takes about $2^{1}/_{2}$ hours to cruise the harbor, while guests indulge in a fine three-course meal and bop away on the dance floor. Adults cost A$89 (U.S.$62.30), and children A$50 (U.S.$35). Reservations are essential.

Matilda Cruises. Departing Aquarium Wharf, Darling Harbour. ☎ **02/9264 7377.** Fax 02/9261 8483.

The modern Matilda fleet is based in Darling Harbour and offers 1-hour sightseeing tours, morning and afternoon coffee cruises, and daily lunch and dinner cruises. One-hour sightseeing cruises leave Darling Harbour six times daily and cost A$16 (U.S.$11.20) for adults and A$8 (U.S.$5.60) for children 5 to 12. Two-hour coffee cruises leave Darling Harbour at 9am and 3:05pm and cost A$24 (U.S.$16.80) for adults and A$12 (U.S.$8.40) for children. Two-hour lunch cruises leave at 12:15pm daily and cost A$48 (U.S.$33.60) for adults and A$24 (U.S.$16.80) for children. Three-hour dinner cruises leave at 7pm and cost A$90 (U.S.$63) for adults and A$45 (U.S.$31.50) for children. All boats dock at Circular Quay's Eastern Pontoon (near The Oyster Bar, before you get to the Sydney Opera House), 20 minutes after picking up passengers at Darling Harbour.

11 Staying Active

CYCLING   The best place to cycle in Sydney is in Centennial Park. Rent bikes from **Centennial Park Cycles,** 50 Clovelly Rd., Randwick (☎ **02/9398 5027**), which is 200 meters (660 ft.) from the Musgrave Avenue entrance. (The park has five main entrances). Standard bikes cost A$6 (U.S.$4.20) for the 1st hour, A$10 (U.S.$7) for 2 hours, and A$14 (U.S.$9.80) for 3 or 4 hours. Mountain bikes can be hired for the day to take on bush trails elsewhere. They cost A$30 (U.S.$21) for 8 hours, or A$40 (U.S.$28) for 24 hours.

Bicycles & Adventure Sports Equipment, Pier 1, The Rocks (☎ **02/9252 2229**), rents mountain bikes from A$5 (U.S.$3.50) per hour, or A$15 (U.S.$10.50) per day. You can rent in-line skates here, too, for A$15 (U.S.$10.50) per day, with all protective clothing.

GOLF   Sydney has more than 90 golf courses and plenty of fine weather. The 18-hole championship course at **Moore Park Golf Club,** at Cleveland Street and Anzac Parade, Waterloo (☎ **02/9663 1064**), is the nearest to the city. Visitors are welcome daily except Sunday mornings and all day Friday. Greens fees are A$18 (U.S.$12.60) Monday to Friday, and A$21 (U.S.$14.70) Saturday and Sunday.

One of my favorites is **Long Reef Golf Club,** Anzac Avenue, Colloroy (☎ **02/9982 2943**). This northern-beaches course is surrounded by the Tasman Sea on three sides and has gorgeous views. Greens fees are A$25 (U.S.$17.50) daily. For general information on courses, call the **NSW Golf Association** (☎ **02/9264 8433**).

FITNESS CLUBS   **The City Gym,** 107 Crown St., East Sydney (☎ **02/9360 6247**), is a busy gym near Kings Cross. It has ground-floor windows looking directly onto staring pedestrians (though you can hide in the back if you prefer). Drop-in visits are A$8 (U.S.$5.60), and it's open 24 hours daily.

JOGGING   The Royal Botanic Gardens, Centennial Park, or any beach are the best places to kick-start your body. You can also run across the Harbour Bridge, though you'll have to put up with the car fumes. Another popular spot is along the sea cliffs from Bondi Beach to Bronte Beach.

PARASAILING   If being strapped to a harness and a parachute 100 meters (330 ft.) above Sydney Harbour while being towed along by a speed boat is your idea of fun, contact **Sydney Harbour Parasailing and Scenic Tours** (☎ **02/9977 6781**). A regular flight will see you in the air for 6 to 7 minutes at the end of a 100-meter (330-ft.) line. It costs A$39 (U.S.$27.30) per adult. For A$49 (U.S.$34.30), you can get 8 to 10 minutes in the air and 150 meters (495 ft.) of line on a "super flight." Tandem rides, for children and adults, are also available. The boat departs next to the Manly ferry wharf in Manly.

SURFING   Bondi Beach and Tamarama are the best surf beaches in the south, while Manly, Narrabeen, Bilgola, Colloroy, Long Reef, and Palm Beach are the most popular on the north side. Most beach suburbs have surf shops where you can rent a board. At Bondi Beach, the **Bondi Surf Co.,** 72 Campbell Parade (☎ **02/9365 0870**), rents surfboards and body boards for A$20 (U.S.$14) for 3 hours. *Caution:* When surfing in the north, watch out for "blue bottles"—small blue jellyfish—or "stingers," the broken-off stinging cells of the same.

SWIMMING   The best place to swim indoors in Sydney is the **Sydney International Aquatic Centre,** at Olympic Park, Homebush Bay (☎ **02/9752 3666**). The pool was described by Juan Antonio Samaranch, the president of the International Olympic Committee, as "the best swimming pool in the world." It's open Monday to Friday from 5am to 9:45pm, and Saturday, Sunday, and public holidays from 7am to 7pm. Entry costs A$4.50 (U.S.$3.15) for adults and A$3.50 (U.S.$2.45) for children.

Another popular place is the **Andrew (Boy) Charlton Pool,** Mrs. Macquarie's Point (☎ **02/9358 6686**)—near the Art Gallery of New South Wales. It has great views over the finger wharves of Wooloomooloo. The pool is open in summer only, Monday to Friday from 6am to 8pm, and Saturday and Sunday from 6am to 7pm. Entry costs A$2 (U.S.$1.40) for adults and A$1 (U.S.70¢) for children.

Another good bet is the **North Sydney Olympic Pool,** Alfred South Street, Milsons Point (☎ **02/9955 2309**). Swimming here costs A$2.90 (U.S.$2.05) for adults and A$1.40 (U.S.$1) for children. By the way, there have been more world records broken in this pool than in any other in the world.

TENNIS   There are hundreds of places around the city to play one of Australia's most popular sports. A nice one is the **Miller's Point Tennis Court,** Kent Street, The Rocks (☎ **02/9256 2222**). It's run by the Observatory Hotel and is open daily from 8am to 9:30pm. The court costs A$20 (U.S.$14) per hour. The **North Sydney Tennis Centre,** 1a Little Alfred St., North Sydney (☎ **02/9371 9952**), has three courts available from 7am to 10pm daily. They cost A$14 (U.S.$9.80) up until 5pm on weekdays, and A$18 (U.S.$12.60) at other times.

WINDSURFING   My favorite spot to learn to windsurf or to set out onto the harbor is at Balmoral Beach, in Mosman on the North Shore. Rent boards at **Balmoral Windsurfing, Sailing and Kayaking School & Hire,** 3 The Esplanade, Balmoral Beach (☎ **02/9960 5344**). Windsurfers cost A$25 (U.S.$17.50) per hour, and lessons cost A$145 (U.S.$101.50) for 5 hours teaching over a weekend. This place also rents fishing boats.

YACHTING   **Balmoral Boat Shed,** Balmoral Beach (☎ **02/9969 6006**), hires catamarans, 12-foot aluminum runabouts, canoes, and surf skis. The catamarans and runabouts cost A$30 (U.S.$21) per hour (with an A$80/U.S.$56 deposit), and go down in price for additional hours (a full day costs A$110/U.S.$77). Other vessels cost

A$10 (U.S.$7) an hour with a A$10 (U.S.$7) deposit. **Sydney by Sail** (☎ 02/9552 7561 or mobile phone 0419/367 180) offers daily introductory sailing cruises on the harbor aboard luxurious 34- and 38-foot yachts. A maximum of six people sail aboard each boat, which leaves from the National Maritime Museum at Darling Harbour. Introductory sails run for 90 minutes and cost A$39 (U.S.$27.30) per person. Reservations are essential.

12   Catching a Cricket Match & Other Spectator Sports

CRICKET   The **Sydney Cricket Ground,** at the corner of Moore Park and Driver Avenue, is famous for its 1-day and test matches, played generally from October through March. Phone the **New South Wales Cricket Association** at ☎ 02/9261 5155 for match details. **Sportspace Tours** (☎ 02/9380 0383) run tours of the stadium, the Sydney Cricket Ground Museum, and the Football (rugby league) Stadium next door. Tours run Monday to Saturday at 10am, 1pm, and 2pm, and cost A$18 (U.S.$12.60) for adults, A$12 (U.S.$8.40) for children, and A$48 (U.S.$33.60) for a family.

FOOTBALL   In this city, "football" means rugby league. If you want to see burley chaps pound into each other while chasing an oval ball, then be here between May and September. The biggest venue is the **Sydney Football Stadium,** Moore Park Road, Paddington (☎ 02/9360 01). Match information is available at ☎ 0055 63 133. Buy tickets at **Ticketek** (☎ 02/9266 4800).

HORSE RACING   Sydney has four horse-racing tracks, Randwick, Canterbury, Rosehill, and Warwick Farm. The most central and most well known is **Randwick Racecourse,** Alison Street, Randwick (☎ 02/9663 8400). The biggest race day of the week is Saturday. Entry costs A$6 (U.S.$4.20) per person. Call the **Sydney Turf Club** at ☎ 02/9799 8000 with questions about Rosehill and Canterbury, and the Randwick number above for Warwick Farm.

SURFING CARNIVALS   Every summer these uniquely Australian competitions bring large crowds to Sydney's beaches, as surf clubs compete against each other in various water sports. Contact the **Surf Lifesaving Association** (☎ 02/9663 4298; fax 02/9662 2394) for times and locations. Other beach events include Iron Man and Iron Woman competitions, during which Australia's fittest struggle it out in combined swimming, running, and surfing events.

YACHT RACING   While sailing competitions take place on the harbor most summer weekends, the start of the Sydney to Hobart Yacht Race on Boxing Day (Dec 26) is something not to be missed. The race starts from the harbor near the Royal Botanic Gardens.

Sydney Strolls

*S*ydney is relatively compact, so it's a wonderful city for exploring on foot. The first walk I've described, through The Rocks, is pretty much a "must-do" for any visitor to Sydney. The second stroll, down George, Pitt, and Macquarie streets, provides a good mix of history and shopping. The third walk starts at Milsons Point CityRail Station at the far end (northern end) of the Sydney Harbour Bridge, runs past the rust-colored Overseas Passenger Terminal on the edge of the Circular Quay, past the Opera House, and through the Royal Botanic Gardens before ending at the Art Gallery of New South Wales.

WALKING TOUR 1
On The Rocks

Start: The Rocks Visitor Centre and Exhibition Gallery, 106 George St.
Finish: George Street.
Time: Allow around 1 hour, but longer if you stop off to shop.
Best time: Any day, though Saturday brings The Rocks Market and big crowds on George Street.

The Rocks is the site of the oldest settlement in Australia. Initially, convict-built timber houses lined the rocky ridge, which gave the area its name, and dockyard buildings lined the water's edge. In the 1840s a range of more permanent stone buildings was erected, including most of the pubs and shops still standing today. Slums grew up, too, and when the bubonic plague came to Sydney in 1900, the government set about demolishing most of the shanty buildings. Between 1923 and 1932 a large portion of the historic stone cottages in the area was pulled down to make way for construction of the Harbour Bridge. In the 1970s the government decided to pull the lot down and replace it with giant "international" office blocks and a hotel. Local residents stood together, though, and following a 2-year "Green Ban" by the Builders' Labourers Federation, during which they refused to touch any historic building, the government relented.

Start your walk at:

1. **The Rocks Visitor Centre and Exhibition Gallery,** 106 George St. (☎ **02/9255 1788**), open daily from 9am to 5pm. This excellent visitor center has plenty of information on Sydney and a whole range of Australiana books, too. Upstairs, on two levels, is a fascinating gallery of photographs, explanatory texts, an audiovisual presentation, and objects relating to The Rocks. The building itself is part of the former Sydney Sailors' Home built in the 1860s.

Outside on George Street, turn left, then turn left again at the first small avenue you come to, and walking down towards the water you'll see:

2. **Cadmans Cottage,** built in 1816. This small white building was the headquarters of the government body that regulated the colony's waterways. It's named after John Cadman, a pardoned convict who became the government coxswain and who lived here from 1827 to 1846. It's interesting to note that before a land-reclamation scheme, the water once lapped at its front door. Turn towards the water, look to the right, and you'll see a row of historic buildings:

3. **The Sailors' Home,** built in 1864, is the first of them. Sydney was a rough old town in those days, and no sooner had a sailor left his ship with his wages than he was likely to lose them in the brothels, pubs, and opium dens; gamble them away; or be mugged by gangs of "larrikins" who patrolled the back lanes. Concerned local citizens built the home to provide stricken sailors with lodging and food.

4. **The Coroners Court** next door, which was built in 1907, used to sit above the now-demolished morgue (or the "Dead House," as it was called). Before the Coroners Court was built, bodies would often be dissected for autopsy on the bar of the Observer Tavern across the street, over a few beers. Notice the exposed original foreshore rocks displayed beneath an arch on the wall.

5. **Mariners Church,** built in 1856, is a neoclassical building mostly obscured by later buildings.

6. **The Australasian Steam Navigation Company Building,** built in 1884, has a fabulous Flemish clock tower that was once used for spotting incoming ships. Take a look inside the Natural Australian Furniture Shop at the amazing wooden rafters. It was

Walking Tour 1: On The Rocks

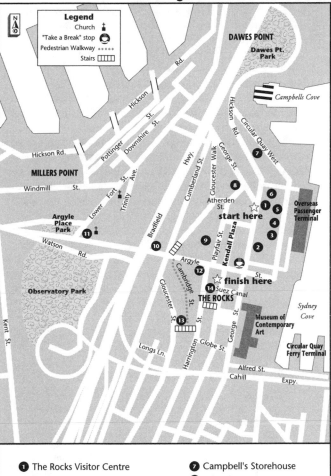

Legend

Church ♱

"Take a Break" stop 🐢

Pedestrian Walkway •••••

Stairs ▭▭▭

DAWES POINT

Dawes Pt. Park

Campbells Cove

MILLERS POINT

Argyle Place Park

Observatory Park

start here

Kendall Plaza

finish here

THE ROCKS

Suez Canal

Sydney Cove

Museum of Contemporary Art

Circular Quay Ferry Terminal

Overseas Passenger Terminal

Circular Quay West

Cahill Expy.

❶ The Rocks Visitor Centre and Exhibition Gallery
❷ Cadmans Cottage
❸ The Sailors Home
❹ The Coroners Court
❺ Mariners Church
❻ Australasian Steam Navigation Company Building
❼ Campbell's Storehouse
❽ Atherden Street
❾ Foundation Park
❿ The Argyle Cut
⓫ Garrison Church
⓬ The Clocktower Building
⓭ Susannah Place
⓮ The Suez Canal

A-1049

used as a storehouse, but before that the location was occupied by the home of the prominent merchant Robert Campbell.

7. **Campbell's Storehouse,** built between 1838 and 1890, was where Robert Campbell stored his tea, sugar, cloth, and liquor, which he imported from Asia. This wonderful pair of gabled buildings now houses four popular restaurants. From here, trace your steps back to a short flight of stairs that take you up to Hickson Road. Turn left onto George Street, then cross the road, and turn left onto:

8. **Atherden Street,** the shortest street in Sydney; it was named after a local landowner. Notice the natural rock wall at its end that gave The Rocks its name. Turn left into Playfair Street. Notice the markings in the rock walls where old slum dwellings used to be fixed. A little way along you'll see some steps. Follow them up to:

9. **Foundation Park,** which is an interesting artist's impression of what it was like inside the remaining structure of an old house in The Rocks. There wasn't much room, as you'll see. Follow the steps up to your right to Gloucester Walk. Follow this along until you get to Argyle Street. Turn to your left and walk down the hill and on the corner you'll find a nice place to:

 TAKE A BREAK   The historic **Orient Hotel.** Upstairs are restaurant eating areas, or you could just refresh yourself with a glass of local beer (order a "schooner" if you're really thirsty, or a smaller "midi").

When you're refreshed, head back up Argyle Street, where you'll find a great archway across the road.

10. **The Argyle Cut** was made by chain gangs chipping away at a mass of solid rock in a bid to link The Rocks to Cockle Bay (now Darling Harbour). The project was started in 1843, but 2 years later the use of convict labor was prohibited for government projects in the colony. In 1859 it was finally blasted through with explosives. At the top of the hill to your right is:

11. **Garrison Church,** built in 1839, a wonderful little Anglican church with stained-glass windows and engraved at the base with the names of children who died prematurely. In the early years, the soldiers sat on one side and the free settlers sat on the other. To keep the riffraff out, people had to pay for their pews, which were then name-tagged. Return back along Argyle Street the way you came and turn right into Harrington Street.

12. **The Clocktower Building,** on the corner of Harrington and Argyle streets, was built on the site of demolished cottages as the government stepped up its plans to clear the area of its historic buildings. After construction, the building lay empty for 5 years as people displayed their displeasure. Ironically, perhaps, it's now the home of Tourism New South Wales, the government tourism-promotion office.

Continue down Harrington Street and take a set of steep stairs to your right. At the top you'll find:

13. **Susannah Place,** 58-64 Gloucester St., a small terrace of four historic houses built in 1844, which give visitors a glimpse into the life of working-class families of the period and later. The houses are all part of the Historic Trust of New South Wales. Guided tours of the houses are offered between 10am and 5pm Saturday and Sunday year-round, and daily between 10am and 5pm in January. Tours cost A$5 (U.S.$3.50) for adults, and A$3 (U.S.$2.10) for children. Call the **Historic Trust** at ☎ **02/9241 1893** for details.

Go back down the stairs, cross Harrington Street, and backtrack on until you spot a thin lane on your left next to a craft shop selling Didgeridoos. The lane is:

14. **The Suez Canal,** which was created in the 1840s and became notorious as a place for prostitutes and the so-called "Rocks Push"—hoodlums who commonly dressed up as dandies in satin waistcoats, tight flared pants, bandannas around their necks, and jaunty hats. Looking good, they'd pounce on unwary sailors and citizens and mug them. Finish the walk on George Street.

WALKING TOUR 2
The City Streets

Start: Town Hall.

Finish: Circular Quay.

Time: You'll need at least half an hour just to walk the 2.5 kilometers (1¹/₂ miles) from start to finish, but it's likely you'll stop off many times along the way.

Best Times: Any time except Sunday, when some of the shops are closed, and rush hours and lunchtimes during the week, when the streets can get really crowded.

Sydney's oldest road, George Street, started off as a walking track, later became a wooden road for horses and carts, and later still took its car-pounded asphalt form. It's busy, full of traffic, and unappealing in most parts, so it's best just to dip in and out of. Running parallel to George is Pitt Street, which is good for shopping, and farther up is Macquarie Street, where history buffs will find some historic benefit.

Begin your walk at:

1. **Town Hall,** built in 1889. Every city has to have somewhere to roll a red carpet into, and this is Sydney's. This impressive sandstone building is home to the lord mayor's council, and it also acts as an exhibition space and a concert hall. Visitors are welcome to have a look around the lower floor. Adjacent to Town Hall is:

2. **The Queen Victoria Building,** built in 1883, a fabulous piece of architecture with some 200 mostly fashion shops on four levels. It's been described as the best arcade in the world by more than a few high-profile architects. Inside it's all arches, filtered light, Romanesque columns, ornate plasterwork, stained-glass windows, and lace ironwork. It started off life as a produce market but fell into disrepair from the 1930s on, before rising phoenixlike from its mothballs in 1986. If you're around on the hour, look out for the amazing clock that displays English history in pop-up book form.

Leaving the building at the far end, cross over the road and walk down Market Street to:

3. **AMP Centerpoint Tower,** which has some good shopping and a cheap food court on its lower levels. If you haven't done it yet, don't miss out on catching an elevator to top (see "Other Top Attractions: A Spectacular View, Sydney's Convict History & More," in chapter 5). Find your way out of the Pitt Street entrance again and you're on:

4. **Pitt Street Mall.** This pedestrian-only shopping street has a couple of excellent record shops and some well-stocked fashion boutiques. At the end of the mall, turn left into:

5. **The Strand Arcade,** built in 1892. This Victorian thoroughfare runs between Pitt and George streets on three levels. There are some interesting shops here.

🍵 **TAKE A BREAK**   **The Old Coffee Shop,** on the ground floor of the Strand Arcade, is a terrifically atmospheric place to rest up and get a cup of reasonable coffee. They serve good cakes, too. When you've had your fill, head back out to George Street and continue walking to:

Walking Tour 2: City Streets

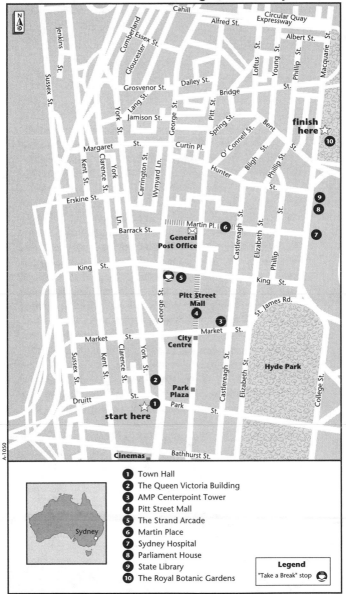

1. Town Hall
2. The Queen Victoria Building
3. AMP Centerpoint Tower
4. Pitt Street Mall
5. The Strand Arcade
6. Martin Place
7. Sydney Hospital
8. Parliament House
9. State Library
10. The Royal Botanic Gardens

Legend
"Take a Break" stop

6. **Martin Place.** This closed-off street is a strange-looking, often wind-blown, "square," but it's all that the city center has to call a plaza. Lunchtime sees crowds munching on sandwiches as they listen to free performances (beginning at 12:15pm) down in a concrete bull pit. The sturdy building to your left as you enter Martin Place is the original, and former, General Post Office. Continue right up to the end and you'll arrive at Macquarie Street. Across the road is the:

7. **Sydney Hospital.** The original hospital on this sight was huge and was known as the "Rum Hospital" following its construction in 1816 because its builders were paid in the form of a 3-year monopoly to import rum into the colony. Notice Il Porcellino, the bronze pig in the front yard; it's supposed to bring good luck if you stroke its nose. Next door is:

8. **Parliament House** (☎ **02/9230 2111**), where the state's politicians argue over how they'll spend the public's money. It was originally a wing of the Rum Hospital but was converted to the more sober business of government in 1828. Visitors can pop in and see the action when parliament is sitting. Question time, starting at 2:15pm on Tuesday, Wednesday, and Thursday, is the best time to visit, but you must book in advance. Free guided tours are available on nonsitting days at 10am, 11am, and 2pm. Bookings are essential. Next to Parliament House is the:

9. **State Library,** which is split into two separate parts, the older sandstone building on the corner of Macquarie and Bent streets holding a wide range of important historical books, while next door the newer section has two levels of reference materials. Continue on Macquarie Street to the entrance just across Bent Street of:

10. **The Royal Botanic Gardens.** At this end of the gardens is the Rose Garden. From here walk downhill to the sea, then follow the sea wall to your left all the way to Circular Quay.

WALKING TOUR 3
The Bridge, the House & the Gardens

Start: Milsons Point CityRail Train Station.
End: The Art Gallery of New South Wales.
Time: Around 2 hours.
Best Times: Anytime but peak traffic hours when the Harbour Bridge becomes a bit too smoggy.

Walking Tour 3: The Bridge, the House & the Gardens

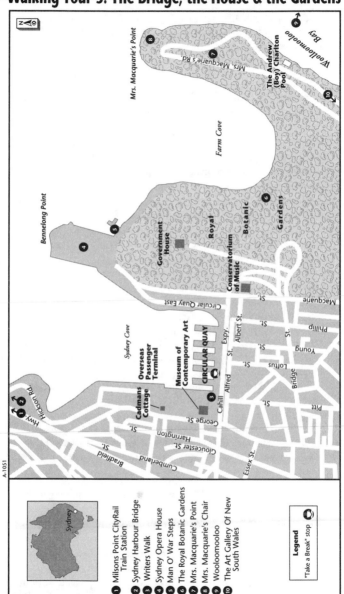

Mrs. Macquarie's Point

Bennelong Point

Farm Cove

Royal Botanic Gardens

Government House

Conservatorium of Music

Woolloomooloo Bay

The Andrew (Boy) Charlton Pool

Mrs. Macquarie's Rd.

Sydney Cove

Overseas Passenger Terminal

Museum of Contemporary Art

Cadmans Cottage

CIRCULAR QUAY

Circular Quay East

Cahill Expy.

George St.

Harrington St.

Gloucester St.

Cumberland St.

Bradfield Hwy.

Essex St.

Alfred St.

Albert St.

Phillip St.

Young St.

Loftus St.

Bridge St.

Pitt St.

Macquarie St.

Hickson Rd.

Sydney

1. Milsons Point CityRail Train Station
2. Sydney Harbour Bridge
3. Writers Walk
4. Sydney Opera House
5. Man O' War Steps
6. The Royal Botanic Gardens
7. Mrs. Macquarie's Point
8. Mrs. Macquarie's Chair
9. Woolloomooloo
10. The Art Gallery Of New South Wales

Legend
C "Take a break" stop

A-1051

135

This is a great walk because it takes in some of Sydney's major icons, the Harbour Bridge and the Opera House, as well as a wander through the Botanic Gardens to the Art Gallery of New South Wales.

Start your walk at:

1. **Milsons Point CityRail Train Station,** which is just one stop from the Wynyard station across Sydney Harbour. Just around the corner from the train station (literally a 20-second walk) you'll find a set of steps that lead to the Harbour Bridge walkway.

    Surprisingly, few tourists attempt the walk across the:

2. **Sydney Harbour Bridge,** though I guarantee the experience will stay in your memory. The walk takes you from one side to the other with spectacular views in between. You could stop off at the Pilon Lookout (see the box "A Bridge to Cross, Mate" in chapter 5). At the end of the walkway on the Sydney side of the bridge, follow the steps down into The Rocks and make your way down to the waterfront to the:

3. **Writers Walk,** which starts just past a fig-tree planter beside the Overseas Passenger Terminal and carries on through Circular Quay and to the Opera House. Along the way is a series of round brass plaques set into the brick footpath that celebrate the achievements of both Australian and overseas writers. Look out for A. B. "Banjo" Patterson, Henry Lawson, D. H. Lawrence, Charles Darwin, David Williamson, Kenneth Slessor, Jack London, and Aboriginal poet Oodgeroo Noonuccal, among others.

    Follow the walk along Circular Quay, taking a break if you feel like it at:

    ☕ **TAKE A BREAK**   **Rossini,** in Circular Quay, an Italian restaurant with chairs out front (see chapter 4). It's a good place for a coffee, an ice cream, or a good-sized lunch if you're hungry.

    After you've refueled, continue along to the:

4. **Sydney Opera House.** The best-looking modern building in the world has its roots firmly in the colonial past. It stands on Bennelong Point, named after an Aborigine befriended by Governor Macquarie. Macquarie built him a hut on the site the Opera House now stands on to encourage other Aborigines to see the benefits of their culture. Bennelong later died in a quarrel with others of his tribe; he had eventually found it impossible to fit in either white or Aboriginal society. The original name for the Point site though was Cattle Point, named after six cows and a

bull kept there. (The herd escaped and ran off into the forest when the convict guarding them fell asleep. They were found 7 years later having bred up into quite a herd.) Walk up the Opera House steps, where you can get a very unusual view of the building's two main shells.

Continue on around the Opera House until you reach the:

5. **Man O' War Steps.** This set of stone steps going down to the water acted as a landing and embarkation point for sailors coming and going in their warships in the early days of the colony.

Next proceed to:

6. **The Royal Botanic Gardens,** entered just by the sea wall. You can follow the sea wall all the way around Farm Cove, or alternatively dip into the middle of the gardens to take advantage of the shady groves and rain-forest walks. The gardens used to be where the First Fleet's vegetable plots were planted.

7. **Mrs. Macquarie's Point,** is at the far end of the sea wall. Up on top of the small cliff here is one of the best spots to see the Opera House and Harbour Bridge together.

8. **Mrs. Macquarie's Chair** is simply a bench cut out of the rock that was used as a resting place for Governor Macquarie's wife on her walks. Find it just up the hill on the asphalt footpath. Walk up to the parking lots and across the headland, where you'll see:

9. **Wooloomooloo.** The long warehouse-type buildings down below are the Finger Wharves; beyond them are the warships of the Australian navy (and visiting American ships when they're in port). From here walk up Art Gallery Road to:

10. **The Art Gallery of New South Wales.** End your trip here with a browse around the galleries. When you've finished, retrace your steps to the far end of the motor bridge where an entry will take you back into the Botanic Gardens. Alternatively, walk across the parkland opposite the gallery, called the Domain, and you'll end up on Macquarie Street near Martin Place CityRail train station.

7

The Shopping Scene

*T*hough not as good as Melbourne, Sydney still attracts a lot of visitors for its extensive shopping. Most shops of interest to the visitor are located in The Rocks, and along George and Pitt streets (including the shops below the AMP Centerpoint Tower and along the Pitt Street Mall). Other shopping precincts worth checking out are Mosman on the North Shore and Double Bay in the eastern suburbs for their exclusive boutique shopping, Chatswood for its general shopping centers, the Sydney Fish Market for the sake of it, and the various weekend markets (listed below).

Nobody should miss the Queen Victoria Building (QVB), on the corner of Market and George streets. This Victorian shopping arcade is one of the prettiest in the world and home to some 200 boutiques on four levels. The arcade is open 24 hours, but the shops do business Monday to Saturday from 9am to 6pm (Thurs to 9pm) and Sunday from 11am to 5pm. Several other arcades in the city center also offer good shopping potential, including the Royal Arcade under the Hilton Hotel; the Imperial Arcade near the AMP Centerpoint Tower; and the Skygarden Arcade, which runs from Pitt Street Mall to Castlereagh Street.

If you're looking for bargains, head to Foveaux Street between Elizabeth and Waterloo streets in Surry Hills for the factory clearance shops. Here you will find end-of-the-run, last-season fashions and seconds for a fraction of the price of clothes bought elsewhere.

Shopping hours are usually 8:30am to 5pm weekdays and 9am to 4pm on Saturday. Many shops stay closed on Sunday, although major department stores and shops aimed at tourists, like opal stores, are open 7 days. Sales tax in Australia is included in the price on the tag, not added at the cash register. Unfortunately, that means that you as a visitor pay tax, too, but jewelry, camera, and electronics stores often have "tax-free" prices for international travelers (you must show your passport and airline ticket).

1 Sydney's Best Buys

By Natalie Kruger

Although shopping in Australia is generally comparable to that in Europe and America, the variety is not always as good and you may think prices are high. Listed below are some good things to purchase in Australia, including some things that you can only buy Down Under.

ABORIGINAL ART & CRAFTS Dramatic, colorful, and intriguing, Aboriginal art is a great memento for visitors to Australia and serious business for international art investors. You can buy a print or an original work on paper, fabric, or bark starting at A$65 (U.S.$45.50), although works by some artists can cost thousands of dollars. Generally expect to pay between A$100 and A$300 (U.S.$70 and $210) for a work approximately 40 centimeters by 30 centimeters (15 in. by 12 in.) and about A$600 to $800 (U.S.$420 to $560) for larger works. All genuine Aboriginal art tells a story, often a Dreamtime creation myth.

An industry has been built up by non-Aboriginal artists sticking a few dots and lines on bark and calling it art, so make sure your work is accompanied by a certificate of authenticity.

JEWELRY Opals, diamonds, and pearls are what to look for Down Under. Jewelry stores, particularly opal stores, abound, so don't buy in the first place you see. A good rule of thumb is to buy only from stores with knowledgeable staff who can answer all your questions. If they can't, there is bound to be a more professional store around the corner that can. Because duty and sales tax together can be as high as 45% on Australian jewelry, there are big savings to be had if you show your passport and airline ticket to claim the "tax-free" price for international shoppers. This discount varies from store to store—another reason to shop around.

Australia supplies most of the world with **opals** from Quilpie, Winton, Lightning Ridge, Andamooka, and the underground desert town of Coober Pedy. What causes the pretty show of color in an opal is light passing through the spheres of silica that make up an opal. Size is not important when it comes to valuing opals. Color and clarity are—the more brilliant the colors in your opal, and the more colors it displays, the better it is. Check to see if it's free of "dead" patches that have no color play.

All That Glitters Isn't Gold
(Sometimes It's Opal)

Australia has around 96% of all the world's known opal deposits, of which there are three main types. The first is boulder opal, found largely in arid regions of western and northern Queensland. These opals are generally flat in appearance and found on the side of large iron-stone boulders. The dark background of the iron stone ensures brightly colored stones. A top-quality Boulder opal could fetch $100,000.

The second type, white opal, is mined primarily in Coober Pedy, 1,000 kilometers (630 miles) north of Adelaide, with smaller deposits found elsewhere. The most expensive white opals are translucent with strong colors and good clarity, while cheaper opals are more milky in color. A quality white opal could fetch A$50,000 (U.S. $35,000).

The third and most sought-after type of opal is the black opal, found mostly in Lightning Ridge in New South Wales near the Queensland border, with small deposits in Black Gate in southern Queensland, and in Mintabie, 30 kilometers (19 miles) from Marla in South Australia. Good-quality stones have a very dark background and lustrous colors, with reds and oranges fetching the best prices. Rare and extremely valuable black opals have recognized patterns, such as checkerboard squares, ribbons, and pinheads of color. Nearly 100% of all good-quality opal is exported to Japan, Korea, and Germany.

As well as these "solid" stones (stones which have been cut and polished but not interfered with in any other way), there are also "doublets," which are usually made by cementing a thin layer of good-quality light opal onto a dark background to bring out the color, and "triplets," which are doublets made with thin traces of opal with a clear dome of quartz or glass cemented to their faces to magnify the pattern. A good-quality doublet can cost as much as some lower-quality solid stones, while triplets are significantly cheaper.

—*Extract from an article published in* Australian Geographic
by the author Marc Llewellyn in July 1998.
© *Marc Llewellyn*

Australia's **South Sea pearls** are the world's best, and are arguably the most coveted item of jewelry among Australian women—next to diamonds, anyway. Farmed off Broome in Western Australia and the Cobourg Peninsula north of Darwin by the Kailis and Paspaley families, these pearls can be *big*—anywhere from 10 millimeters to 15 millimeters across. A pearl over 15 millimeters is rare and extremely valuable. A lot of jewelry uses half-pearls, or "mabe" pearls, which form on the inside edge of the pearl shell. The most important thing to look for in a pearl is a fine, thick luster, followed by a good surface or "complexion." Small flaws are not necessarily a bad thing—a pearl with a smooth complexion but poor luster will not fetch as much as one with rich luster and some surface imperfections. Contrary to what most of us think, color and shape do not affect the price, although fashions for a certain color or shape can put a premium on those kinds. The rule is, buy what looks good against your complexion. Australian South Sea pearls come in white (and white-pink), silver (and silver-pink or silver-blue), gold, and fancy (champagne, peach, and so on). Misshapen pearls are just as valuable as perfectly round ones. Bigger is better, although the smaller 2-millimeter to 10-millimeter "keshi" pearls are desirable because they formed without an initial "seed" in the oyster shell, which means they are solid nacre. Pearls are weighed in "momme"—1 momme equals 3.75 grams.

The world's biggest **diamond** mine is the Argyle mine in the Kimberley region of Western Australia. Along with white diamonds, it produces rare "champagnes" and cognacs, and is the only mine anywhere to commercially produce the world's rarest diamond, the pink, which can reach A$1 million (U.S.$700,000) a carat. Word is that the mine will run out of pinks in the early 2000s, according to one leading jeweler, so if you have a spare million big ones burning a hole in your pocket, get in quick! Argyle diamonds are widely available in jewelry stores appointed to stock them; call **Argyle Diamonds** (☎ **1800/640 056** in Australia or 08/9482 1150) for store locations.

OUTBACK CLOTHING   If you want to look like a rugged Outback Aussie, there is no shortage of stores to help you do it. Queensland grazier, saddlier, and bush poet R. M. Williams has put his name to a chain of stores that outfit city folk who want to emulate country folk. R. M. Williams is famous for his sturdy elastic-sided riding boots, just as popular as weekend wear for city stockbrokers as they are among bushmen who actually wear them riding.

The look is not complete without a classic Aussie bush hat, the Akubra. (made from rabbit pelts, not the skin of "akubras"). There are quite a few copycat brands sold in souvenir stores, but purists should hold out for the real thing. To complete the Aussie stockman look, get a Driza-bone oilskin raincoat from selected souvenir stores or R. M. Williams.

WINE   Any liquor store is happy to sell you wine, but shipping it overseas is another matter. Wine merchants are limited to exporting six bottles of wine per customer to the United States, and a mere one bottle to California. If you are buying inexpensive stuff, the freight of around A$100 (U.S.$70) can easily cost more than the wine—and on top of that, your home country may charge duty. **Inter-Liquor** (☎ **1800/252 008** in Australia) stocks and delivers a select range of good wines up to the six-bottle limit. If you are serious about getting your hands on larger quantities of a particular label, keep a note of the wine's maker, vintage, and name and ask a liquor merchant in your home country to import it. He or she has a liquor license, so the six-bottle restriction will not apply.

2   Shopping A to Z

ABORIGINAL ARTIFACTS & CRAFTS

Aboriginal & Tribal Art Centre. 1st Floor, 117 George St., The Rocks. ☎ **02/9247 9625.** Fax 02/9247 4391.

This center carries a wide range of desert paintings and bark paintings, mostly of very high quality. Collectibles such as Didgeridoos, fabrics, books, and boomerangs are on sale, too.

Coo-ee Aboriginal Art Gallery and Shop. 98 Oxford St., Paddington. ☎ **02/9332 1544.** Fax 02/9360 1109.

The proprietors of Coo-ee collect artifacts and fine art from more than 30 Aboriginal communities and dozens of individual artists throughout Australia. They also stock the largest collection of limited-edition prints in Australia. There are also plenty of hand-painted fabrics, T-shirts, Didgeridoos, boomerangs, sculpture, bark paintings, jewelry, music, and books. Don't expect it to be cheap, however.

Original & Authentic Aboriginal Art. 79 George St., The Rocks. ☎ **02/ 9251 4222.**

Quality Aboriginal art is on offer here from some of Australia's best-known painters, among them Paddy Fordham Wainburranga whose paintings even hang in the White House in Washington, and Janet

Forrester Nangala, whose work has been exhibited in the Australian National Gallery in Canberra. Expect to pay in the range of A$1,000 (U.S.$700) to A$4,000 (U.S.$2,800) for the larger paintings. There are some nice painted pots here, too, ranging from A$30 (U.S.$21) to A$80 (U.S.$56).

ART PRINTS & ORIGINALS

Done Art and Design. 123-125 George St. The Rocks. ☎ **02/9251 6099.** Fax 02/9235 2153.

The art is by Ken Done (he's well known for having designed his own Australian flag, which he hopes to raise over Australia should it abandon its present one following the formation of a republic). The clothing design is by his wife Judy. It's basically designer fashion with printed sea- and beachscapes, the odd colorful bird, and lots of pastels. There is another Done store in the Queen Victoria Building.

Ken Duncan Gallery. 73 George St., The Rocks (across from The Rocks Visitor Centre). ☎ **02/9241 3460.** Fax 02/9241 3462.

This photographer-turned-salesman is making a killing from his exquisitely produced large-scale photographs of Australian scenery.

BOOKS

Abbey's Bookshop. 131 York St. (behind the Queen Victoria Building). ☎ **02/9264 3111.**

This interesting, centrally located bookshop specializes in literature, history, crime, and mystery, and has a whole floor on language and education.

Dymocks. 424-428 George St. (just north of Market St.) ☎ **02/9235 0155.**

The biggest of four book department stores in the city, Dymocks has three levels of general books and stationary. There's a reasonable travel section here with plenty of guides.

Gleebooks Bookshop. 49 Glebe Point Rd., Glebe. ☎ **02/9660 2333.**

Specializing in art, general literature, psychology, sociology, and women's studies, Gleebooks also has a secondhand store (with a large children's department) down the road at 191 Glebe Point Rd.

✪ **Goulds Book Arcade.** 32-38 King St., Newtown. ☎ **02/9519 8947.**

Come here to search for unusual dusty volumes. Located about a 10-minute walk from the Newtown CityRail station, the place is bursting at the seams with many thousands of secondhand and new books. You can browse for hours here.

✪ **Travel Bookshop.** Shop 3, 175 Liverpool St. (across from the southern end of Hyde Park, near the Museum CityRail station). ☎ **02/9261 8200.**

Hundreds of travel guides, maps, Australiana titles, coffee-table books, and travel accessories line the shelves of this excellent bookshop.

CRAFTS

Australian Craftworks. 127 George St., The Rocks. ☎ **02/9247 7156.**

This place showcases some of Australia's best arts and crafts, collected for sale from some 300 Australian artists from around the country. It's all displayed in a former police station built in 1882, a time of economic depression when mob riots and clashes with police were common in this area. The cells and administration areas are today used as gallery spaces.

✪ **The puppet shop at the rocks.** 77 George St., The Rocks. ☎ **02/9247 9137.** Fax 02/9418 4157.

I can't believe I kept walking past the sign outside for so many years without looking in. Deep down in the bowels of a historic building, I eventually came across several cramped rooms absolutely packed with puppets, costing from a couple of dollars to a couple of hundred. The owners make their own puppets—mostly Australian in style (emus and koalas and that sort of thing)—as well as import things from all over the world. Wooden toys abound, too. It's the best shop in Sydney!

Telopea Gallery. Shop 2 in the Metcalfe Arcade, 80-84 George St., The Rocks. ☎ **02/9241 1673.**

This shop is run by the New South Wales Society of Arts and Crafts, which exhibits work made by its members, all of whom are NSW residents. There are some wonderful glass, textiles, ceramics jewelry, fine metals, spinning, weaving, and wood-turned items for sale.

DEPARTMENT STORES

The two big names in Sydney shopping are David Jones and Grace Bros. **David Jones** (☎ **02/9266 5544**) is the city's largest department store, selling everything from fashion to designer furniture. You'll find the women's section on the corner of Elizabeth and Market streets, and the men's section on the corner of Castlereigh and Market streets. **Grace Bros.** (☎ **02/9238 9111**) is along the same lines, and is located on the corner of George and Market streets.

DUTY-FREE SHOPS

Sydney has several duty-free shops selling goods at a discount. To take advantage of the bargains, you need a passport and flight ticket, and you must export what you buy. The duty-free shop with the best buys is **Downtown Duty Free,** which has two city outlets, one on the basement level of the Strand Arcade, off Pitt Street Mall (☎ **02/9233 3166**), and one at 105 Pitt St. (☎ **02/9221 4444**). It has five more stores at Sydney's Kingsford Smith Airport.

FASHION

The best place to go for fashionable clothes is the Queen Victoria Building, otherwise the major department stores and Pitt Street Mall outlets will keep you busy for hours.

Extremely fashionable in Australia, Japan, and elsewhere are the jewelry and housewares of Australian company **Dinosaur Designs.** They make a range of modern resin, silver, and ceramic items with bold colors. Find their shops at 339 Oxford St., Paddington (☎ **02/9361 3776**); on the ground floor of the Argyle Department Store, Argyle Street, The Rocks (☎ **02/9251 5500**); and Shop 73, first floor, The Strand Arcade, City (☎ **02/9223 2953**).

If you're in the market for traditional Australian Outback clothing, head to **R. M. Williams,** 389 George St. (☎ **02/9262 2228**). Moleskin trousers may not be the height of fashion at the moment, but you never know. R. M. Williams boots are famous for being both tough and fashionable. Akubra hats, Drizabone coats, and kangaroo-skin belts are for sale here, too.

FOOD

The goodies you'll find in the food section of the David Jones department store on Castlereagh Street (the men's section) will be enough to tempt anyone off their diet. It sells the best of local and imported products to the rich and famous.

Darrell Lea Chocolates. At the corner of King and George streets. ☎ **02/9232 2899.**

This is the oldest location of Australia's most famous chocolate shop. Pick up some wonderful handmade chocolate and lots of unusual candy, including the best licorice this side of the Kasbah.

GIFTS & SOUVENIRS

The shops at the Taronga Zoo, the Oceanarium in Manly, the Sydney Aquarium, and the Australian Museum are all good sources for gifts and souvenirs. There are many shops around The Rocks worth browsing, too.

National Trust Gift and Bookshop. Observatory Hill, The Rocks. ☎ **02/ 9258 0173.**

You can pick up some nice souvenirs, including books, Australiana craft, and indigenous foodstuffs, here. An art gallery on the premises presents changing exhibits of paintings and sculpture by Australian artists. Often pieces are for sale. There's also a cafe.

MARKETS

If you're in Sydney on the weekend, you should try to get to one of the colorful street markets. The most touristy, but not necessarily the best, is **The Rocks Market** (☎ 02/9255 1717), held every Saturday and Sunday on George Street in The Rocks. The main street is closed to traffic from 10am to 4pm to make it easier to stroll around stalls filled with arts and crafts, jewelry, clothes, and the like.

Saturday is also a good time to head to Paddington, where the **Paddington Bazaar** is held on the grounds of St. John's Church on Oxford Street (just follow the crowds). Here you'll find everything from essential oils and designer clothes to new-age jewelry and Mexican hammocks. Expect things to be busy from 10am to 4pm. Take bus no. 380 or 389 from Circular Quay.

Another popular Saturday market is **Balmain Market,** on the grounds of St. Andrew's Church, Darling Street, Balmain. It's active from 8:30am to 4pm, with some 140 stalls selling craft work, jewelry, and knickknacks. Take the ferry to Balmain (Darling Street); the market is a 10-minute walk up Darling Street.

Paddy's Markets (☎ 1300/361589 in Australia), on the corner of Thomas and Hay streets in Haymarket, near Chinatown, is a Sydney institution, with hundreds of stalls selling everything from cheap clothes to chickens. It's open Friday to Sunday from 9am to 4:30pm. Above Paddy's Market is **Market City** (☎ 02/9212 1388), which has 3 floors of fashion stalls, food courts, and specialty shops. Of particular interest is the largest Asian-European supermarket in Australia, on level 1, and the Kam Fook yum cha Chinese restaurant on level 3, also the largest in Australia.

MUSIC

HMV Music Stores. Pitt Street Mall. ☎ **02/9221 2311.**

This is one of the best music stores in Sydney. The jazz section is impressive. CDs in Australia are not cheap, with most new releases costing around A$30 to $35 (U.S.$21 to $24.50).

Sounds Australian. Shop 33, upstairs in The Rocks Centre, 10-26 Playfair St. (near Argyle St.), The Rocks. ☎ **02/9247 7290.** Fax 02/9241 2873.

Anything you've ever heard that sounds Australian you can find here. From rock and pop to Didgeridoo and country, it's all here. Fortunately, if you haven't a clue what's good and what's bad, you can spend some time listening before you buy. The management is extremely knowledgeable.

OPALS

ANA House Sydney. 37 Pitt St. ☎ **02/9251 2833.**

When buying good opal, it's always a good idea to bargain. This is one of the best city stalls to do it in. It sells some good stones, as well as all the usual touristy trinkets. There's a special VIP viewing room off to the side of the main sales floor if you're interested in buying real quality. Upstairs is a pretty good souvenir shop.

Australian Opal Cutters. Suite 10, Level 4, National Building, 250 Pitt St. ☎ **02/9261 2442.**

Learn more about opals before you buy at this shop. The staff gives you lessons about opal to help you compare pieces.

WINE

Australian Wine Center. 1 Alfred St., Shop 3 in Goldfields House, Circular Quay. ☎ **02/9247 2755.** Fax 02/9247 2756.

This is one of the best places in the country to pick up some Australian wine by the bottle or the case. A large range of wines from all over Australia is stocked on the premises, including bottles from small boutique wineries you're unlikely to find anywhere else. Individual tastings are possible at any time, though there are formal tastings every Thursday and Friday afternoon between 4 and 6pm. Wine is exported all over the world from here, so if you want to send home a crate of your favorite, you can be assured it will arrive in one piece.

8

Sydney After Dark

*T*he best way to find out what's on is to get hold of the "Metro" section of the Friday *Sydney Morning Herald* or the "7 Days" pullout from the Thursday *Daily Telegraph*.

1 The Performing Arts

For details on Sydney's most famous performing-arts venue, you know, that Opera House, see "The Opera House & Sydney Harbour" in chapter 5.

Half-price tickets to theater, music, and dance performances (usually that night's performance) are available from the **Halftix** booth at the top of Martin Place, near Macquarie Street, from noon onwards. Call ☎ **0055 26655** after 11am daily for information on available shows. Tickets must be paid for in cash only.

THEATERS

Sydney's blessed with plenty of theaters, many more than we have space for here—check the *Sydney Morning Herald,* especially the Friday edition, for information on what's currently in production.

Belvoir Street Theatre. 25 Belvoir St., Surry Hills. ☎ **02/9699 3444.** Tickets around A$34 (U.S.$23.80)

The hallowed boards of the Belvoir are home to Company B, which pumps out powerful local and international plays upstairs in a wonderfully moody main theater, formerly part of a tomato-sauce factory. Downstairs a smaller venue generally shows more experimental productions, such as Aboriginal performances and dance.

Capital Theatre. 13-17 Campbell St., Haymarket (near Town Hall). ☎ **02/9320 5000.** Tickets prices vary.

Sydney's grandest theater plays host to major international and local productions like, cough, Australian singing superstar Kylie Minogue. It's also been the Sydney home of musicals such as *Miss Saigon* and *My Fair Lady.*

Her Majesty's Theatre. 107 Quay St., Haymarket (near Town Hall). ☎ **02/9212 3411.** Ticket prices average A$45–$65 (U.S.$31.50–$45.50).

A quarter of a century old, this large theater is still trawling in the big musicals. Huge productions that have run here include *Evita* and *Phantom of the Opera*. At press time *The Boy from Oz* was on stage.

Wharf Theatre. Pier 4, Hickson Rd., The Rocks. ☎ **02/9250 1700.** Ticket prices vary.

This wonderful theater is situated on a refurbished wharf on the edge of Sydney Harbour, just beyond the Harbour Bridge. The long walk from the entrance of the pier to the theater along old creaky wooden floorboards builds up excitement for the show. The Sydney Theatre Company is based here, a group well worth seeing whatever production is running. Dinner before the show at the Wharf's restaurant offers special views of the harbor.

2 A Casino

Star City. 80 Pyrmont St., Pyrmont (adjacent to Darling Harbour). ☎ **02/9777 9000.** Free admission. Open 24 hours. Ferry: Pyrmont (Darling Harbour). Monorail: Casino.

This huge entertainment complex opened in 1997 has 15 main bars, 12 restaurants, two theaters—the Showroom, which presents Las Vegas–style revues, and the Lyric, Sydney's largest theater—and a huge complex of retail shops. All the usual gambling tables are here, in four main gambling areas, and there are several private gambling rooms. The four gaming rooms each have a different color scheme reflecting various areas of Australia. The "desert" gaming room features a man-made rock with a bar beneath a tumbling waterfall. In all, there are 2,500 slot machines in which to get rid of your change.

3 The Club & Music Scene

ROCK

Metro. 624 George St. ☎ **02/9264 2666.** Cover varies.

A medium-sized rock venue with space for 1,000, the Metro is the best place in Sydney to see local and international acts. Tickets sell out quickly.

JAZZ, FOLK & BLUES

✪ **The Basement.** 29 Reisby St., Circular Quay. ☎ **02/9251 2797.** Cover A$9–$10 (U.S.$6.30–$7) for local acts, A$20–$25 (U.S.$14–$17.50) for international performers.

Australia's hottest jazz club also manages to squeeze in plenty of blues, folk, and funk, too. Pick up a leaflet at the front door that shows who's playing when. A new Blue Note Bar specializing in jazz opened in July 1998. Acts appear every night.

The Bridge Hotel & Brasserie. 135 Victoria St., Rozelle. ☎ **02/9810 1260.**
Cover A$5–$25 (U.S.$3.50–$17.50).

Come on a Sunday afternoon and you're assured of getting the
blues. Friday and Saturday nights offer either blues, rock, or house
music, depending on their whim. The three-level beer garden out
the back is nice on a sunny day.

The Harbourside Brasserie. Pier 1, Hickson Rd., Walsh Bay (behind The
Rocks). ☎ **02/9252 3000.** Cover A$8–$20 (U.S.$5.60–$14) depending on
performer.

Eat to the beat of soul and rhythm and blues at this not-bad eatery.
Comedy nights attract big acts. Drinks are expensive.

Round Midnight. 2 Roslyn St., Kings Cross. ☎ **02/9356 4045.** Cover A$5
(U.S.$3.50) Tues–Thurs, A$10 (U.S.$7) Fri–Sun.

Come here to see live jazz New Orleans–style. At this small, smoky,
cozy joint, groups of two and three squeeze around small round
tables. It's reminiscent of New York's Cotton Club.

Soup Plus. 383 George St., (near the Queen Victoria Building). ☎ **02/9299
7728.** Cover A$5 (U.S.$3.50) Mon–Thurs; A$20 (U.S.$14) Fri and Sat, including 2-course meal.

It seemed such a pity on my last visit to this cavernous jazz bar that
the cover charge forced me to eat—the bistro-style food really was
poor. However, some mellow blues cheered our nonplused group in
the end.

DANCE CLUBS

Bourbon & Beefsteak Bar. 24 Darlinghurst Rd., Kings Cross. ☎ **02/9358
1144.** Cover A$5 (U.S.$3.50) Fri–Sat.

Right in the middle of the red-light district, this 24-hour restaurant
and nightspot freaks-out to dance music downstairs nightly from
11pm to 5am. It's popular with both younger backpackers and the
25-to-35 crowd.

Riche Nightclub. In the Sydney Hilton, 259 Pitt St. ☎ **02/9266 0610.**
Cover: hotel guests free; nonguests A$12 (U.S.$8.40) Fri and Sun, A$15
(U.S.$10.50) Sat.

This hot spot for dancing is popular with the local over-25 club set,
as well as hotel guests wanting to shake their booty to typical
"dance" music.

GAY & LESBIAN CLUBS

With Sydney having the largest gay community outside San Francisco, no wonder there's such a happening scene here. The center of

it all is Oxford Street, though Newtown has established itself as a major gay hangout, too. For information on news and events concerning gays and lesbians, pick up a copy of the *Sydney Star Observer,* available at art-house cinemas and many cafes and stores around Oxford Street.

✪ **Albury Hotel.** 2-6 Oxford St. (near Barcom Ave.). ☎ **02/9361 6555.**

An institution, the Albury is a grande dame offering drag shows nightly in the public bar, and knockout Bloody Marys in the cocktail lounge.

✪ **Imperial Hotel.** 35-37 Erskineville Rd., Erskineville (near Union St.). ☎ **02/9519 9899.** No cover.

A couple of minutes' walk from King Street in Newtown, the Imperial is a no-attitude gay venue with a pool and cocktail bar out front and a raging cabaret venue out back. Sydney's best full-production drag shows happen late on Thursday, Friday, and Saturday nights, with dancing in between.

Midnight Shift. 85 Oxford St. (near crown St.). ☎ **02/9360 4319.**

The beat here is sleazy, groovy, and dance party. A favorite with the denim and leather set, and the odd drag queen, this place gets more energetic as night becomes day.

Newtown Hotel. 174 King St., Newtown. ☎ **02/9557 1329.**

The octagonal bar here is the center of a casual drinking and cruising scene. The place kicks up its heels during late-night drag shows and powerfully camp discos.

77. 77 William St., East Sydney. ☎ **02/9361 4981.** Cover A$5 (U.S.$3.50) Thurs, A$7 (U.S.$4.90) Fri, A$6 (U.S.$4.20) Sat, A$5 (U.S.$3.50) Sun.

This basement venue, beneath a tower block and prestige car salesroom, is an odd one out location-wise, but its moody interior is a hot spot for alternative, dance, progressive house, and jungle music.

Taxi Club. 40 Flinders St., Darlinghurst (near Taylor Sq., Oxford St.). ☎ **02/9331 4256.** Cover A$10 (U.S.$7) Fri–Sat.

"Tacky Club," as it's affectionately known, is good for commercial dance music and midweek cabaret shows. It's open 24 hours.

4 The Bar Scene

Bondi Hotel. 178 Campbell Parade, Bondi Beach. ☎ **02/930 3271.**

This huge, whitewashed conglomerate across the road from Bondi Beach offers pool upstairs, a casual beer garden outside, and live jazz on weekend afternoons in the front bar. Watch yourself—too much drink and sun turns some people nasty here.

The Friend in Hand. 58 Cowper St., Glebe. ☎ **02/9660 2326.**

In the same location as the fantastically cheap Caesar's No Names spaghetti house, The Friend in Hand offers cheap drinks, poetry readings on Monday evenings, trivia night on Tuesday evenings, and the distinctly unusual Crab Racing Party on Thursdays. The entertainment starts at 7pm—they supply the crustaceans.

Henry the Ninth Bar. In the Sydney Hilton, 259 Pitt St. ☎ **02/9266 0610.**

This mock Tudor drinking hole gets very busy on Friday and Saturday nights when Irish bands take the stage. They serve up some good dark ales in an oaky atmosphere.

Hero of Waterloo Hotel. 81 Lower Fort St., The Rocks. ☎ **02/9252 4553.**

This sandstone landmark was once allegedly the stalking ground of press gangs, who'd whack unsuspecting landlubbers on the head, push them down a trapdoor out the back, and cart them out to sea. The beer does a similar thing.

Jacksons on George. 178 George St., The Rocks. ☎ **02/9247 2727.** Cover A$5 (U.S.$3.50) Fri and Sat after 10pm.

A popular drinking spot, this place has four floors of drinking, eating, dancing, and (expensive) pool playing. A haunt for suits and tourists. Drinks go up in price without warning on band nights.

✪ **Lord Nelson Hotel.** At Kent and Argyle sts., The Rocks. ☎ **02/9251 4044.**

Another Sydney sandstone landmark, the Lord Nelson rivals the Hero of Waterloo for the title of "Sydney's oldest pub." A drink here is a must for any visitor. The drinks are sold English-style, in pints and half pints, and the landlord even makes his own prize-winning beers.

✪ **Marble Bar.** In the Sydney Hilton, 259 Pitt St. ☎ **02/9266 0610.**

Once part of a hotel demolished in the 1970s, the Marble Bar is unique in that it's the only central Europeanish grand-cafe–style drinking hole in Australia. With oil paintings, marble columns, and brass everywhere, it's the very picture of 15th-century Italian Renaissance architecture. It's a tourist attraction in itself. Live music, generally jazz or soul, is played here Tuesday to Saturday beginning at 8:30pm. Dress smart on Friday and Saturday evenings, when it's full of suits.

The Mercantile. 25 George St., The Rocks. ☎ **02/9247 3570.**

Sydney's original Irish bar is scruffy and loud when the Irish music's playing in the evening, but it's an essential stop-off on any self-respecting pub crawl of The Rocks. The Guinness is a goodly drop.

✪ **Watsons Bay Hotel.** 1 Military Rd., Watsons Bay. ☎ **02/9337 4299.**

If it's a sunny afternoon, don't waste it: Get over to Watsons Bay for the best food you'll find in the sun anywhere. The beer garden serves very good seafood and BBQ meat dishes, while you sip your wine or beer overlooking the harbor. Nearby are the fabulous Doyles Wharf Restaurant and Doyles at the Beach take-away.

5 Movies

You can find the city's major movie houses, **Hoyts** (☎ **13 27 00**), **Greater Union** (☎ **02/9267 8666**), and **Village** (☎ **02/9264 6701**), right next to each other on George Street just past Town Hall. They tend to show big-budget movie releases. For something different, head to one of Sydney's best art-house cinemas. Eat "Jaffas," round candy-coated chocolates, if you want to fit in.

Academy Twin Cinema. 3A Oxford St., Paddington. ☎ **02/9361 4453.** A$12 (U.S.$8.40) adults, A$7.50 (U.S.$5.25) children. Tues all tickets A$7.50 (U.S.$5.25).

A good cinema to check out for its new-release art-house films. As the name suggests, there are two movie screens here.

✪ **Hayden Orpheum Picture Palace.** 380 Military Rd., Cremorne. ☎ **02/ 9908 4344.** Tickets A$11.50 (U.S.$8.05) adults, A$7.50 (U.S.$5.25) children. Tues A$7.50 (U.S.$5.25) adults, A$4.50 (U.S.$3.15) children.

This movie house—the best in Sydney, with six screens—is an experience in itself, especially on Saturday and Sunday evenings when a Wurlitzer pops up from the center of the Cinema 2 stage, and the musician in a tux gives a stirring rendition of times gone by. The whole place is wonderfully art deco.

Valhalla. 166 Glebe Point Rd. (between Bridge Rd. and Hereford St.) ☎ **02/ 9660 8050.** A$11.50 (U.S.$8.05) adults, A$6 (U.S.$4.20) children. A$30 (U.S.$21) transferable 5-ticket booklet valid Mon–Thurs.

The movie-going world cried when they removed the reclining seats from one of the best art-house cinemas in Sydney. Popular with students. Buy an institutional "choc top" ice cream for A$2.50 (U.S.$1.75).

Side Trips from Sydney

1 The Central Coast

Gosford, 84km (52 miles) N of Sydney

The Central Coast is an area of natural beauty worth exploring if you're heading up the coastline or plan to visit the wineries of the Hunter Valley. The area encompasses the city of Gosford, a picturesque town on the edge of Brisbane Water National Park, where you can boat, fish, and bushwalk; the Entrance, famous for its pelican feedings at 3:30pm every day; Terrigal, with its beautiful beaches and diving with gray nurse sharks; and Old Sydney Town in Somesby.

ESSENTIALS

GETTING THERE To reach Gosford by car, take the Pacific Highway and the Sydney-Newcastle Freeway (F3). It takes about an hour. **CityRail** trains (☎ **13 15 00**) leave from Central Station for Gosford every 30 minutes. Round-trip fares are A$12 (U.S.$8.40) for adults and A$6 (U.S.$4.20) for children during commuter times, and A$7.50 (U.S.$5.25) and A$2.50 (U.S.$1.75), respectively, off-peak. **Central Coast Airbus** (☎ **02/4332 8655**) picks up passengers at the international and domestic terminals at the Sydney airport and at Chalmers Street, near Central Station, nine times daily. From Central Station, the fare is A$11 (U.S.$7.70) one-way and A$22 (U.S.$15.40) round-trip. **Busways** (☎ **02/4368 2277**) meets most trains at Gosford station from Sydney and goes to Terrigal, Ettalong, Avoca, Woy-Woy, and the attractions at Somesby. The one-way fare to Terrigal is A$3.30 (U.S.$2.30) for adults, and A$1.60 (U.S.$1.10) for children. Seaplanes also fly to the area.

VISITOR INFORMATION The **Gosford City Visitors Information Centre** is at 200 Mann St. (☎ **02/4323 2353**); it's open daily. Alternatively, **Central Coast Tourism** (☎ **1800/806 258** in Australia or 02/4385 4430) provides information on the area over the telephone.

Sydney & Environs

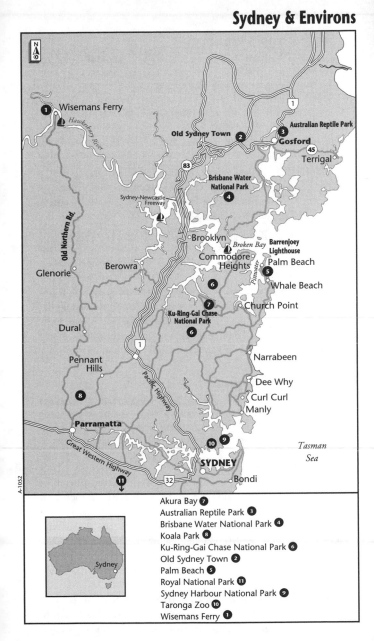

Akura Bay ❼
Australian Reptile Park ❸
Brisbane Water National Park ❹
Koala Park ❽
Ku-Ring-Gai Chase National Park ❻
Old Sydney Town ❷
Palm Beach ❺
Royal National Park ⓫
Sydney Harbour National Park ❾
Taronga Zoo ❿
Wisemans Ferry ❶

SEEING THE TOP ATTRACTIONS

Australian Reptile Park. Pacific Hwy., Somersby. ☎ **02/4340 1022.** Admission A$10.95 (U.S.$7.65) adults, A$5.50 (U.S.$3.85) children. Daily 9am–5pm. Closed Christmas Day. From Gosford, take the bus marked AUSTRALIAN WILDLIFE PARK (10-minute ride).

What started off as a one-man operation supplying deadly snake antivenom in the early 1950s has ended up a nature park teeming with the slippery-looking creatures. But it's not all snakes and lizards here. You'll also find Eric, a 15-foot-long saltwater crocodile; an alligator lagoon with some 50 American alligators; as well as plenty of somewhat cuddlier creatures, such as koalas, platypus, wallabies, dingoes, and flying foxes. The park is set in beautiful bushland dissected by nature trails.

✪ **Old Sydney Town.** Pacific Hwy., Somesby. ☎ **02/4340 1104.** Admission A$17 (U.S.$11.90) adults, A$10 (U.S.$7) children. Wed–Sun 10am–4pm; daily during school holidays. From Gosford, take the bus marked OLD SYDNEY TOWN (15-minute ride).

You can spend quite a few hours here on a nice day wandering around this outdoor theme park bustling with actors dressed up like convicts, sailors, and the like. You'll see plenty of stores, buildings, and ships from the old days of the colony, and performances are put on throughout the day. It's the Australian version of an American Wild West theme town.

WHERE TO STAY & DINE

Crowne Plaza Terrigal. Pine Tree Lane, Terrigal, NSW 2260. ☎ **1800/02 4966** in Australia, or 02/4384 111. Fax 02/4384 5798. 196 units. A/C MINIBAR TV TEL. A$300–$360 (U.S.$210–$252) double; A$500–$1,800 (U.S.$350–$1,260) suite. Additional person A$35 (U.S.$24.50) extra. Children under 19 stay free in parents' room. AE, BC, DC, MC, V. Free parking. From Sydney, take the train or a bus to Gosford (free pickup to resort can be arranged).

This beachfront resort is a popular spot for weekending Sydneysiders and tourists making the road trip up the north coast. All rooms except six have ocean views, with the least expensive standard rooms having partial views. Rooms are very comfortable and come with either two queen-size beds or a queen and a double sofa bed. Children are not allowed on the 7th floor, where for an extra A$45 (U.S.$31.50) you get champagne, canapés, and continental breakfast with your room.

Dining/Entertainment: Breakfast is served in either the delightful Conservatory or the Florida Beach Bar and Grill. The top-ranking restaurant is La Mer, which specializes in seafood and

French cuisine. The Norfolk Brasserie is more casual. A nightclub, which is also on the premises, can really kick-off on Friday and Saturday nights in summer.

Amenities: Concierge, 24-hour room service, laundry, valet, nightly turndown, complimentary daily newspaper on request, babysitting, massage, large health club, gym, sauna, spa, children's club, children's center, hair salon, gift shop, newsstand, saltwater pool.

2   The Blue Mountains

Today, the escape valve for the residents of the humid and heavily populated city of Sydney and its western suburbs, the Blue Mountains formed one of the most difficult barriers to early exploration of the interior in the fledgling days of the colony. In 1813, three explorers—Blaxland, Wentworth, and Lawson—managed to conquer the sheer cliffs, valleys, and dense forest, and cross the mountains to the plains beyond. The Great Western Highway and Bells Line of Road are the access roads today—winding and steep in places, they are surrounded by the Blue Mountains and Wollemi National Parks. The views from some of the cliff tops, into the valleys of gum trees and across to craggy outcrops that tower up from the valley floor, are spectacular. It's colder up here than down on the plains, and the clouds can sweep in and fill the canyons with mist in minutes, while waterfalls cascade down sheer drops, spraying the dripping fern trees that cling to the gullies.

The Blue Mountains derive their name from the ever-present blue haze that is caused by light striking the droplets of eucalyptus oil that evaporate from the leaves of the dense surrounding forest.

VISITOR INFORMATION   Information is available and accommodations can be booked at **Blue Mountains Tourism,** with locations at Echo Point Road, Katoomba, NSW 2780 (☎ **02/4739 6266**) and on the Great Western Highway at Glenbrook (☎ **02/ 4739 6266**). The first of these information centers is an attraction in itself, with giant glass windows overlooking a gum forest and the cockatoos and colorful lorikeets feeding on the seed dispensers. Make sure you pick up a copy of the *Blue Mountains Pocket Guide,* a free guide to dining, accommodations, bushwalking, and entertainment in the area. Both offices are open from 9am to 5pm daily (the office at Glenbrook closes at 4:30pm on Sun).

The **National Park Shop,** Heritage Centre, at the end of Govetts Leap Road, Blackheath (☎ **02/4787 8877**), is run by the National

Parks & Wildlife Service and offers detailed information about the Blue Mountains National Park itself and its bushwalking options. It also sells a wide range of nature-based gifts and can arrange personalized guided tours of the mountains and spotlighting tours at night in search of native animals.

KATOOMBA: GATEWAY TO THE BLUE MOUNTAINS

114km (71 miles) W of Sydney

Katoomba (population 11,200) is the largest town in the Blue Mountains and the focal point of the Blue Mountains National Park. It used to be a hard journey by horse and cart up here from Sydney in the 1870s, but these days it's a far easier $1^1/_2$- to 2-hour trip by train, bus, or car.

ESSENTIALS

GETTING THERE   If you decide to drive, the journey will take you around $1^1/_2$ hours (longer during rush hours). From Sydney, travel along Parramatta Road and turn off onto the M4 motorway (pay a A$1.50/U.S.$1.05 toll). Frequent rail services connect Sydney to Katoomba from Central Station (this route is covered by CityRail and Countrylink). The train trip takes 2 hours, leaving from platforms 12 and 13 of Central Station. Trains leave almost hourly, stopping at Katoomba and then at Mt. Victoria and Lithgow. An adult day-return round-trip ticket costs A$12.40 (U.S.$8.70) off-peak and A$20.80 (U.S.$14.55) during commuter hours. A child's day-return round-trip ticket costs A$2.40 (U.S.$1.70).

Many private bus operators offer day trips from Sydney, but it's important to shop around because some offer a guided coach tour where you just stretch your legs occasionally, while others let you get the cobwebs out of your lungs with a couple of longish bushwalks. Tours with **The Wonderbus** (☎ 02/9555 9800) include most of the major sites and a short bushwalk. Day tours leave Sydney at approximately 7:45am and return after 7pm and cost A$48 (U.S.$33.60). Overnight packages, with accommodation in the YHA hostel, are also available.

Cox's River Escapes, P.O. Box 81, Leura, 2780 (☎ 02/ 4784 1621 or mobile phone 015/400 121; fax 02/4784 2450), offers highly recommended tours for those wanting to get off the beaten track. Operator Ted Taylor picks up at the Rivercat ferry stop at Parramatta, or from Blue Mountains accommodations, and transports his clients around in air-conditioned four-wheel–drive vehicles seating a maximum of six. Half-day tours visit remote areas and

New South Wales

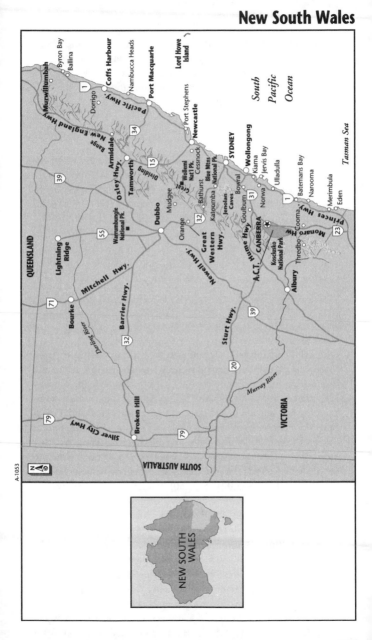

travel through private property in and around the Megalong Valley. Full-day tours travel either around the Megalong Valley, the Garden of Stone National Park, and along the edge of wilderness areas (a 2^1/$_2$-hour bushwalk is optional), or through areas of the Blue Mountains in search of remote lookouts. Half-day trips with morning or afternoon tea cost A$95 (U.S.$66.50); full-day trips with morning tea, lunch, and afternoon refreshments cost A$150 (U.S.$105).

AAT Kings, Shop 1, corner of Alfred Street and ferry wharf no. 1, Circular Quay (☎ **02/9252 2788**; fax 03/9274 7400), runs a typical big-bus tour of the mountains, taking in all the usual sights, with a couple of short walks included. It costs A$66 (U.S.$46.20) for adults, and A$33 (U.S.$23.10) for children. Another large operator, **Australian Pacific Tours,** 102 George St., The Rocks (☎ **02/9252 2988;** fax 02/9247 2052), offers a similar trip with a visit to the Australian Wildlife Park (part of Australia's Wonderland Complex; see "Other Top Attractions: A Spectactular View, Sydney's Convict History & More" in chapter 5) and a quick visit to the Sydney Olympic site at Homebush Bay. This tour costs A$78 (U.S.$54.60) for adults and A$39 (U.S.$27.30) for children.

GETTING AROUND   If you take the train to Katoomba from Sydney, walk up the stairs from the station; across the street and to your left you'll see the Savoy Theatre. Coaches operated by **Mountain Link** (☎ **1800 801 577** in Australia) meet most trains from Sydney outside this theater and take passengers to the main Blue Mountains attractions, including Echo Point, the Three Sisters, Leura Village, the Gordon Falls, and Blackheath, as well as other drop-off points for good views. Between 14 and 17 buses run each way daily. Single-ride tickets to one destination cost between A$1.70 (U.S.$1.20) and A$3.60 (U.S.$2.50) depending on the distance.

Alternatively, you can connect with the **Blue Mountains Explorer Bus.** This red double-decker bus leaves from outside Katoomba train station at 9:30am, 10:30am, 11:30am, 12:20pm, 1:40pm, 2:30pm, 3:30pm, and 4:40pm on weekends and public holidays only. It stops at 18 major attractions between Katoomba and Leura, including the Three Sisters, the Scenic Railway & Skyway, Echo Point, Katoomba Falls, Leura Cascades, Gordon Falls Reserve, the MAXVISION cinema, and various resorts, arts and crafts galleries, and tearooms. You can get on and off as often as you want. It costs A$18 (U.S.$12.60) for adults, A$8 (U.S.$5.60) for children, and A$45 (U.S.$31.50) for a family of five. Between Monday and Friday you have the option of the 3-hour "Blue Mountains Highlights Tour," which costs A$32 (U.S.$22.40) for adults, A$16 (U.S.$11.20) for children, and A$80 (U.S.$56) for a family. The tour leaves Katoomba train station Monday to Friday at 10:30am, 11:30am, and 2pm. Both are operated by **Fantastic Aussie Tours** (☎ **1300/300 915** in Australia or 02/4782 1866). Combined rail/bus tours from Sydney can be purchased at any **CityRail** (☎ **13 15 00** in Australia) station and cost a couple of dollars less than buying the tickets separately.

An alternative, and thrilling, way to see the mountains is on the back of a chauffeur-driven Harley-Davidson with **Blue Thunder Motorcycle Tours** (☎ **02/4571 1154**). Trips cost A$60 (U.S.$42) for 1 hour, A$115 (U.S.$80.50) for 2 hours, A$165 (U.S.$115.50) for 3 hours, A$210 (U.S.$147) for half a day with lunch, and A$300 (U.S.$210) for a full day with lunch.

SEEING THE TOWN

The most visited and photographed attractions in the Blue Mountains are the unusual rock formations known as the **Three Sisters.** The best place to view these astonishing looking pinnacles is from Echo Point Road, right opposite the Blue Mountains Tourism office. Other good lookouts include Evans Lookout, Govetts Leap, and Hargreaves Lookout (all at Blackheath).

One thing you have to do in the Blue Mountains is take a ride on the **Scenic Railway,** the world's steepest. It consists of a carriage on rails that is lowered 415 meters (1,370 ft.) down into the Jamison Valley at a maximum incline of 52°. Originally it was used to transport coal and shale in the 1880s from the mines below. The trip only takes a few minutes there and back; at the bottom there are some excellent walks through forests of ancient tree ferns. Another popular attraction is the **Skyway,** a cable car that travels 300 meters (990 ft.) above the Jamison Valley. The trip takes 6 minutes round-trip. Both the Scenic Railway and Skyway (☎ **02/4782 2699**) cost A$4.50 (U.S.$3.15) round-trip for adults and A$2 (U.S.$1.40) for children, and operate from 9am to 5pm (last trip at 4:50pm).

Travel Tip

If you can, try to visit the Blue Mountains on weekdays, when most Sydneysiders are at work and the prices are lower. Note, too, that winter is the busiest period in the Blue Mountains.

The **MAXVISION Cinema,** 225-237 Great Western Hwy., Katoomba (☎ **02/4782 8900** or 02/4782 8928), is a giant-screen cinema showing a movie called *The Edge,* which portrays dramatic natural views of the Blue Mountains, including canyons, waterfalls, and underground rivers. The special effects shown on the screen 18 meters (59 ft.) high and 24 meters (79 ft.) wide make you feel as if you're actually participating in the action. *The Edge* runs for 38 minutes. Session times are 10am, 11:45pm, 12:30pm, 1:15pm, 3pm, and 5:15pm. It costs A$12 (U.S.$8.40) for adults, A$8 (U.S.$5.60) for children, and A$35 (U.S.$24.50) for a family. Other movies (titles vary) are shown between each screening of *The Edge.* The cinema is a 5- to 10-minute walk from the train station. The cinema is open daily from 9am to 11pm, with recent release movies shown on part of the giant screen in the evenings. There are a restaurant and a snack bar on the premises.

BUSHWALKS & OTHER ACTIVE ENDEAVORS

The Blue Mountains area is one of Australia's best-known adventure playgrounds. Rock climbing, caving, abseiling, bushwalking, mountain biking, horseback riding, and canoeing are all practiced here throughout the year. Whereas almost every other activity costs money, bushwalking (hiking) is the exception to the rule that nothing in life is free. There are some 50 walking tracks in the Blue Mountains, ranging from routes you can cover in 15 minutes to the 3-day Six-Foot Track trip that starts just outside Katoomba and finishes at Jenolan Caves. If you are planning to do some bushwalking, I highly recommend picking up a copy of *Sydney and Beyond—Eighty-six Walks in NSW,* by Andrew Mevissen. It features eight walks in the Blue Mountains, from easy 1-hour treks to 6-hour tramps, including a walk around the Ruined Castle at Katoomba; a less well-known hike to Walls Cave; and walks at Govetts Leap, the Grand Canyon at Blackheath, and into the Grose Valley. Buy it at bookshops and tourist information centers, such as The Rocks Visitors Centre in Sydney.

Great Australian Walks, Suite 2, 637 Darling St., Rozelle, NSW 2030 (☎ **1800/242 461** in Australia or 02/9555 7580; fax 02/9810 6429), is a superb operator offering walks in the Blue Mountains. I had great fun on their 3-day Six-Foot Track Walk from Katoomba to Jenolan Caves. Though not a wilderness trek, it goes through nice pockets of rain forest and open gum forests and traverses pretty farming country. The trip includes transport, guides, all food and drink, four-wheel–drive support vehicle to carry your luggage,

1-night hut accommodations, a 2nd night camping with all gear supplied, and a cave tour at Jenolan Caves. It costs A$340 (U.S.$238) for adults. Young children are allowed only on school holidays, for A$189 (U.S.$132.30).

One of the best adventure operators in the area is the **Blue Mountains Adventure Company,** P.O. Box 242, Katoomba, NSW 2780 (☎ **02/4782 1271** or mobile phone 0418/210743; fax 02/4782 1277). Find it in Katoomba at 84a Main St. (above Elders Real Estate). Another well-known operator is the **Australian School of Mountaineering,** 166b Katoomba St., Katoomba, NSW 2780 (☎ **02/4782 2014**; fax 02/4782 5787). Both operators can organize rock-climbing, abseiling, and canyoning expeditions, while the Blue Mountains Adventure Company also offers caving and mountain biking, and the Australian School of Mountaineering offers bushcraft and survival training. Expect to pay around A$95 (U.S.$66.50) for a full-day's introductory rock-climbing course including abseiling, and between A$95 (U.S.$66.50) and A$125 (U.S.$87.50) for a day's canyoning.

If you feel like adventuring on your own, you could always hire a mountain bike from **Cycletech,** 3 Gang Gang St., Katoomba (☎ **02/4782 2800**). Bikes cost A$15 (U.S.$10.50) for half a day and A$25 (U.S.$17.50) for a full day (superior front-suspension mountain bikes cost A$40/U.S.$28 a day). Cycletech can supply you with a regional map with bike trails marked for A$4.95 (U.S.$3.45). This company was also gearing up to do guided cycle tours.

WHERE TO STAY

There are plenty of places to stay throughout the Blue Mountains, including historic guesthouses, B&Bs, resorts, motels, and homestays.

Blue Mountains YHA Hostel. 66 Waratah St. (at Lurline St.), Katoomba, NSW 2780. ☎ **02/4782 1416.** Fax 02/4782 6203. 80 beds in 16 units, most with bathroom. A$13–$18 (U.S.$9.10–$12.60) dorm bed; A$50 (U.S.$35) double/twin. Family rates available and guests under 18 half-price. BC, MC, V.

This former guesthouse is fine for a couple of nights, if you don't mind things a little less than luxurious. It's friendly, clean, comfortable, well located, and has log fires in the living areas, a communal kitchen and dining room, and a laundry. The double rooms are simple, with either a double, twin, or bunk beds and not much else but a small bathroom. The dorm rooms accommodate from 4 to 12 people; the cheaper dorm rooms on the top floor share bathrooms.

✪ **Echoes Guesthouse.** 3 Lilianfels Ave., Echo Point, Katoomba, NSW 2780.
☎ **02/4782 1966.** Fax 02/47 823707. 12 units. MINIBAR TV TEL. Weekend
$660 (U.S.$462) double for 2 nights, including 1 dinner and 2 breakfasts; midweek A$260 (U.S.$182) double with breakfast. AE, BC, DC, MC, V. Free parking. Children are not allowed.

Despite being less expensive than Lilianfels Blue Mountains (see below) across the road, Echoes has got by far the superior views. It's
right on the edge of the dramatic drop into the Jamison Valley, and
most guests can sit on their balcony and simply draw in their breath
at the fantastic scenery. Rooms are smaller than at Lilianfels and
quite simply furnished. All have underfloor heating, and two corner
rooms have Jacuzzis. Upstairs is a large deck offering more legend-
ary views, plus a lounge with an open fire, a restaurant serving
French cuisine, and a bar—all with large windows. The property
also has a sauna.

Lilianfels Blue Mountains. Lilianfels Ave., Echo Point, Katoomba, NSW 2780.
☎ **1800/024 452** in Australia or 02/4780 1200. Fax 02/4780 1300. 86 units,
1 cottage. A/C MINIBAR TV TEL. A$290–$345 (U.S.$203–$241.50) double;
A$420–$550 (U.S.$294–$385) suite; A$850 (U.S.$595) cottage. Additional person A$40 (U.S.$28) extra. Ask about off-season packages. AE, BC, DC, MC, V.
Free parking.

Set just over a road from Echo Point, this Victorian country-house
hotel has some impressive views. Remarkably, it's also managed
to combine both the facilities of a top-class resort and the coziness
of a guesthouse. Rooms are very spacious and stocked with
antique furnishings. Most come with king-size beds and both a
tub and shower. Those with views are more expensive. The living
areas are just as grand, with roaring log fires and more antiques.
The lounge, which overlooks the Jamison Valley, is the property's
best feature. On the grounds is a free-standing 1889 cottage,
which was originally the servants' quarters. Meant for two, it has
 a sitting room and bedroom with a four-poster bed, a spa, intimate
log fires, and its own private gardens. Lilianfels also has a billiards
room, a library and reading room, a tennis court, and a French
bowls lawn.

   Dining/Diversions: Darley's Restaurant is set in historic sur-
rounds and offers very good meals. Lilian's is more casual but equally
good, while the Lobby Lounge is perfect for light meals and teas.

   Amenities: A heated indoor pool; a health club with floatation
tank, herbal bath, gym, sauna, and Jacuzzis; room service; dry clean-
ing/laundry; nightly turndown; secretarial services; massage therapist
and beautician; mountain bikes.

WHERE TO DINE

Katoomba Street has many ethnic dining choices, whether you're hungry for Greek, Chinese, or Thai. Restaurants in the Blue Mountains are generally more expensive than equivalent places in Sydney.

Lindsay's. 122 Katoomba St., Katoomba. ☎ **02/4782 2753.** Reservations recommended. Main courses A$16–$23.50 (U.S.$11.20–$16.45). AE, BC, JCB, MC, V. Wed–Mon noon–3pm and 6pm–midnight. INTERNATIONAL.

Swiss chef Beat Ettlin has been making waves in Katoomba ever since he left some of the best European restaurants behind to try his hand at dishes such as pan-fried crocodile nibbles on pumpkin scones with a ginger dipping sauce. The food in this upmarket New York speakeasy is as glorious as its decor—Tiffany lamps, the sketches doodled by Australian artist Norman Lindsay, and the booths that line the walls. The three-level restaurant is warmed by a cozy fire surrounded by an antique lounge stage and resounds every night to piano or classical music or a jazz band. The menu changes every few weeks, but a recent popular dish was grilled veal medaillons topped with Balmain bugs (small saltwater crayfish), with potato and béarnaise sauce.

Paragon Café. 65 Katoomba St., Katoomba. ☎ **02/4782 2928.** Most menu items A$5.50–$15 (U.S. $3.85–$10.50). AE, MC, V. Tues–Fri 10am–3:30pm; Sat–Sun 10am–4pm. CAFE.

The Paragon has been a Blue Mountains institution since it opened for business in 1916. Inside, it's decked out with dark wood paneling, bas-relief figures guarding the booths, and chandeliers. The homemade soups are delicious. The cafe also serves pies, pastas, grills, seafood, waffles, cakes, and a Devonshire tea of scones and cream.

The Pavilion at Echo Point. 35 Echo Point Rd., Katoomba. ☎ **02/4782 7055.** Main courses A$10.95–$16.50 (U.S.$7.65–$11.55). AE, BC, DC, JCB, MC, V. Sun–Fri 10am–4:30pm; Sat 10am–7:30pm. MODERN AUSTRALIAN/ SNACKS.

This miniature version of Sydney's Queen Victoria Building is so close to Echo Point that it looks like a shove will send it tumbling over the edge. Light fills the three-story building through a rooftop

Bushwalking Safety Tip

Before setting off on a bushwalk, always tell someone where you are going—plenty of people get lost every year.

glass atrium and huge windows on the top two floors. On the ground level are a few stores; on the middle level is a food court with a burger/pie outlet, a bakery, and an ice cream counter; and on the top level is a cafe serving dishes such as baked camembert in puff pastry, battered fillets of trout on a vegetable fritter, and oven-baked baby barramundi with lemon and parsley butter. The food is good for the price, but the views from the terrace and balcony are even better.

TrisElies. 287 Main St., Katoomba. ☎ **02/4782 4026.** Reservations recommended. Main courses A$12–$19.50 (U.S.$8.40–$13.65). Daily noon–midnight. BC, MC, V. TRADITIONAL GREEK.

Perhaps it's the belly dancers and plate smashing, or the smell of moussaka, but as soon as you walk through the door of this lively eatery you feel like you've been transported around the world to an authentic Athenian taberna. The restaurant folds out onto three tiers of tables, all with a good view of the stage where every night Greek or international performances take place. The food is solid Greek fare, such as souvlaki, traditional dips, fried haloumi cheese, Greek salads, casseroles like mother could have made, whitebait, and sausages in red wine. If it's winter, come in to warm up beside one of two log fires.

LEURA

107km (66 miles) W of Sydney; 3km (2 miles) W of Katoomba

The fashionable capital of the Blue Mountains, Leura is known for its gardens, its pretty old buildings (many of them holiday homes for Sydneysiders), and its cafes and restaurants. Just outside Leura is the Sublime Point Lookout, which has spectacular and unusual views of the Three Sisters formation in Katoomba. From the southern end of Leura Mall, a cliff drive takes you all the way back to Echo Point in Katoomba while revealing some spectacular views over the Jamison Valley.

WHERE TO STAY

Fairmont Resort. 1 Sublime Point Rd., Leura, NSW 2780. ☎ **1800/786 640** in Australia or 02/4782 5222. Fax 02/4784 1685. 230 units. A/C MINIBAR TV TEL. Weekend A$174–$246 (U.S.$121.80–$172.20) double; A$302–$530 (U.S.$211.40–$371) suite. Midweek A$136–$210 (U.S.$95.20–$147) double; A$258–$472 (U.S.$180.60–$330.40) suite. Additional person A$35 (U.S.$24.50) extra. Children under 16 stay free in parents' room. Ask about cheaper rates through Aussie auto clubs. 2-night minimum stay on weekends. AE, BC, DC, JCB, MC, V. Free parking.

If the more personalized attention of a B&B or guesthouse is not your scene, then you could always opt for this award-winning resort.

It opened in 1988 as the Blue Mountains only deluxe-hotel–style accommodation. Rooms are pretty luxurious and come with either twins, queen-size, or king-size beds. The valley-view rooms on the upper floors have the best outlooks and cost the most. The resort is popular with Sydneysiders who come up to enjoy the recreational facilities and the Blue Mountain's best golf course, which is just across the road.

Dining: Both Misty's and the Terrace offer exquisite fine dining with excellent service. There's also a bistro.

Amenities: Indoor and outdoor swimming pools, health club, gym, spa, sauna, four floodlit tennis courts, two squash courts, adjacent Leura Golf Course, children's center and supervised activity program, concierge, 24-hour room service, laundry, valet, nightly turndown, massage, baby-sitting, business center, gift shop.

The Little Company Retreat. 2 Eastview Ave., Leura, NSW 2781. ☎ **02/ 4782 4023.** Fax 02/4782 5361. 35 units, 6 cottages. TV TEL. Fri–Sat A$220 (U.S.$154) standard double, A$240 (U.S.$168) deluxe double, A$280 (U.S.$196) premier double; Sun–Thurs A$180 (U.S.$126) standard single, A$200 (U.S.$140) deluxe single, A$240 (U.S.$168) premier single. Cottages A$450–$1,000 (U.S.$315–$700). Rates include breakfast. Ask about special packages. Rates increase during Yulefest (approximately the 3rd weekend in June to the 2nd weekend in Aug). Reduced rates for children under 12. AE, BC, DC, MC, V. Free parking.

This country house—formerly used as a retreat for the nuns of the Little Company of Mary for 50 years—is set in parklike grounds shaded by giant pine trees. Ten homey rooms inside the Nunnery itself come with country-style furniture, bathrooms, queen-size beds, and good views of Mt. Wilson and Mt. Hay. Deluxe rooms are larger than the standard rooms, though similarly furnished, and the premier rooms come with a spa. One room is set up to accommodate travelers with disabilities. Breakfast and dinner are served in the cozy, turn-of-the-century–decorated dining room or the historic chapel. There are also six four-room cottages suitable for small groups or families. All have lounges with open fireplaces and kitchens, and some have spa baths. On the grounds are a heated pool, a croquet lawn, a tennis court, and a volleyball court. Regular evening meals are available for nonguests.

A TEAROOM

Bygone Beautys Tea Room. 20-22 Grose St., Leura. ☎ **02/4784 3117.** Devonshire teas A$5.50 (U.S.$3.85); light meals around A$8 (U.S.$5.60); afternoon tea A$12.50 (U.S.$8.75) per person or A$22 (U.S.$15.40) for 2 people. BC, MC, V. Daily 10am–5pm. Closed Christmas Day and New Year's Day. LIGHT MEALS/DEVONSHIRE TEAS.

Everyone has to try a Devonshire tea in the Blue Mountains. It's just part of the experience. This is one of the more unusual places to partake. It's set in the midst of the largest private antique emporium in the Blue Mountains, yet it's still cozy in an Edwardian kind of way. As well as your scones and cream, you can treat yourself to a light lunch—such as soup, a chicken casserole, or a beef curry and rice—or a traditional afternoon tea, with sandwiches, scones, home-made biscuits and cakes, all served on fine china and silver. What's more, you can browse over the antiques when you finish dining.

BLACKHEATH

114km (71 miles) W of Sydney; 14km (9 miles) W of Katoomba

The Three Brothers at Blackheath are not as big as their more fa-mous Three Sisters in Katoomba, but you can climb two of them for fabulous views. Or you could try the Cliff Walk from Evans Lookout to Govetts Leap, where there are magnificent views over the Grose Valley and Bridal Veil Falls. It's about a $1^1/2$-hour tramp through a banksia, gum, and wattle forest, with spectacular views of peaks and valleys.

GETTING THERE   The Great Western Highway takes motorists west from Katoomba to Blackheath. CityRail trains also stop at Blackheath.

WHERE TO STAY & DINE

✪ **Cleopatra.** 118 Cleopatra St., Blackheath, NSW 2785. ☎ **02/ 4787 6238.** Fax 02/4787 6238. 3-course meal A$75 (U.S.$52.50). AE, BC, DC, MC, V. Mon–Sat 7:30pm–11pm; Sun from 1–3:30pm. FRENCH.

The *Sydney Morning Herald*'s "Good Food Guide" consistently rates this restaurant as the best outside Sydney. It's also won the Ameri-can Express restaurant award for the best restaurant in western New South Wales for 6 years. The dining room, in a hidden treasure of a National Trust house, is comfortable and warm and furnished with tasteful antiques. Chef Dany Chouet has been preparing marvelous provincial French food here for 15 years. On the menu you could find appetizers such as duck-neck sausage of duck and pork, flavored with truffle juice and cognac; or a salad of mussels, baby squid, and prawns with fresh borlotti beans. A standout among the main courses is the Tasmanian salmon covered with a purée of black ol-ives, with spring onions, olive oil, and lemon juice. A classic dessert is the hot chocolate pudding with a liquid chocolate center served with fresh-mint sauce. Lunch in summer is served in the garden. If you anticipate being too full to move after dinner, then you can stay in one of the house's five cozy rooms and apartments. Midweek they rent for A$180 to $230 (U.S.$126 to $161) per person including dinner and breakfast, and on weekends from A$385 to $495 (U.S.$269.50 to $346.50) per person including 2-night accommodation, two dinners, and one lunch.

✪ **Jemby-Rinjah Lodge.** 336 Evans Lookout Rd., Blackheath, NSW 2785. ☎ **02/4787 7622.** Fax 02/4787 6230. 10 cabins, 3 lodges. Fri–Sun A$180–A$130 (U.S.$126–91) per cabin (occupied by up to 2 adults and 2 children); Mon–Thurs A$133–A$95 (U.S.$93.10–$66.50) per cabin; additional adult A$15 (U.S.$10.50) extra, additional child A$10 (U.S.$7) extra. A$55 (U.S.$38.50) per person in lodge including breakfast. AE, BC, MC, V. Free parking.

The Blue Mountains National Park is just a short walk away from these 10 deluxe cabins (two one-bedroom and eight two-bedroom) and three pole-frame lodges. If you like hiking, come here, because the nearby walking tracks take you to the spectacular Grand Canyon, the Grose Valley Blue Gum forests, and Walls Cave, a resting place for local Aborigines 10,000 years ago. The cabins are right in the bush, can sleep up to six people, and are well spaced. Each has a slow combustion heater, carpets, a bathroom, a fully equipped kitchen, and a lounge and dining area. There are also an automatic laundry and barbecue areas nearby. The lodges each have five bedrooms, two bathrooms, and a common lounge area with a circular fireplace. Composting toilets, walkways, and solar heating help protect the environment. You can rent linens, but bring your own food. Free pickup can be arranged from Blackheath train station.

The new Treetops Retreat Cabin is two stories high with a balcony and verandah. It's larger and plusher than the standard cabins and is already a favorite with American guests who tend to snap it up as soon as they see it. It has a fireplace, kitchen, solar-powered TV and VCR, and a Japanese-style tub supplied with heated rainwater.

WENTWORTH FALLS
103km (64 miles) from Sydney; 7km (4.3 miles) from Katoomba

This pretty little town has numerous craft and antique shops, but the area is principally known for its magnificent 935-foot-high waterfall, situated in Falls Reserve. On the far side of the falls is the National Pass Walk—one of the best in the Blue Mountains. It's cut into a cliff face with overhanging rock faces on one side and sheer drops on the other. The views over the Jamison Valley are spectacular. The track takes you down to the base of the falls to the Valley of the Waters. Climbing up out of the valley is quite a bit more difficult, but just as rewarding.

WHERE TO STAY

If you want to stay in a historical cottage, then consider **Bygone Beautys Cottages,** 20-22 Grose St., Leura, NSW 2780 (☎ **02/ 4784 3117;** fax 02/47813078). Nine of the 17 totally self-contained cottages the group owns are in Wentworth Falls; the others are in Leura and Bullaburra. Prices range from A$62 to $90 (U.S.$43.40 to $63.00) per person midweek, and A$75 to $120 (U.S.$52.50 to $84) per person on weekends (with a minimum 2-night stay).

✪ **Whispering Pines & The Sandpatch.** 178-186 Falls Rd., Wentworth Falls, NSW 2782. ☎ **02/4757 1449.** Fax 03/4757 1219. 4 units in main building, 1 4-bedroom cottage at Sandpatch. TV TEL. Whispering Pines: Weekend A$90–$200 (U.S.$63–$140) double; midweek A$90–$135 (U.S.$63–$94.50) double. Sandpatch: A$180 (U.S.$126) per couple per night plus A$25 (U.S.$17.50) each extra person (minimum of 4 people). Both properties require a minimum 2-night stay on weekends. AE, BC, DC, MC, V. Free parking.

Whispering Pines is a grand heritage mountain guesthouse set in 4 acres of rambling woodland gardens right at the head of Wentworth Falls. Built in 1898, it continues to foster that kind of Victorian luxury that attracted visitors to this guesthouse a century ago. Rooms are cozy and filled with period antiques. If you really want to get away from it all, then the Sandpatch property just down the road is perfect. It offers two large bedrooms, plus guest living rooms, with Persian rugs, polished floorboards, and all the antiques and added modern luxuries you could ask for. Two people can rent the cottage, but they must pay A$50 (U.S.$35) on top of the price above (in other words, two people have to pay for four people, even if only two stay). The cottage sleeps eight people. There's a full kitchen, a CD player, and a VCR.

A NICE SPOT FOR LUNCH

Conservation Hut Café. End of Fletcher St., Wentworth Falls. ☎ **02/4757 3827.** Menu items A$6–$12 (U.S.$4.20–$8.40). BC, MC, V. Daily 9am–5pm. LIGHT MEALS.

This pleasant cafe is in the national park itself on top of a cliff overlooking the Jamison Valley. It's a good place for a bit of lunch on the balcony if you're famished after the Valley of the Waters walk, which leaves from just outside. It serves all the usual cafe fare—burgers, salads, sandwiches, and pastas. There are plenty of vegetarian options, too. There's a nice log fire inside in winter.

MEDLOW BATH

150km (93 miles) W of Sydney; 6km (3.7 miles) E of Katoomba

A cozy place, with its own railway station, a secondhand bookstore, and a few properties hidden between the trees, Medlow Bath has one claim to fame—the **Hydro Majestic Hotel** (☎ **02/4788 1002**), a must-do stop for any visitor to the Blue Mountains. The historic and huge Hydro Majestic has fabulous views over the Megalong Valley; the best time to appreciate the views is at sunset with a drink on the terrace. Also, drop into Medlow Bath's Old Post Office, now a musty secondhand bookshop and antique store, where you can interrupt your browsing with freshly brewed coffee among the bookshelves.

A PLACE TO STAY

The Chalet. 46-50 Portland Road, Medlow Bath, NSW 2780. ☎ **02/4788 1122.** Fax 02/47881064. 8 units, 4 with shared bathroom. TV TEL. Weekend $A240–$280 (U.S.$168–$196) per person for 2-night stay in double, including dinner and breakfast; weekdays A$50–$60 (U.S.$35–$42) per person with breakfast. Restaurant open Wed–Sat. AE, BC, DC, MC, V. Free parking.

Built in 1892, this recently renovated guesthouse is far from your average drive-in motel. When you stay at the Chalet, you are buying a bit of a bygone era. The heritage-listed cottage is set away from the main road through the Blue Mountains in 3 acres of gardens and lawns. Inside, it is split in two by a long chessboard-tiled hallway. On one side is a grandma's lounge with a fireplace, flowery sofas, lace curtains, doilies, and arrangements of plastic flowers. Next door is an impressive wood-paneled dining room, with a beamed ceiling and crisp linen tablecloths, another blazing fireplace, and jazz on Saturday evenings. Guests also have the use of the clay tennis court outside. Four of the eight rooms are suitable for families, and four have private bathrooms. The Chalet prides itself on its contemporary food, and although the menu is small and lacks a vegetarian option, it's excellent. The Chalet is strictly BYO (bring your own) when it comes to alcohol.

JENOLAN CAVES

182km (113 miles) W of Sydney; 70 W (43 miles) of Katoomba

The winding road from Katoomba eventually takes you to a spur of the Great Dividing Range and a series of underground limestone caves considered to be some of the world's best. Known to the local Aborigines as "Binoomea," meaning "dark place," millions of people have come to see the amazing stalactites, stalagmites, and underground rivers and pools since the caves were opened to the public in 1866.

GETTING THERE   It's a 1½-hour drive from Katoomba to the caves. CityRail trains run to Katoomba and link up with daily Jenolan Caves excursions run by **Fantastic Aussie Tours** (☎ 02/

4782 1866). The CityRail combination train/bus tour costs A$60
(U.S.$42) for adults and A$30 (U.S.$21) for children—on top of
that add the train fare from Sydney to Katoomba. The tour alone
from Katoomba costs A$64 (U.S.$44.80) for adults and A$32
(U.S.$22.40) for children. These prices include cave entry. You can
purchase the train/bus combination tickets at any rail station.

One-day round-trips from Sydney are operated by **AAT Kings**
(☎ 02/9252 2788; fax 03/9274 7400) and **Australian Pacific
Tours** (☎ 02/9252 2988; fax 02/9247 2052). Coach tours depart
the coach terminal at Circular Quay. If you can handle 6 hours on
a coach that's fine, but I really recommend staying overnight in either Jenolan Village or somewhere else in the Blue Mountains.

EXPLORING THE CAVES

There are nine caves open to the public, with guided tours conducted by staff employed by the **Jenolan Caves Reserves Trust**
(☎ 02/6359 3311). The first cave tour starts at 10am weekdays and
9:30am weekends and holidays. The final tour departs at 4:30pm
(5pm in warmer months). Tours last 1 to 2 hours, and each costs
A$12 to A$25 (U.S.$8.40 to U.S.$17.50) for adults, and A$8 to
A$20 (U.S.$5.60 to U.S.$14) for children under 15. Family conces-
sions and multiple-cave packages are available. The best all-round
cave is Lucas Cave; Imperial Cave is best for seniors. **Adventure
Cave tours,** including canyoning, last from 3 hours to all day and
cost from A$40 to $100 (U.S.$28 to $70) per person.

WHERE TO STAY & DINE

The Gatehouse Jenolan. Jenolan Caves Village, NSW 2790. **02/6359 3042.**
21 units. Weekends A$60 (U.S.$42) double; weekdays A$50 (U.S.$35) double.
Dorms sleeping 6 people cost A$90 (U.S.$63) weekends and $80 (U.S.$56)
weekdays; if you want to share a dorm it costs A$20 (U.S.$14) weekends and
A$15 (U.S.$10.50) weekdays. AE, BC, MC, V. Free parking.

The Gatehouse is a clean and cozy budget-style lodge opposite the
caves themselves. It sleeps 66 people in all, in seven six-bed rooms
and six four-bed rooms. There are also two common rooms, lockers, washing machines and dryers, basic kitchen facilities, and a barbecue area. There are also four family rooms with a double bed and
a set of bunk beds. There are outdoor barbecues on the premises,
and apparently at least one ghost.

Jenolan Caves House. Jenolan Caves Village, NSW 2790. ☎ **1800/068 050**
in Australia or 02/6359 3322. Fax 02/6359 3227. 99 units, 43 with bathroom.
TV TEL. Weekend A$120 (U.S.$84) double without bathroom, A$170 (U.S.$119)

Classic and Mountain Lodge doubles; midweek A$110 (U.S.$77) double without bathroom, A$150 (U.S.$105) Classic and Mountain Lodge doubles. A$50 (U.S.$35) budget rooms. Family rooms also available. AE, BC, DC, MC, V. Free parking.

This heritage-listed hotel was built between 1888 and 1906 and remains one of the most outstanding pieces of architecture in New South Wales. The main part of the enormous three-story building is constructed of sandstone and fashioned in a Tudor-style black-and-white. Around it are several scattered outhouses, cottages, and former servants' quarters. Rooms vary within the main house from simple budget-style bunk rooms to "Traditional" rooms with shared bathrooms and "Classic" rooms with private bathrooms. The traditional and classic rooms are both old-world and cozy, with heavy furniture and views over red-tile rooftops or steep vegetated slopes. Mountain Lodge rooms are found in a separate building behind the main house and are more motel-like in fashion. The lodge's bar fills up inside and out on summer weekends; Trails Bistro sells snacks (bring your own if you're a vegetarian, though), milk, and bread. Chisolms at Jenolan is a fine-dining restaurant serving very good Modern Australian cuisine.

Index

See also separate Accommodations and Restaurant indexes, below.
Page numbers in italics refer to maps.

ACCOMMODATIONS

FROMMER'S® COMPLETE TRAVEL GUIDES

(Comprehensive guides to destinations around the world, with selections in all price ranges—from deluxe to budget)

FROMMER'S® DOLLAR-A-DAY GUIDES

(The ultimate guides to comfortable low-cost travel)

Australia from $50 a Day	Israel from $50 a Day
California from $60 a Day	Italy from $50 a Day
Caribbean from $60 a Day	London from $70 a Day
England from $60 a Day	Mexico from $35 a Day
Europe from $50 a Day	New York from $75 a Day
Florida from $60 a Day	New Zealand from $50 a Day
Greece from $50 a Day	Paris from $70 a Day
Hawaii from $60 a Day	San Francisco from $60 a Day
Ireland from $50 a Day	Washington, D.C., from $60 a Day

FROMMER'S® PORTABLE GUIDES

(Pocket-size guides for travelers who want everything in a nutshell)

Acapulco, Ixtapa/ Zihuatenejo	Dublin	Puerto Vallarta, Manzanillo & Guadalajara
Bahamas	Las Vegas	San Francisco
California Wine Country	London	Sydney
Charleston & Savannah	Maine Coast	Tampa Bay & St. Petersburg
Chicago	New Orleans	Venice
	New York	Washington, D.C.
	Paris	

FROMMER'S® NATIONAL PARK GUIDES

(Everything you need for the perfect park vacation)

Grand Canyon	Yosemite & Sequoia/ Kings Canyon
National Parks of the American West	
Yellowstone & Grand Teton	Zion & Bryce Canyon

FROMMER'S® IRREVERENT GUIDES

(Wickedly honest guides for sophisticated travelers)

Amsterdam	Manhattan	San Francisco
Boston	New Orleans	Walt Disney World
Chicago	Paris	Washington, D.C.
London		

FROMMER'S® MEMORABLE WALKS

(Memorable neighborhood strolls through the world's great cities)

Chicago	New York	San Francisco
London	Paris	

THE COMPLETE IDIOT'S TRAVEL GUIDES

(The ultimate user-friendly trip planners)

Cruise Vacations	Las Vegas	New York City
Planning Your Trip to Europe	Mexico's Beach Resorts	San Francisco
Hawaii	New Orleans	Walt Disney World